T0350125

A Most Enterprising Country

A Most Enterprising Country

North Korea in the Global Economy

Justin V. Hastings

Cornell University Press
Ithaca and London

First published 2016 by Cornell University Press
Printed in the United States of America

Library of Congress Cataloging-in-Publication Data

Names: Hastings, Justin V. (Justin VanOverloop), author.
Title: A most enterprising country : North Korea in the global economy / Justin V. Hastings.
Description: Ithaca ; London : Cornell University Press, 2016. | Includes bibliographical references and index.
Identifiers: LCCN 2016026646 | ISBN 9781501704901 (cloth : alk. paper)
Subjects: LCSH: Korea (North)—Economic conditions. | Korea (North)—Foreign economic relations. | Korea (North)—Politics and government—1994–2011.
Classification: LCC HC470.2 .H37 2016 | DDC 337.95193—dc23
LC record available at https://lccn.loc.gov/2016026646

Cloth printing   10   9   8   7   6   5   4   3   2   1

Contents

Figures

PREFACE

Any serious study of North Korea has to contend with the fundamental problem that the North Korean government is not particularly eager to be studied, and what little official information it does release often has a dubious connection to reality. It is traditional in prefaces of books about North Korea to bemoan the lack of reliable data about the country, but then to exclaim that North Korea is not nearly as opaque as one would think, and that there has been an mini-boom in the information available in recent years, information that can now be used to present a more balanced and comprehensive picture.[1] It is true: the proliferation of blogs and South Korean news websites in particular that are focused on North Korea, the ability of people in North Korea to move back and forth across the border, and to report from within North Korea using Chinese mobile phone towers, and the access that certain NGOs have had to North Korea in recent years have all had the effect of making North Korea a little less opaque. There is actually a fair amount of information in the public domain about how North Koreans do business, and in the interests of not reinventing the wheel and to take advantage of the new data sources available, I relied extensively on secondary sources that have arisen in recent years. Much of this book is thus a reinterpretation of what outsiders know (or think they know) about North Korean trade networks.

At times I was able to collect information not otherwise found in secondary sources, none of which are necessarily concerned with North Korea's trade networks per se, as opposed to North Korea's external economic relations overall.[2] There are various ways to go about this. Traditionally, books and articles about North Korea often rely, explicitly or implicitly, on information from North Korean defectors living in South Korea.[3] Given that the book is largely about business being done outside of North Korea or, if within North Korea, between North Koreans and outsiders, I had less reason to rely on defector interviews than have many other books. With that said, I did rely on defector interviews to the extent that my secondary sources relied on them to provide insight into North Korea's domestic situation over the years. Besides English and Korean (which was the province of my research assistant Haneol Lee), the research for this book was conducted in Chinese, and because of this, the book necessarily disproportionately reflects views of North Korea by Chinese people and sources. While Chinese sources arguably have a better picture of what is happening in North Korea than those from any other country except perhaps South Korea, they introduce their own biases, particularly Chinese government sensitivity about North Korean issues.

While I emphasize the ambiguous nature—the blurring of licit and illicit—of much North Korean trade, for trade that was clearly illicit or under sanction by the international community, I relied on United Nations sanctions committee reports and court documents from the United States (in the case of Taiwanese criminal cases involving North Koreans) and Australia (in the case of the *Pong Su* incident). Strangely, the section on post-2005 North Korean drug trafficking networks in chapter 3 was also the easiest to research. Between 2006 and 2011, the Chinese government appears to have sanctioned reporting by northeastern Chinese newspapers on drug trafficking cases involving North Koreans (always referred to obliquely as *jingwairen*—people from outside [China's] borders). One can speculate on the reasons for this—possibly the Chinese government was using the reports to express its annoyance with the drugs emanating from North Korea, and to indirectly pressure the North Korean government to stop the flows—but the reports can get quite detailed (they are clearly taking their information from police and court documents) and are thus useful in parsing out the process and networks used by drug traffickers during that period. The sections on drug trafficking in chapters 1 and 3 are taken, with modification, from Justin V. Hastings, "The Economic Geography of North Korean Drug Trafficking Networks," *Review of International Political Economy* 22 no. 1 (2015): 162–93, and are used with permission from Taylor & Francis.

I partly addressed data issues by the focus of the book itself: while many books about North Korea are about North Korean society and domestic politics, which are difficult for outsiders to view directly (much less talk to North Koreans about), this book is by and large about events happening outside of North Korea, which are more easily observable. It is also about trade networks that, while they emanate from within North Korea, eventually must involve North Koreans talking to non–North Koreans. And these non–North Koreans are willing to talk. I also attempted to address data issues by the design of the book: chapters 2, 3, and 4 begin with overviews of conditions in North Korea and elsewhere, and broad generalizations about North Korean trade networks, then hone in on specific illustrative case studies for which more detailed information was available. While the case studies are useful in demonstrating how certain types of trade networks *can* function, I am unable to claim that they are representative, although I have no specific evidence that they are atypical of the North Korean experience.

I rely on discussions and interviews with perhaps a hundred people knowledgeable on some aspect of the North Korean economy or trade. These include academic and think-tank experts in China, Hong Kong, South Korea, and the United States, as well as businessmen and government officials in China and Hong Kong. My research assistant Yaohui Wang conducted additional interviews under my direction with Chinese businessmen, officials, and academics in Beijing, Dandong, Shenyang, Dalian, Yanbian, Hunchun, Baishan, and Changbai. The interviews were largely used for three purposes: as background, to guide the research and provide context; as the basis for summarizing knowledgeable experts' understanding of North Korean political economy (as seen in the section on the food chain in chapter 3); and to piece together the structure and behavior of trade networks used by North Korean traders by talking to those who do business with them (as seen with the case study of the

Dandong traders in chapter 2, and the survival strategies used by Chinese businessmen in chapter 4). There were also instances where firms that had dealt with North Koreans went public with their (usually negative) experiences, and I took advantage of those narratives (for instance, in the case of the Xiyang debacle analyzed in chapter 4).

In this my approach could be considered a qualitative version of how North Korea's trade data is often collected, through mirror statistics—the data about trade with North Korea that are reported by its counterparties. Indeed, the quantitative trade data in this book are taken from the United Nations Comtrade database and the Chinese Ministry of Commerce. While relying on formal trade sources no doubt leaves out a large portion of North Korean trade—the high portion of goods that are smuggled through Dandong makes this almost certain—I am more interested in the magnitudes and trends in North Korean trade, which presumably can be represented in official statistics despite imprecision, and none of my arguments rest on specific trade numbers.

The relatively poor data make it all the more important that the analysis be based on a theoretical framework that can structure what little we know and help to fill in the gaps in our knowledge. One of the tasks of much of this book is to map out North Korean trade networks, to see where they do business outside of North Korea, and between North Korea and the rest of the world, how they do business, who is involved (and who is actually making money), and how and where they interact with non–North Korean people, governments, and businesses. As such, throughout the book, but with a light touch, I draw inspiration from the extensive literature on global economic networks, and frame North Korean trade networks as global value chains.[4] North Korean trade networks are rather unusual examples of these globalized economic networks, but are examples nonetheless. The global value chain framework and its predecessor, the global commodity chain,[5] have been criticized on the grounds that their emphasis is on linear flows and processes for adding value, when the reality is much more complex and dynamic.[6] Nonetheless, if our goal is to understand the networks that move profits, goods, and labor into and out of North Korea, a linear framework makes sense and has the benefit of being relatively parsimonious.

We can think of North Korean trade networks as chains with nodes physically located in both North Korea and elsewhere, connected by the bidirectional flows (both into and out of North Korea) of information, material goods, and financial resources. These flows are coordinated and configured through relationships among networks' nodes, which can consist of individuals, actual firms, and North Korean state institutions. These chains are in turn embedded in social, political, and economic networks at every stage that help or hinder their activities.[7]

Thinking of North Korean trade networks as value chains allows us to answer a number of questions about their structure and operation. What is being bought and sold, and how is it moved about? In the case of North Korean trade networks, the input-output structure is simply the nodes involved in the process by which North Korea, and North Koreans, obtain supplies, produce goods, distribute and retail them, and capture value. With both licit and illicit trade, we would expect the input-output structures themselves to look much like their counterparts in other countries, although some revision of how we think about the input-output structures of North Korean value chains will be necessary because of unique North Korean governance structures and institutional frameworks.

Where are the nodes in the network located, and how are they linked? In the case of North Korean trade networks, it is useful to think of the physical locations of the nodes in the networks not only relative to each other, but also relative to North Korea. Within North Korea, levels of economic development, and attention from the state, vary dramatically, with Pyongyang at the pinnacle, and the northeastern provinces traditionally at the bottom. Institutional conditions also vary in the special economic zones within North Korea as well as, informally, within Pyongyang, and along the border with China (and to a lesser extent Russia). Outside of North Korea, it would be useful to categorize the territories by their proximity to North Korea itself, allowing us to think about the different geographic scales at which networks may operate, and the varying logistical resources, business knowledge, and social and government connections they would need to operate at each scale.[8] In terms of increasing distance from North Korea, these territories would consist of: northeastern China, particularly the provinces of Jilin and Liaoning; the rest of China, including Hong Kong and Macau; the rest of northeast Asia, including Japan, South Korea, and Taiwan; and the rest of the world.

Who controls the networks? Who captures value in the chain, and where and how is it captured? How is control exercised over the networks?

What is the governance structure of the networks, or the "authority and power relationships between firms that determine how financial, material, and human resources are allocated and flow" through the networks?[9] These are perhaps the most critical questions for understanding the evolution of North Korean trade networks. Within North Korea are a panoply of private citizens, state officials at all levels, and state, hybrid, and private organizations. Originating from and often physically located outside of North Korea are North Korean trade networks' foreign partners: individuals and private firms looking to make money from doing business with North Korean traders, investors who sink money into North Korean enterprises (for whatever reason), and foreign states seeking goods from North Korean suppliers or providing goods to North Korean buyers for political, security, and economic reasons.

Actors within the networks engage in economic transactions and build formal and informal relationships designed to move goods from supplier to buyer, ensure the maintenance of their operations, and make a profit. The relationships between nodes fall into categories that range from arms-length market relationships, which may persist over time but where the costs of finding new partners are low, to hierarchical relationships, in which the buyers and suppliers (or nodes in the network) have an in-house managerial relationship (that is, one in which they are part of the same organization).[10] Aside from market relationships and hierarchical relationships, we can also think of relational connections, in which the two nodes interact on the basis of trust, reputation, and noneconomic linkages such as ethnicity or social ties.[11] The specific type of connection between two nodes in the network depends on the institutional environment in which they find themselves, and the nature of the actors themselves.

What are the rules under which different nodes in the network operate? Which "local, national, and international conditions and policies shape the globalization process" at different points in the networks?[12] North Korean trade networks operate within the context of the laws and regulations of state institutions in multiple countries, especially but not limited to North Korea, as well as sanctions regimes put in place by the United Nations, Japan, South Korea, and various Western nations, and enforced by a number of other countries. While typical analysis envisions institutional frameworks as designed to encourage and support certain types of firms, their operations, and more generally development, institutional frameworks relative to North Korean business networks are designed to both encourage and discourage economic activities. The general political and economic characteristics of the territory surrounding a node, such as favorable government regulations, legitimate production and transportation infrastructure, political stability (or instability), and the local availability of technology conducive to network operations also shape what the nodes can accomplish in their trading, how they make money, who they can contact and with whom they can make deals, and how they can move their trading goods around.

Outside of North Korea, the institutional environment may be indifferent (for North Korean businesses operating legally in China, for instance), or outright hostile (for North Korean illicit activities in China, or for most operations in countries with sanctions against North Korea), with specific state institutions, such as monetary authorities, customs agencies, intelligence agencies, and foreign ministries, actively attempting to subvert North Korean commerce.

Within North Korea itself, given the irrelevance of the rule of law, the specific laws and regulations in place are perhaps beside the point. Of perhaps equal or greater relevance is the ever-shifting informal power networks that determine what is allowed, encouraged, discouraged, or stamped out at any given time, lubricated with patron-client networks and rents. As a result, the environmental conditions in which trade networks inside of and emanating from North Korea are likely to operate will depend to a large extent on the attitude of the central state and local state officials toward trade, and the informal networks in which those engaged in trade are embedded. Both are apt to change over time, and shape the manner in which the trade networks are structured to take advantage of state prerogatives or avoid the state entirely.[13]

Acknowledgments

Given the subject matter, most of the people who contributed to the research and writing of this book must remain unnamed, but their help is much appreciated. James Goymour, Edward Morris, Haneol Lee, and Yaohui Wang provided research support at various stages of the process. Yaohui in particular was a self-starter whose interest in North Korea was so strong that he went to northeastern China and conducted many of the interviews in chapter 4 himself. Without his help, it would not have been possible to write this book in anything like the detail it has.

A significant portion of this book was written during visiting fellowships in 2014 at Nanyang Technological University's S. Rajaratnam School of International Studies in Singapore, with support from Kumar Ramakrishna, and the East-West Center in Honolulu, where I was hosted as a POSCO Visiting Fellow by Denny Roy. Stephan Haggard and Charles Armstrong provided much needed feedback on earlier drafts of the manuscript. The two anonymous reviewers also made valuable suggestions, as did the participants in a number of presentations. Parts of this book or research related to this book were presented at the International Studies Association 2013 Annual Meeting in San Francisco, the East-West Center in Honolulu, the Department of Nuclear and Quantum Engineering at KAIST in Daejeon, South Korea, the Institute of Peace and Unification Studies at Seoul National University in Seoul, South Korea, the Sam Nunn School of International Affairs at the Georgia Institute of Technology in Atlanta, the Myanmar Institute of Strategic and International Studies in Yangon, Myanmar, and the China in the World/Lowy Institute China Forum at the Australian National University in Canberra, Australia.

The research for the book was conducted with generous grants from the University of Sydney, the Australian Research Council (grant DP140102098), and the John D. and Catherine T. MacArthur Foundation (grant 100981). Roger Haydon, my editor at Cornell University Press, was enthusiastic about this project from the very beginning, and waited patiently for years while it moved from hazy idea to reality.

Finally, I dedicate this book to my wife, Tiffany, and to Zephyr, whose impending birth spurred writing as little else could.

A Most Enterprising Country

Introduction

The Enterprising Country

> "Let's be clear. The regime in Pyongyang is dangerous. Its behaviour is often
> unpredictable. But one thing about it we can predict is it being hell-bent
> on building a nuclear arsenal. We should not be lulled into a false sense of
> security by the dire state of the country's economy. In fact, North Korea's
> weapons programs are a source of funding for the regime. It sells its weapons
> secrets for hard currency that keeps the regime's coffers stocked. Countries
> like Syria and Iran are buyers. Make no mistake the North Korean regime
> is armed and dangerous. It has a long history of brinkmanship and has
> shown that it is prepared to lash out. A cruel totalitarian state, it has no
> regard for the welfare of its people, much less world opinion."
>
> — Kevin Rudd, Australian Minister for Foreign
> Affairs and Trade, 2011

In 2011, when then–Australian Minister of Foreign Affairs and Trade
Kevin Rudd warned of the security threat posed by North Korea to Australia, it was primarily in the context of the threat North Korea posed to
regional stability, and the increasing range of North Korean missiles.[1]
While these are all traditional concerns about North Korea, one line stood
out—quite aside from nuclear weapons, Rudd was also worried about
North Korean weapons sales as a way of boosting its moribund economy.
That North Korea has sold and sells weapons abroad is not new information or even particularly surprising. In his statement, Kevin Rudd was possibly thinking of incidents such as the one that occurred in December 2009,
when a Ukrainian-registered, Russian-made cargo plane was intercepted

in Bangkok with thirty-five tons of North Korean–produced rockets, missile parts, and small arms bound for Iran.[2]

Yet what often goes unremarked upon is the juxtaposition of the security threats North Korea poses in part because of its commercial dealings around the world, and the other reason it has attracted attention from outside observers—its totalitarian, autarkic, politically isolated regime. Several months after his statement about the threat posed by North Korea, in another op-ed Rudd described North Korea as "reclusive, isolated, and paranoid," and "a throwback to a former era. A bizarre mix of 1984-style state control, personality cult, wacky ideology, and military bravado," a common assessment among Western observers.[3] In other words, a country so isolated that it has not consistently released economic statistics since the 1960s, that still does not allow the vast majority of its citizens to access the Internet, and that is often colored gray on statistical world maps because of its lack of cooperation with information-gathering international institutions such as the World Bank and United Nations, is also one where at least some people are able to access the global economy with seeming ease. As Rudd noted, "Its leaders sip cognac and whisky, smoke Cuban cigars and dine on caviar and lobster while their subjects go unfed."[4]

While the cognac that North Korea's elites drink, and the Cuban cigars they smoke, are certainly signs of their depraved indifference to the suffering of their population, the cognac and Cuban cigars had to come from somewhere, and North Koreans had to have the ability to find sellers, order and pay for the goods, and then get them back to North Korea. Likewise, when North Korea sells weapons abroad, it has to find willing buyers and make suitable contracts, and then find ways to get those weapons from North Korea to the buyer in one piece, under the surveillance of the United States and other hostile powers. The desire to engage in elite indulgences and irresponsible weapons sales are perhaps necessary corollaries of what it means to be a "rogue state." The continued *ability* to engage in what is fairly sophisticated international commerce, particularly in the face of one of the more comprehensive sanctions regimes ever created, is not.

Yet it is not just cognac and missiles that North Korea buys and sells. It is also involved in more prosaic commercial endeavors. On a frigid day in October 2012, I happened to be in Shenyang in northeastern China, and went to Xita, the ethnic Korean neighborhood in Shenyang. There was clear evidence of a North Korean presence: dour middle-aged men in the ill-fitting, oversized Mao suits favored by North Korean officials walked the streets of the neighborhood. There were also two North Korean restaurants across from each other on the main street in Xita, both sporting giant North Korean flags on their storefronts and young women in immaculate makeup and traditional Korean dresses standing at the doors, waiting to usher customers inside. That North Korea runs restaurants throughout East Asia is not surprising to North Korea watchers. The restaurants have occasionally been featured in journalistic accounts, often as an example of how odd North Korea is, or as a way (for locals) to experience North Korean culture.[5] Yet the existence of the restaurants leads to more questions: What kind of "reclusive, isolated, and paranoid" regime runs its own chain of restaurants around the world? What does what seems to be a fairly extensive North Korean business presence outside of North Korea say about North Korea's actual isolation?

Several details of the restaurants in Shenyang stood out. On the same street, several buildings down, was a branch of Angel-in-us, a well-known South Korean coffee, ice cream, and waffle chain, suggesting that Xita is at least one place where South Koreans, North Koreans, and ethnic Korean Chinese are theoretically free to mix, and that some North Korean businesspeople may not be as isolated as many analysts assume. As to the potential competitive advantage of North Korean restaurants, under the North Korean flag fronting one of the restaurants was a sign in Chinese: *Pingyang xiangrou guan.* The restaurant was apparently one that served dog meat. While eating dog is a legal gray area in South Korea, at least one North Korean restaurant seemed willing to advertise its willingness to cater to a taste that is otherwise stigmatized by many South Koreans. Perhaps, in doing business, North Koreans are not nearly as isolated or as unacquainted with markets as one would think.

This book explores the seeming puzzle at the heart of how so many observers think about North Korea: the most politically isolated state in the world, and one notorious for isolating its own citizens from all sources of outside information, nonetheless sustains itself in large part by international trade and integration into the global economy, albeit in a quantity and of a quality that would be unrecognizable to many other states in the international system. It is not just the Kim family, or even elites, that access trade networks, but also private North Korean citizens. The transnational trade networks that crisscross the region and the world, and sustain the global economy by producing, distributing, and selling goods, labor, and information, have been accessed in different ways by the North Korean state, and North Koreans in general, in the face of a hostile political environment. In accessing the global economy, in contrast with their paranoid, isolated image, both the North Korean state and North Korean citizens have proven pragmatic, entrepreneurial, and adaptable. The world's last Stalinist state is also one of the most enterprising.

North Korea's Economic Survival

It was not always obvious North Korea would survive. In the decade following the Cold War, analysts argued that North Korea's economic collapse would precipitate a more general collapse of the state.[6] Although North Korea's economy did in fact collapse in tandem with the great famine of the mid-1990s, described by North Korean state propaganda as the Arduous March, the state bent but did not give,[7] and North Korea's economy ostensibly grew from 2000 (with significant downturns) to recover by 2012 to Cold War levels.[8] While one should never take numbers coming out of the country too seriously, it appears that North Korea actually ran a current-account surplus in foreign trade in 2011 and 2012.[9]

Why is North Korea is still here? North Korea trundles on, despite its seeming unwillingness (or inability) to play by the rules generally accepted by the rest of the world. One theory, based on a political logic, argues that since the fall of the Soviet Union, China has propped up North Korea by sending food and fuel aid, and by running interference for the DRPK during crises.[10] While China has demonstrated increasing impatience with North Korea over its nuclear provocations, it has been unwilling to abandon North Korea to the full consequences of its actions. North Korea, for its own part, extracts aid from other countries through its nuclear program and its steady litany of provocations.[11] Through skillful brinksmanship, North Korea has created a situation where these provocations (and the accompanying *status quo*) are preferable to its collapse for all of the relevant external actors, notably China, South Korea, and the United States.[12] Within the country, North Korea's leadership has perfected the tools of authoritarian stability by restricting outside information, establishing stringent controls over movement and social mobility, coup-proofing institutions, and playing elites off each other.[13]

Yet a political logic for North Korea's survival cannot be the only explanation. The concessions extracted by North Korea's provocations have typically come in dribs and drabs, with unpredictable frequency and quantity, and after the 2006 nuclear test have fallen off as the United States, South Korea, and China have become tired of the incessant blackmail (although aid has continued nonetheless). Moreover, making other countries afraid to take the risk of toppling the regime for fear that what will happen next would be worse does not translate into affirmative steps to help North Korea grow economically. Instead, another set of theories argues that North Korea's survival has been predicated on fundamental changes in the North Korean economy, and in the relationship between the population and the state at all levels. Three (mutually reinforcing) threads in understanding the post–Cold War North Korean economy argue that North Korea has survived, in these understandings, precisely because it is no longer *in reality* an autarkic, centrally planned command economy.

In one thread, the formal command economy collapsed following the withdrawal of Soviet aid, and parallel economies requiring less coordination by the central state eventually emerged. The specific nature of these economies is up for debate. Habib divides North Korea's economy into five parallel economies: the first, the remnants of the formal command economy; the second, the military economy; the third, the "illicit economy," the largely state-led effort to bring in hard currency through the production and sale of drugs, counterfeit cigarettes, counterfeit money, and the like; the fourth, the "court economy" that provides imported luxury goods to the central state elite; and the fifth, the informal, marketized economy, by which ordinary people unconnected to the state survive.[14] Chung likewise divides the economy into the formal and informal sectors, although he goes further and argues that the party-run "court economy" is in fact specifically designed to put substantial goods and foreign exchange under the control of the supreme leader.[15] In this thread, the fates of the North Korean regime and its people have diverged, with the regime dependent on proceeds generated from the military and party economies, while the population's survival depends on the informal economy and the remnants of the formal economy that still function.

A second thread emphasizes the rise of the informal domestic economy as a coping mechanism to deal with the collapse of the formal economy. After the Public Distribution System ground to a halt during the

Arduous March, and ceased to provide enough food to avoid starvation, and state social control mechanisms loosened up, ordinary North Koreans who survived did so in part by engaging in informal trading, often in markets that sprang up around the country to sell food and consumer goods, and that were run by women (since the men were still required to attend their state-assigned jobs).[16] While the state initially tolerated the markets during the Arduous March because it had little other choice, and officially embraced some aspects of the market in its 2002 reforms,[17] it was deeply uncomfortable with the implications of market activity for social, economic, and political control, and eventually cracked down, beginning with an attempted return to the Public Distribution System in 2005, increasing restrictions on markets and who could use them in 2008 and 2009, and culminating in the November 2009 currency reform that was apparently designed to destroy the assets of *won*-based private traders, and force workers back to their work units.[18] Despite the crackdowns, the markets have not disappeared,[19] and indeed some aspects of the informal economy, such as the level of bribes paid by traders to operate, seem to have remained relatively stable.[20]

The third thread focuses on North Korea's trade, both licit[21] and illicit,[22] with the outside world. North Korea maintains formal trade connections with many countries, although in the years since United Nations and Japanese sanctions took hold following North Korea's first nuclear test in 2006, followed by suspension of the growth in South Korean investment in 2008, the country has found it increasingly difficult to maintain a wide range of these relations.[23] The result is increasing reliance on market-oriented trade relations with China specifically,[24] and dependence on mineral exports (which were not sanctioned, even partially, until 2016).[25] Despite Chinese government encouragement, Chinese companies themselves have been wary of investing in North Korea, and large companies have mostly avoided the country in the absence of a favorable institutional framework for governing trade and protecting investments,[26] and lack of infrastructure in northeastern China, particularly in Yanbian, the ethnic Korean autonomous prefecture bordering North Korea.[27] Yet North Korea appears to be growing its trade even in the face of sanctions.

The threads produce a picture of a North Korean economy that, whatever its formal designation and however it is described by journalists and politicians, has evolved into something that is neither autarkic nor all that centrally planned. One aspect of the often unwilling and largely unplanned changes to the North Korean economy of the past twenty years—North Korea's trade networks—is implicated in all three threads. Both the state and nonstate actors engage in trade, both to export goods to earn hard currency, and to import goods for consumption within North Korea. They are forced by circumstances at different points to become like the other to survive, suggesting that the parallel state and nonstate, formal and informal economies are intertwined: nonstate actors within North Korea must co-opt, avoid, or be subsumed within the state, while state actors outside of North Korea lose (or abandon) most of the privileges they had domestically and face a hostile environment, with governments frequently attempting to hound them out of existence. What would be considered standard business activities in the rest of the world become illegal and questionable precisely because North Koreans are involved, blurring the line between licit and illicit. Furthermore, the trade networks themselves stretch from inside North Korea to the outside world, connecting the domestic economy with the global economy, leading to the question of how isolated North Korea actually is, and the extent to which the networks serve as an entrée into understanding a country that experiences the buffeting wind of globalization in most unusual ways. As such, they may represent the very first, most tentative means by which North Korea (or, more specifically, its population) can be brought, however slowly, into the global community.

Doing Business as North Korea

The argument of this book is simply this: while North Korea overall remains a disaster in all dimensions—socially, economically, and politically—both for its own population and for the region, North Korean trade networks have been surprisingly effective. What follows is not a paean to the brilliance of North Korean economic planning. Rather, by effective, I mean nothing but that at the basest level North Korean trade networks have been able to continue operating despite the ever-shifting roadblocks put in their way, both inside of North Korea and outside it, and are able to raise income and acquire goods to support the people involved in the networks. Indeed, the networks have shown surprising resilience despite (or perhaps because of) their ambivalent reception by the North Korean central state, and throughout the fraught relationship between North Korea and the rest of the world. For many average North Koreans, trade allows them to survive, or even to acquire lifestyles that the state is unable to provide. For the North Korean state, trade networks are partially responsible for keeping elites in power. Certainly trade is not the only arrow in the Kim dynasty's quiver: aside from diplomatic maneuvering, domestically, North Korea maintains a personality cult around whichever Kim is in power, and a totalizing, if frayed, ideological system that prevents organized political opposition from arising. The Kim dynasty has also traditionally played the military, the civilian government, and the Korean Workers Party off each other, preventing any faction from overwhelming the others.[28] Nonetheless, the fruits of trade, and the economic opportunities that trade presents, allow the Kim dynasty to pay off elites for their support.

Moreover, the effectiveness of North Korea's trade networks does not depend on them playing a particularly large role in North Korea's overall economy. It is true that formal trade probably represents only a small part of North Korea's formal economy, and trade of all kinds—licit or illicit—no doubt represents only a small part of North Korea's overall formal and informal economies; but trade networks are qualitatively different from other forms of economic activity in North Korea precisely because they are required by their very nature eventually to interact with non–North Koreans. As such, they form the lion's share of both the North Korean state and North Korean citizens' interaction with the outside world. Trade, in other words, is how a politically isolated country deals with other countries.

What explains the effectiveness of North Korean trade networks? At the most basic level, North Korean trade networks are ruthlessly pragmatic and adaptable, operating with something approaching Darwinian economic logic, as if their survival is at stake, because it often is. Many of the explanations for North Korea's political survival revolve around showing the pragmatism and clear-headedness of North Korean elites: however outrageous their outward-facing behavior, however bizarre their personality cults, however isolated from the outside world, when it comes to maintaining their own survival, they are able to discern how best to survive (either through playing foreign powers off each other, or by oppressing their own population) and to put those plans into action.[29] Paradoxically, as with political survival, the harsh political and economic environments that North Korean enterprises experience both overseas and within North

Korea encourage pragmatism, as ideological trappings are stripped away. As in nuclear brinkmanship, in trade networks, North Koreans have become adept at navigating hostile conditions not under their control.

What drives this pragmatism, and why does it work (relatively) well? North Koreans have by and large been forced by their circumstances to become entrepreneurial, although the form of that entrepreneurialism varies by the relationships among actors, trade networks, and the North Korean state. From the 1970s onward, North Korean officials posted overseas were expected both to provide for both themselves and the regime back home, by whatever means necessary, while, from the 1980s, state companies received permits to engage in foreign trade. In the face of the famine and the collapse of the formal economy in the 1990s and early 2000s, private citizens were also forced to become entrepreneurial in order to survive, leading to the private markets that sprung up across the country. Hybrid trading networks that mixed private agency and state resources in turn emerged from state and private entrepreneurialism by providing goods for the private market through the cooptation of state actors. State entities themselves have also become hybrid entrepreneurs as they have been forced to provide for themselves and the state, and as state officials have used their positions to engage in creative private income generation even as the formal economy broke down.

When they operate between North Korea and overseas, these entrepreneurial North Korean trade networks take advantage of local support systems. For private, hybrid, and state networks alike, these systems are built up in part by taking advantage of relationships up and down the North Korean state apparatus, and using local social and ethnic ties, such as those with South Koreans and ethnic Koreans in China, that stretch across political cleavages. For central state–driven trade networks, much official trade is done through multifunctional diplomatic outposts, state-owned company branches, and the like, and through the strategic use of state prerogatives (although these advantages are gradually being stripped away) and of foreign and North Korean brokers who are able to navigate the logistics of international trade. In both cases, North Koreans prefer to establish long-term trading relationships if at all possible. Yet at the same time, the networks are responsive to changing business environments. They are highly risk-acceptant, and have become experts at operating in the blurred zones between licit and illicit, or between formal and informal trade, at least as defined by the outside world. They are adept at identifying and operating in jurisdictions that provide a combination of technological development, logistical connections, market and nonmarket ties to foreign trade networks, and friendly (or at least neutral) political and legal environments. They have also been willing (and in some cases forced) to shed many of the trappings of the state and become like commercial enterprises as a means of surviving. The networks are opportunistic, with a willingness to engage in a series of one-off trades across a diverse range of goods and services, using a variety of trading relationships and serving different market niches, with anyone willing to do business with them.

In essence, these networks are a result of the decentralization of economic activity that took place during and after the Arduous March. Since the Arduous March, more people in and from North Korea are capturing value in more locations along different sections of trade networks as they move within North Korea, and as they stretch from North Korea to the outside world. While the central state can shape the contours of the trade—by selectively cracking down on or ignoring market activity in North Korea, and by giving out licenses for formally permitted trade overseas—and can profit from trade through imported goods, bribes, taxes, fees, and loyalty payments up the food chain, the extent to which it actually controls what happens on the ground to any but the most centrally directed networks is unclear.

Blurring the Lines

North Korean trade networks are not uniquely creative or adaptable. Many transnational organizations, such as Western multinationals like Apple, Google, and Siemens, are flexible and resourceful in reinventing themselves, crafting new strategies, and arbitraging different jurisdictions in order to maximize profitability, minimize tax liability, make their supply chains more efficient, and obtain access to new markets. Yet unlike Western (or even Chinese) multinationals, North Korean trade networks have adapted to operate in business environments that are not only ambiguous and fraught with economic and political risk, but often outright hostile to their activities and existence. The manner in which North Koreans do business confounds definitions and expectations about what "normal" economic integration is, in large part by blurring the boundary lines for defining actors and the nature of economic activities. State actors become like nonstate actors, and vice versa, and new actors arise that call into question the boundary between state and nonstate. Activities change from licit to illicit and back again, and to the extent that the formal institutions in North Korea work at all, it is because of informal economic activities and informal (if semi-institutionalized) relationships.

This can be seen when we look at the variety of economic actors operating from North Korea. The actors within the North Korean trade community can be categorized by the scale of their business operations, the sophistication of their transactions, and the nature of their relationships with the North Korean state and with each other. At the peak are the trading companies of the central state—the highest levels of the military, party, and cabinet, and the agencies, such as Offices 38 and 39, specifically tasked with exporting weapons, natural resources, and mundane goods for foreign currency, and importing luxury goods, consumer items, and components for weapons programs to support the top echelon of North Korean society.[30] Next are state-owned entities with trading licenses. State entities must fend for themselves, or more specifically, they must engage in profit-making enterprises that can both support themselves and provide revenue to the central state. The result is that state-associated organizations (that is, party, state, and military organizational units) often have subordinated trading corporations that can be quite entrepreneurial and use state connections to make money through anything sellable. Some can export resources, build partnerships with foreign investors, or establish enterprises outside of North Korea, subject to the central state's power to grant licenses to do business overseas.[31] Others can rent out to private actors the legal ability to engage in foreign trade.[32]

At the bottom, furthest from the central state, are private traders (mostly women) who do business in North Korean *won* in the informal markets that have sprung up as survival mechanisms in the North Korean countryside.[33] Aside from bribes to local officials when necessary, they probably have little connection to the state. Larger private traders who do business in hard currencies, such as Chinese *yuan*, US dollars, or euros, and who may actually provide the link between local markets and foreign buyers and suppliers (especially in China), may have to pay more substantial bribes to, and establish relationships with, local and mid-level officials to operate.[34]

In the middle are what might be called hybrid traders: actual state officials who use their position to go into business for themselves, and private traders with more substantive connections to state institutions, either because they have formed networks with local officials seeking rents in exchange for permission to operate and access to certain state resources, or because they have bought their way to state status. These hybrid traders may formally be state entities, but often act as if they were privately owned, thus using both state prerogatives and private sector flexibility to their advantage.[35]

North Korean trading networks adapt to changes in the political and economic conditions they face by changing their locations (thus perhaps changing the conditions), switching the goods they trade, and changing how the networks are controlled and coordinated, with whom they interact, and the manner in which connections with the outside world are established and maintained. The specific strategies that North Korean trade networks adopt depend in part on their access to state prerogatives and resources—diplomatic outposts (and diplomatic immunity), trading licenses, shipping companies, and the like—which serve as both a blessing and a curse to networks. State prerogatives and resources allow trading networks to operate across a wider span of the globe, as they use diplomatic outposts and state trading company branches as launch pads for trade, and allow the central state to capture more value further from North Korea. Networks with access to state prerogatives also likely face a friendlier, somewhat more stable institutional environment inside of North Korea.

At the same time, state-associated assets draw the unwanted attention of sanctions enforcers, even when transactions are otherwise licit, potentially limiting their usefulness. Networks that are overly reliant on overseas state assets may also be limited in where they can operate by where North Korean outposts are. Paradoxically, it may be the private trade and hybrid networks—those with minimal access to the North Korean state—that are most creative in establishing ties with the global economy, even if they themselves are located closer to North Korea.

Given the complex relationships between the state and traders in North Korea, it is less useful to ask whether a trade network emanating from North Korea is "state"—or "nonstate"—centric, or formal versus informal, than to look at how state institutions at various levels are involved as actors, what their role is in the governance of the network, and how they are involved in setting the institutional environment in which the network is operating. As state entities are set adrift to survive on their own, or adopt private commercial forms and methods to evade scrutiny, and hybrid traders are often state-owned in name only, the difference between state and nonstate commerce emerging from North Korea is blurred. The North Korean state (at all levels) is not only—through its state-owned enterprises—an economic actor, but also sets the rules under which all North Korean economic actors operate, as well as creates many of the structures that control North Korean economic networks, both inside and outside of North Korea. The actual ground rules, enforced through both formal institutions and informal networks and understandings, are often unrelated to what the law says. The result is that the North Korean state and North Korean state officials depend on activities that are technically illegal even within North Korea. Moreover, to the extent that North Korean state actors are able to operate outside of North Korea, they are often able to do so by shedding the forms of state institutions, giving up access to state assets, and taking on the appearance and behavior of private companies. It may as a result be more useful to think of trade networks less as state or nonstate actors, and more in terms of their access to state prerogatives, resources, and political favor.

The distinction between licit and illicit trade is also blurred. While geographers generally assume that global economic networks are composed of legitimate firms engaging in legitimate production, with much of the empirical literature being focused on legitimate industries (such as automobiles and textiles), there is nothing per se that prohibits the basics of analytical frameworks from being applied to "illicit" industries.[36] Licit and illicit economic activities are not only not mutually exclusive, but have little meaning to a state like North Korea, which after all denies the fundamental legitimacy of much of the international system. Conceptually, many studies of the North Korean economy (or, more generally, studies of North Korea's survival strategies and assessments of the threat North Korea may or may not pose) separate North Korea's extramural activities into legitimate and illicit categories.[37] Many North Korean smuggling and money laundering activities are, after all, considered "illicit" because of sanctions and because North Koreans are involved, not because of any quality inherent to the activities themselves, and would likely be considered "legitimate" in most other contexts. "Illicit" ' activities can be accounted for not by categorizing any particular good or activity as "illicit" or "licit" but by varying the institutional hostility to networks' activities as goods, people, and information move from one place to another. "Illicit" activities would necessarily face markedly more hostile state attention (outside, and occasionally inside North Korea), restrictive regulations, and even active attempts to shut them down. "Licit" North Korean trade, on the other hand, may still face obstacles outside of North Korea due to the stigma of sanctions and the inability of many North Korean firms to access international financing.

All of this blurring has consequences for trade. As with North Korea's skillful diplomatic brinksmanship, North Koreans engaged in business are adept at maneuvering within hostile environments not of their making or choosing. The antagonistic environment outside North Korea, and the uncertain environment inside North Korea, force North Korean trade networks to be adaptable and follow a ruthless economic logic. Yet while North Koreans operate with legal ambiguity, find ways to take advantage of their terrible situation, and are comfortable with informality, those on the outside looking in experience North Korea as an unpredictable business environment rife with semiformalized corruption and capriciousness, making North Korea an unattractive prospect for many foreign investors, and sabotaging the formal domestic economy.

North Korea in Context

North Korea is not the only Cold War communist holdover to have survived, although it chose perhaps the strangest path. Some countries saw the writing on the wall early on as their command economies reached their logical endpoint of stagnation and decrepitude: China began reforming and opening up in 1979, and Vietnam its own similar *doi moi* in 1986. Their economic reforms, and the growth they led to, combined with a continued willingness to crush political dissent, allowed them to survive and prosper well into the twenty-first century.

Others had their own period of deprivation and muddled through via a combination of grudging reform, self-help, opening up, and finding new patrons. Cuba lost Soviet aid with the collapse of the Soviet Union just as North Korea did. As with North Korea, Cuba also went through what it called a "Special Period" from 1990 to 1995, in which caloric intake declined substantially, agricultural output dropped (as Cuba was cut off from the Communist Bloc's provision of fertilizer), and industry and transportation virtually ground to a halt because of a lack of fuel and thus electricity.[38] Cuba's response, as with North Korea, was to attempt to mentally prepare its population for deprivation, and the society that had become used to subsisting on subsidies from sympathetic countries was forced to transform dramatically. Organic agriculture replaced fertilizer-driven industrial agriculture, and sugar fields were shifted to production of fruits and vegetables. Cuba also turned to cultivation of a fairly substantial tourist industry as a means of attracting foreign currency, and began opening up its economy (very tentatively) to private enterprises and informal entrepreneurship. Conveniently, with the election of Hugo Chavez as president of Venezuela in 1998, Cuba was also able to receive oil shipments in exchange for supplying doctors to Venezuela.[39]

While North Korea accepted aid from other countries (eventually), the government officially refused to even consider "reform and opening up,"[40] because of its climate had little ability to make a Cuban-style shift to sustainable agriculture and sun-drenched tourism, and for its part adopted a strategy that seemed almost designed to alienate allies and further isolate itself politically from the rest of the world. Instead, the way in which it survived can be seen in part as the growth and eventual dominance of economic networks that shared some similarities with other transition economies.

While North Korea is often thought of by casual observers as sui generis—a bizarre country where ersatz Disney characters dance for a laughing, pudgy dictator—it has a great deal in common with many other countries that double as economic disaster zones, particularly other socialist command economies. Much like North Korea, the economies of Cold War–era socialist countries in Eastern Europe, whatever their conceits, depended on "second economies," the black and gray markets that served as the safety valves for the rank inefficiencies and hypocrisies of the formal state economy. Participation in the second economies allowed regular citizens to acquire food and consumer goods they needed through barter and other commerce in black and gray markets, bring in hard currency, and cut through choking bureaucracy with bribes. They also allowed the formal command economy to limp along without bringing the whole country down with it.[41]

Hungary, for instance, developed a strong second economy with private actors, and public actors involved in private business (with a mix of formal regulations and informal understandings).[42] While Hungary's communist bureaucracy legalized aspects of the second economy as a remedial measure for the failures of the formal economy, state firms found it easiest to subcontract business to their own workers and organizations, in effect creating hybrid networks and siphoning off time and workers from the formal economy.[43] As will be seen, North Korea was no different in this regard: informal markets already existed in some respects in the 1980s, and the Arduous March forced a large portion of the population to create and participate in an even more expansive second economy with both private and hybrid networks as the formal economy ground to a halt.

What separated North Korea from other communist states, and even other transition economies, was the extent to which the parts of the overall economy that allowed North Korea to survive were based on foreign trade. While other communist countries' second economies were partially or even mostly illegal (and thus informal), they were also primarily domestic in nature. Even before the end of the Cold War, North Korean state trading companies and diplomats abroad, freed from the shackles of the planned economy within the country, roamed the globe looking for trading opportunities and were surprisingly cognizant of how to take advantage of the global economy created by capitalism. Private and hybrid actors who arose during the 1990s and early 2000s also often survived by engaging in trade with other countries, notably China. Unlike Cold War–era Soviet and Eastern European second economies, North Korea's second economy, in essence, was both internationally oriented and came of age in a time when post–Cold War globalization was the driving force in both political and economic change.

Because informal and formal, state and nonstate, licit and illicit lines are blurred in how North Korea taps into the global economy, the nature of much of North Korea's engagement is not picked up by trade statistics or accounts that rely on traditional understandings of international trade.[44] North Korean economic engagement with the outside world does not operate in a manner familiar to many Western observers. Recorded, formal North Korean trade is not large in absolute terms: according to an estimate by South Korea's Bank of Korea, North Korea's 2012 real GDP was approximately US$23 billion, with external trade (including trade with both South Korea and the rest of world) amounting to a little less than

US$9 billion. Trade is approximately equal to 40 percent of North Korean GDP, which is on the low end of trade dependency among the world's nations, but does not per se make North Korea an unusually isolated country.[45] Yet a key thread in this book is to ask how large the numbers need to be for the trade networks to be effective. Regular citizens and even state entities engage in trade as a means of survival, navigating within the environment imposed by the central state. The central state engages in trade to keep itself in power, doling out benefits (both luxury goods and economic opportunities) to elites in exchange for their support, and bringing in the material it needs for its military projects. The absolute numbers needed may not be huge; the trade networks are effective because they allow their participants to survive (and perhaps even prosper), and because they are able to adapt under changing, challenging conditions.

Outside of North Korea, North Korean businesses face (in a very general sense) the same environment as everyone else, but the ways in which they choose to operate, and the forms they adopt, challenge the conventional wisdom about the paths to integration in the global economy, and more generally, our thinking about the way the global economy works in fact, if not in theory. In this, delving into North Korea's experience with the global economy contributes to our understanding of what might be called "exotic" economic globalization, where the actors are not simply state and transnational corporations, and where trade does not only consist of movements of legitimate labor, goods, money, and information between formal actors. The "illicit" aspects of economic globalization are often ignored or moved into their own discrete category.[46] Transnational criminal organizations' structure and behavior are likened to transnational corporations, with criminals seen as violent entrepreneurs operating in differently regulated environments.[47] Yet North Korean trading networks' operations extend to both licit and illicit activities, often with the same entities engaged in both at the same time, depending on the relative costs and benefits.[48] State regulations are often assumed to be designed to bring in business, or at least encourage certain types of economic development.[49] Yet North Korean trade networks, even the ones engaged in legitimate commerce, often operate in a deeply uncertain regulatory environment, or even, outside of North Korea, environments designed to discourage them from operating at all. Not all North Korean traders are attempting to engage in what the outside world calls "illicit trade," but given the stigma associated with

North Korea, particularly since 2006, whether what they are doing is "illicit" or not may not have a strong effect on the conditions they face. Even the separation between state and nonstate globalized economic actors is not so clear, inasmuch as North Korean state-owned enterprises, formally very similar to state companies in other socialist and transitional economies, often operate effectively as private or hybrid businesses.

North Korea is not the only country where we can see the ability of trade, particularly illicit trade, to integrate people who would otherwise be disconnected into the global economy: poppy farmers in Afghanistan are connected to global trade even if they never leave their village.[50] Nor is North Korea's political economy the only one where state actors and private actors, licit and illicit trade, blur together: the Bosnian war saw the rise of a wartime economy in Sarajevo that made trading bedfellows of local thugs, United Nations officials, and Bosnian and Serbian politicians.[51] But it is rare to see so many aspects of "exotic" economic globalization wrapped up in one country, particularly one that is generally thought not to be very globalized at all. Here is where the value of studying the surprising effectiveness of North Korean trade networks lies.

Tracing the Trade Networks

The book examines what North Korea, and North Koreans, are doing economically between North Korea and the rest of the world, and *outside* of North Korea. The four main chapters trace the evolution, structure, and operation of North Korean trade networks over two periods in time: between the end of the Cold War and 2005, and since 2005. The two time periods represent a relatively sharp break in the institutional environment faced by North Korean trade networks, allowing for a comparison of their structure and behavior in response to changes in the ability or desire of the state to stop or encourage trade within North Korea and between North Korea and the rest of the world; the relationship between the state and international trade; and attitudes of the rest of the world toward North Korean trade.

North Korea's modern trade networks began developing in the early 1990s, soon after the collapse of the Soviet Union in 1991, when the North Korean famines were at their height, the Public Distribution System for food broke down, North Korean state entities became increasingly enterprising in using trade to survive (and fulfill central state financial mandates), and illicit, informal networks sprung up within North Korea, and between North Korea and China to provide ways for North Korean private citizens to obtain food and hard currency. Chapter 1 covers networks' growth during this Arduous March, an event that brought North Korea to the brink of collapse, fundamentally rearranged the relationship between the North Korean state and the population, and between both and the outside world, and laid the groundwork for the trade networks that emerged later. The central state had no choice but to engage in foreign commerce, and to tolerate private commerce inside of North Korea. Yet while North Korea's formal economy collapsed, it faced a relatively benign international environment for trade. While the United States and South Korea maintained some sanctions, with the Cold War over, North Korea was theoretically able to trade with almost every other country in the world.

I then lay out the structure of North Korea's economic integration with the outside world during the long, slow recovery from the Arduous March, from 2005 until the present, during which time the North Korean state attempted to reinstate the Public Distribution System (and thus the expectation that citizens would obtain food solely from the state), seemingly pulled back from some state-centered illicit trade in favor of less contentious trade, attempted to dismantle private markets, and cracked down on illegal border crossings,[52] before finally grudgingly acquiescing to the continued existence of a semiformal private sector intertwined with corrupt state officials and entities.[53] Chapters 2, 3, and 4 focus on how trade and the realities of North Korean economic survival have influenced the structure and behavior of networks with different types of relationships with the North Korean state (or more specifically, with different levels of access to North Korean state resources), ranging from state-centered networks to hybrid and private traders, and how they have in turn influenced North Korean political and economic development, such as it is. Following North Korea's nuclear test in 2006, the increasingly harsh financial and trade sanctions regime put into place have created a hostile climate for North Korean trade, particularly outside of China, allowing us to see how the country's networks have adapted compared to the relatively open environment of the 1990s.

North Korea's top-down state trade networks have adapted in their own way to hostility. Chapter 2 discusses the state agencies whose job it is to raise money directly for the central state and to bring in the goods the central state depends on for political support. They are the most tightly controlled in North Korea, and make the full use of the panoply of North Korean state resources. This results in geographically far-flung operations and relatively well-resourced support structures but also forces the networks to bear the full force of economic sanctions. While much of North Korean state trade depends on China, often it only passes through China on the way to and from other destinations, and North Korea is clearly attempting to diversify away from dependence on Chinese trade. State trade networks have also responded to hostility by adapting their product offerings, moving toward commercial, nonstate forms and methods, making creative use of brokers, and if anything integrating themselves more deeply into global trade. I focus particularly on the import of nuclear components and dual-use goods, and the export of weapons, among the few goods that remain exclusively the province of North Korean state trading networks.

A culture of entrepreneurialism has sprung up in the "new" North Korea, a development I cover in chapter 3. Largely deprived of access to state prerogatives, private trade networks are small in scale (although growing) and geographically concentrated in North Korean border areas and northeastern China. These networks serve as the link between the private markets within North Korea and the outside world, and make use of social and ethnic ties in China in more creative ways than many of the state-owned enterprises. The chapter also looks at those caught in the middle: hybrid networks that have a more complex relationship with the North Korean state. Low and even mid-ranking officials of state organizations have been left to fend for themselves, and they often function essentially as private traders, using their positions and connections to make money, sometimes setting off into China, sometimes attempting to bring in foreign investment, and sometimes extracting rents in creative ways. Actual private traders can also buy a legal status and even positions and ranks within state organizations, and set off on their own, leading to a curious combination of corruption and entrepreneurialism. The state indirectly profits off both through a food chain that has developed in North Korea wherein different levels of the North Korean state are encouraged to become both entrepreneurial and predatory, resulting in a business culture that is at once informal and relatively institutionalized in its push for private citizens and state officials alike to be enterprising. Both private and hybrid economic actors are implicated in two illustrative types of trade networks emanating from North Korea: those engaged in drug trafficking, and those that run North Korean restaurants outside of North Korea.

In the subsequent chapter, I examine a seeming paradox within a paradox. Despite the (relative) success of North Korea's trade activities in bringing in hard currency and sustaining the regime and the population, foreign companies that have invested in North Korea have often come to tears. The foreign companies who survive do so by investing in operations with low capital costs, adapting the nature of their business and transactions to North Korea's institutional environment, building social networks to mitigate risk and provide opportunities, and minimizing their footprint inside of North Korea. The contrast between North Korea's entrepreneurialism and foreign trade and its encounters with foreign investors inside of North Korea is a product of the very qualities that have made North Korean trade networks relatively successful. Comfortable as they are dealing with ambiguity, showing as they do both flexibility and creativity in extracting money from terrible situations, straddling the line between state and nonstate, formal and informal, all of these things work well for North Koreans dealing with a harsh environment. They work less well for foreign investors, who are at best able only to mimic North Korean networks and practices even as they face confusing investment conditions.

In the final chapter, I close with an examination of what North Korean trade networks may mean for the potential for economic reform, denuclearization, and the future of North Korea. The surprising entrepreneurialism of North Korean trade gives clues as to why the regime has been so intransigent in its nuclear program—it may believe that developing a nuclear weapons program is compatible with trade. The implications of the trade networks' "success" for economic reform or the future of the state are ambiguous. North Korea's trade networks are the primary means by which outside influence enters North Korea, and they are the ones developing experience in business that may serve North Korea in the future.[54] At the same time, the nature of the networks—the manner in which they do business, and the environment to which they are adapted—has created winners who survive apart from the state, and large numbers of people who use the blurred, confusing business environment of North Korea to survive, which does not necessarily portend good things for any formal economic reforms or for the future of North Korea itself.

1

Surviving the Arduous March through Enterprise

The story of the Arduous March and its effect on North Korea's political economy has been recounted in great detail elsewhere,[1] and it is not my intention to repeat the able work done by previous writers. This chapter instead traces the origin and development of North Korean entrepreneurialism, and the underlying trading networks, from North Korea's fumbling attempts at survival during the Cold War through to the collapse of trade and the economy at the end of the Cold War, the famine that followed, the desperate responses of the state and the people of North Korea, and finally to the eve of North Korea's attempted retrenchment in 2005 and the international sanctions in the wake of the 2006 nuclear test.

Survival has always been a priority (and perhaps even the central preoccupation) of the North Korean state and, once they realized that the state would no longer take care of their needs, the North Korean population. *How* to survive is a separate question, and one that has not always been adequately answered by either the state or its citizens. The survival imperative has led to a glimmer of pragmatism in actual North Korean economic behavior, regardless of the rhetoric emanating from official propaganda outlets or even stated policies on the ground within the country. This flexibility in reality, if not in ideology, has not always been successful in keeping the North Korean state strong or much of the population alive (especially during the darkest years of the Arduous March), but it has been apparent in North Korean trade for decades.

The survival mechanisms adopted during the Arduous March did not spring fully formed, as if from the forehead of Zeus, after the Cold War. Both top-down and bottom-up trading networks had origins in the Cold War itself; the end of the Cold War drastically increased the scope and importance of those networks, but they were not wholly new. In turn, the ecosystem of state, nonstate, and hybrid trading networks that have enmeshed North Korea in the global economy (however unwillingly) since the international sanctions regime began in 2006 are outgrowths of the top-down and bottom-up coping mechanisms that began to mature and become semi-institutionalized during the relatively "liberal" years of the Arduous March itself and those that followed. This chapter thus provides the background to how North Korea became the surprisingly enterprising country that it is today.

The business environment that North Korean state enterprises faced in the immediate aftermath of the Cold War was harsh, unforgiving, and (with the collapse of the Soviet Union) something of an uncomfortable surprise, but it was not unfriendly specifically to North Korean trade. North Korean companies faced few major international sanctions, and isolation from global economic networks was an artifact of North Korea's self-imposed hermit status, its terrible credit rating, and a lack of things to sell to the rest of the world. Private trading networks, while officially banned, also faced a relatively benign operating environment, inasmuch as the famine impaired the state's ability to crack down on citizens doing whatever it took to survive. At the same time, both top-down and bottom-up trading networks had to navigate environments that were not entirely friendly: what North Korean state enterprises did sell was often illicit in other countries, such that the trade networks moved from state supported to "criminal" simply by crossing international borders, while nonstate networks had to operate, both inside and outside North Korea, in an environment that was almost entirely informal, politically changeable, and individually capricious.

State entities and private citizens alike eventually responded to such conditions with trading networks that were adaptable and flexible in where and how they operated, but not infinitely so. Their spread depended to a large degree on access and territorial proximity to logistical infrastructure and networks that were themselves integrated with the outside world. Outside of Northeast Asia, North Korean trade network nodes clustered around diplomatic and commercial outposts of the North Korean state, leading to networks that were extensive in territorial scope but not particularly dense. Within Northeast Asia, both top-down and bottom-up trade networks preferred to access outside markets, both for purchasing goods and obtaining capital, through networks of ethnic Korean businesspeople around the region. In practice, this funneled the activities of North Korean trade networks without access to state outposts (and even some with such access) through informal networks in northeastern China, Japan, and to a much lesser extent South Korea.

With its own economic survival of paramount importance (to itself), the North Korean central state attempted to extract as much value as it could from state-centered trading networks. In practice, this meant the central state maintained in-house control over the nodes in the chains stretching from North Korea, and reverted to dealing with outside businesspeople only when extending control further down the chain was untenable (notably when North Koreans were either not allowed to trade in specific goods or in particular locations, or when North Korean state traders did not have their own suppliers or buyers). The brokers at the edge of central state control themselves often preferred to deal with firms with which they had nonmarket (often ethnic) ties, but showed themselves capable of delving into global markets when necessary.

The private citizens who went into business during the Arduous March did not have many of the advantages of state-centered networks, particularly access to state resources and, given that what they were doing was technically illegal, political cover. The trade ties of private networks were in some sense the inverse of those of state-centered networks: private traders used markets to sell their goods, but if they imported goods from outside North Korea, they often relied on family and ethnic ties across the border in China or in Japan. To make up for a lack of dependable access to infrastructure or political cover, private (and hybrid) networks also built up ties with state officials, who themselves were often desperate for ways to survive. It was these networks that would be normalized and even semi-institutionalized by the time the central state attempted to crack down in 2005.

In the sections that follow, I find the origins of both state and nonstate North Korean trade networks in pragmatic strategies adopted by the North Korean state and citizens during the Cold War. After a discussion of the collapse of the North Korean economy and the famine that followed the end of the Cold War, I move on to coping mechanisms taken by different segments of North Korean society as they faced economic collapse and starvation, looking first at top-down coping mechanisms of state trading networks, and then at those adopted by private citizens and networks that operated on the boundary between state and nonstate. The chapter concludes with the end of North Korea's "liberal" period in 2005 and 2006 as the central state began cracking down on wayward enterprise, and as the United States and the international community began to take steps to curb North Korea's international trade.

The Cold War

Among communist leaders during the Cold War, Kim Il-sung was perhaps the keenest student of Joseph Stalin. North Korea not only did not follow along with the Soviet Union's de-Stalinization in the late 1950s, it pressed forward with versions of Stalinist political and economic policies that were, if anything, even more extreme than those advocated by Stalin himself. The cult of personality built for Kim Il-sung was perhaps the most notable example, but economic policies were also highly Stalinist: fertilizer-intensive collectivized agriculture, rapid industrialization, a centralized command economy, and a distribution system that provided nearly all the food for the entire North Korean population continued through the end of the Cold War.[2] Yet, as Stalinist as North Korea was, and as opposed to foreign infiltration as its elites were, even during the Cold War, North Korea was remarkably nimble in its foreign trade. The manner in which it engaged with the global economy (however tentatively) betrayed many of the trading methods that North Korean firms would use after the end of the Cold War. Despite the sharp divide between the relatively comfortable isolation of North Korea before the collapse of the Soviet Union and the disasters of the Arduous March, North Korea's trade behavior was not totally new.

As North Korea fell behind the South beginning in the 1960s, the North began pursuing alternative strategies for supporting itself financially and acquiring the goods it wanted from the outside world. These strategies followed two tracks: one in which North Korea extracted concessions from its allies to support its economy, and a second, hedging, strategy in which North Korea began to build trading networks that could bring in income and goods apart from what it could obtain from China and the Soviet Union.

On the first track, North Korea signed friendship treaties in 1961 with both China and the Soviet Union within weeks of each other, in the midst of the Sino-Soviet split. Thereafter, it played China and the USSR off each other in order to maximize financial benefits, one-sided trade, and technical aid.[3] It was a game that China and the USSR played willingly. North Korea benefited from the willingness of its Communist Bloc allies to provide subsidies as a means of propping up a fellow socialist economy for strategic reasons.[4] Up to the end of the Cold War, in a bid to compete with China for influence, the Soviet Union served as North Korea's primary benefactor, sending technical advisors who helped to keep its power generation and industry functioning, providing fertilizer for North Korea's agricultural sector, and accepting barter payment for exports to North Korea at concessionary rates. In this, the North Korean state displayed the same penchant for walking diplomatic tightropes as it would later display in confrontations with the United States and other adversaries.[5]

North Korea also pursued an economic hedging strategy that was designed to establish trading networks outside Soviet or Chinese control, and to provide income and goods directly to North Korea on its own terms. One of the critical aspects of the strategy was the dual political and economic use of North Korean outposts around the world. In the early 1970s, the North Korean central government began treating its embassies and consulates as revenue centers. Rather than receiving operating funds from the state, diplomatic outposts were required not only to provide for their own costs but also to meet quotas for revenue on a yearly basis and transfer it back to Pyongyang. It was here that many of the characteristics that would distinguish North Korean trade networks in later decades emerged. How North Korean officials met these quotas seems to have been left up to the individual diplomats (or rather the outposts), leaving room for a certain desperate creativity. Not all of the trade conducted by North Korean diplomats was illicit, although enough of it was that North Korea became associated with illicit trading. The diplomats were indifferent to the legality of the goods they were trading in the countries in which they were operating—it was not uncommon for both gray market and black market goods (or the proceeds from their sales) to pass through the same outposts. The year 1976, for instance, saw a spate of North Korean diplomats caught smuggling various contraband. In May, North Korean diplomats were caught by Egyptian authorities while trying to smuggle hashish, but were released on account of their diplomatic status. In October the same year, Danish police expelled the entire North Korean diplomatic staff (four people) after they were caught handing off 147 kilograms of hashish to local drug dealers. They had previously been spotted passing suspicious bags into a shady jewelry store from their official embassy Mercedes. Later that month, Swedish, Norwegian, and Finnish police all broke up North Korean diplomatic smuggling rings. The North Koreans had taken advantage of the price differential of liquor and cigarettes between the Soviet Union and Scandinavian countries to bring in large quantities of goods—four thousand bottles of liquor in Norway, for instance—in their diplomatic luggage for resale.[6]

Interestingly, the drug and liquor smuggling incidents, among others, were cases where North Korean diplomats essentially served as brokers, connecting buyers and sellers, both of whom were outside of North Korea. This had several implications for how North Korea was hooked into the global economy. First, by serving as brokers, North Koreans did not actually need to ship anything out of (or into) North Korea itself, allowing the home country to continue to isolate itself from the global economy even as they used the same economy as a source of income. Second, and paradoxically, because they were connecting other nodes within an often illicit trade network and presumably minimizing risk and search costs for other parties, North Korean "businessmen" of the Cold War both needed relatively extensive prior contacts and built new contacts with the outside world as a result of doing business. The manner in which North Koreans did business, in other words, actually required them to become more integrated into global trade networks than simple trade into and out of North Korea would have.

Beginning in the early 1970s, North Korea also established a number of central state–owned trading companies in Europe and Asia. Zokwang Trading Company was set up in Macau in 1974, and Golden Star Bank, an apparent subsidiary of Daesong Bank in Pyongyang, was established in Austria in 1982. Zokwang and Golden Star did in fact do what they were theoretically supposed to do: serve as a trading outpost and a bank, respectively. Zokwang seems to have served as the main hub outside of North Korea for buying and selling goods around East Asia. Regular Air Koryo flights between Macau and Pyongyang primarily worked to move cargo into and out of North Korea. Golden Star Bank seems to have served as a hub in Europe for North Korea's financial dealings, making deals for goods to be shipped to North Korea, serving as a broker for business deals taking place entirely outside of North Korea, and managing North Korean financial accounts.[7] But North Korean trading entities were also used for political ends: Kim Hyun-hee, one of the North Korean intelligence operatives who bombed Korean Airlines flight 858 in 1987, claimed to have trained for several months in Zokwang's offices in Macau.[8]

North Korea's nuclear weapons program, not coincidentally, also intensified in the 1970s.[9] While all of the usual security and political motivations of the program were clear—North Korea's desire for an effective deterrent against the United States and South Korea, lack of trust in Soviet and Chinese security guarantees, domestic prestige, and the like—what often goes unremarked was the trade connections North Korea had to make outside the Communist Bloc in its bid for the bomb. The Soviet Union built a research reactor for North Korea in 1967, but by the 1980s was insisting that North Korea sign the Non-Proliferation Treaty (NPT) in exchange for further nuclear cooperation and assistance. In December 1985, North Korea did sign the NPT, and within weeks signed an agreement for the Soviet Union to provide it with a nuclear power reactor by 1990, a reactor that never materialized.[10] China, meanwhile, also cooperated with North Korea's nuclear program, but reportedly pulled all technicians and aid in 1987 after it became convinced (not without justification) that North Korea may have had less than peaceful aims for its nuclear program, particularly the Yongbyon research reactor.[11] North Korea, in fact, found itself rebuffed by essentially all of its Communist Bloc allies in its quest for nuclear technology and nuclear weapons.[12]

As a result, North Korea pursued other avenues for acquiring nuclear technology. Within the region, in 1987, it tasked the association of Korean residents of Japan sympathetic to North Korea, Chongryon, with putting together a team of technicians and scientists who would collect nuclear information. The next year, it apparently tried to obtain technical equipment, including vacuum tubes, from Japan.[13] From Europe, five blasting furnaces manufactured by the German company Leybold AG apparently ended up in North Korea in 1987. Although the furnaces may have been reexported from East Germany, or Pakistan or India, Leybold employees were, according to Western intelligence sources, in North Korea between 1987 and 1990.[14] At the same time, Degussa AG, a West German company, sourced zirconium (which is used in manufacturing uranium fuel rods) from the United States, and shipped it to North Korea.[15] Nuclear information originating from the European nuclear research agency Urenco may have also been transferred to North Korea via Pakistan in the 1980s (possibly one of Abdul Qadeer Khan's earlier outings into nuclear proliferation).[16] These networks were, compared to the formal nuclear assistance from Communist Bloc countries, probably minute, but they demonstrated that North Korea was able and willing to build new foreign trade links around the world (with the help of social and ethnic networks such as those in Japan) to further its goals, even before the end of the Cold War.

The networks were not confined to solely state-centered trade; in its own way, North Korea encouraged entrepreneurship relatively early on. After a joint venture law was passed in 1984, North Korea also encouraged joint ventures with foreign companies in a bid to bring in foreign currency. In practice the reluctance of the North Korean state to deal with anyone but other Koreans created an odd situation in which the residents in the best positions to establish joint ventures were ethnic Koreans who were regarded with some suspicion by the rest of society: Korean Chinese, and ethnic Koreans from Japan. Tens of thousands of ethnic Koreans had repatriated to North Korea from Japan in the 1960s and 1970s. Although they were treated poorly (as member of suspect classes), they did bring with them Japanese business sensibilities, Japanese currency, and the promise of more of both from their relatives in Japan. These remittances came not only in the form of consumer goods unheard of among other North Koreans, but also the ability to buy their way (through "donations") to a better status: the right to live in Pyongyang and to obtain better jobs as well as seed money to start private enterprises.[17] They were in a sense some of the first international private entrepreneurs in North Korea.

With the passage of the joint venture law, the North Korean government looked to Chongryon to deliver joint venture investments. Between 1986 and 1992, there were only sixty-five actual investments made, all small and nearly all by Chongryon members.[18] In 1985, ethnic Koreans from Japan and the North Korean government set up the joint venture Rakwon Department Store, which was allowed to accept foreign currency in Pyongyang. Within a few years, most localities had at least one foreign currency–accepting store. Despite some retrenchment, Pyongyang by the early 2000s had twenty to thirty foreign currency shops. The shops were originally set up to cater to ethnic Koreans from Japan who had Japanese yen to spend, but later began targeting Western (and presumably Chinese) shoppers as well. As a result, most of the products came from Western and Japanese sources, and the Rakwon chain in particular was run according to Japanese business sensibilities.[19]

Collapse of the North Korean Economy

The collapse of the North Korean economy in the early 1990s was directly tied to the end of the Cold War and the collapse of formal trade with North Korea's communist partners. In 1990, the Soviet Union diplomatically recognized South Korea, and informed North Korea that, from 1991, North Korea would be required to pay in hard currency for goods, particularly oil and natural gas. Kim Il-sung responded by snubbing Soviet ambassadors and declaring the Soviet Union on par with Western countries in its villainy. The Soviet Union's 1990 shipments of oil amounted to 410,000 metric tons, but dropped to 100,000 metric tons in 1991. After the collapse of the Soviet Union at the end of 1991, Russia demanded that North Korea repay its debts in hard currency, and withdrew its technical advisors from North Korean defense facilities. From 1992, many of the goods that North Korea did export to the former Soviet Union were re-exports of consumer goods it had imported from other countries. Even this trade had collapsed by 1994.[20]

China quickly stepped in to take the place of Russia. It also normalized relations with South Korea in August 1992. Unlike Russia, however,

China rescheduled or effectively cancelled much of the debt owed it by North Korea. China also allowed cross-border trade between North Korea, and Jilin and Liaoning provinces in China. It was trade that would be vital to North Koreans during the hard years of the Arduous March.[21] At the same time, China asked for hard currency in any future trading with North Korea. North Korea was thus thrust rather suddenly into the US-dominated global economy by the very partners that it had previously used to stay isolated from that economy. Despite North Korea's hedging since the 1970s, it was strategically caught off guard by the withdrawal of support from China and Russia, and had little ability to access formal trade networks in a competitive environment with hard currency.

What followed was a disaster. North Korea's agricultural system was based on intensive fertilizer usage and irrigation. Such a system does not work well without fertilizer or electricity, and North Korea had problems providing either to its farms, leading to shortages. These problems were exacerbated by the withdrawal of Soviet technical aid in 1991. China picked up some of the slack, and was soon estimated to be providing approximately three-quarters of North Korea's food and fuel supplies.[22] But even this was not enough. In 1992, the North Korean government began promoting a campaign to eat only two meals a day, on the grounds that three meals were overindulgent and unhealthy.[23] In 1993, China had its own grain shortages, and severely cut supplies. Floods in 1994 and 1995 (particularly in July and August) destroyed much of the country's food crop (as well as many food reserves), and swamped hydroelectric plants. In 1994, the Public Distribution System began breaking down in some rural areas. Droughts in 1996 and 1997 caused many of the remaining hydroelectric plants to cease operating, resulting in electricity shortages that cut off power to sanitation facilities and caused the country's rail system to grind to a halt, which in turn meant that coal could not be transported to the remaining coal-fired plants, and supplies could not be shipped by rail around the country.[24]

While estimates of the number of people who died as a result of the famine during the Arduous March vary widely, it was large enough to cause fundamental changes in North Korean society. Because the Public Distribution System essentially stopped functioning, average citizens and even many government officials and soldiers were forced to find their own food sources, or starve. Because factories and workplaces were unable to

produce anything because of a lack of supplies or electricity, workers remained idle. Those who could afford to leave to look for food or other
sources of income did. Trade became a vital lifeline for private citizens,
state officials, and the state itself.

Top-down Coping Mechanisms

Central state enterprises were better placed than most other entities in
North Korea to cope with the fallout from the Arduous March. The top
officials within these organizations were in no danger of starving, being
among the central elite who did receive what handouts existed from the
Public Distribution System. The officials who were stationed overseas
were not only part of the elite as well, but were long accustomed to providing financially (and one presumes nutritionally) for themselves. The central state enterprises also had the advantage of being able to use North
Korean diplomatic outposts that were pre-positioned in strategic (and not
so strategic) locations around the world. What they did not have was much
of anything to sell.

North Korea's initial lack of foreign currency–earning industries, the
outsized economic and social effects of natural disasters, and the relative
disconnect from the global economy were almost entirely due to the failure
of North Korea's political economic system. As such, how the North Korean state, and North Korean citizens, attempted to cope with the disaster
of the 1990s, in part by dealing economically with the outside world, helps
us understand how North Korean trade networks were positioned once
they did face a harsher external political environment from 2006 onward.

A Relatively Benign Environment

Within North Korea, the institutional environment for central state enterprises, and state-owned enterprises in general, changed markedly with
the onset of the Arduous March. The transfer of funds from the central
state to state agencies to cover operating costs (which would normally be
considered a given for most countries) actually began to flow in reverse,
as state entities were expected to cover their own costs (including providing for their workers), and provide sums to the central state for its own

upkeep. While the practice had been standard for diplomatic outposts since the 1970s, it now spread to enterprises within the country. North Korea thus became one of the few states in the world where nearly all state organizations—not just those involved in revenue collection (for what does that mean in a country that officially lacks private ownership?)—came to function as profit centers. The food, gifts, and luxury goods that were historically handed out by the central state on public holidays to demonstrate the magnanimity of the Kim family disappeared with the onset of the Arduous March, and were replaced by requirements for state entities to provide money and gifts of a specified amount to the Kim family as a demonstration of their loyalty.[25] The central state enterprises that had been explicitly set up to bring in revenue and certain goods (whether military items or luxury goods) from outside continued to be expected to do so.

Outside of North Korea, the country did not only face economic problems in the early 1990s because the country had almost no means to provide the hard currency that China and Russia demanded. The first Korean nuclear crisis stretched from February 1993, when North Korea refused to permit an IAEA inspection team access to two undeclared nuclear facilities in violation of its commitments to the Non-Proliferation Treaty, until October 1994, when the United States and North Korea signed the Agreed Framework. The effects of the tensions during the crisis, which resulted in official IAEA censure of North Korea in April 1993, and United Nations Security Council Resolution 825 in May 1993, were mainly diplomatic. UNSCR 825 did not actually impose any economic sanctions on North Korea, and the trade impact of North Korea's lack of cooperation with the IAEA was (understandable) reluctance by other countries to approve the transfer of nuclear components or technology to North Korea. The brief flicker of hope for an improvement in relations between the two Koreas that had started in 1992, and which included talks on economic cooperation, also faded during the nuclear crisis.

Yet once the nuclear crisis was resolved, while conditions inside of North Korea remained dire (inasmuch as the Arduous March was at its peak), the international conditions for North Korea to engage in foreign trade were probably never better than from 1994 to 2006, when United Nations sanctions were first imposed. Once the Agreed Framework was signed in October 1994, North Korea enjoyed relatively good relations with the United States and Japan (or as good as ties can be when there are no actual formal diplomatic relations) until 2001. The Sunshine Policy that began under South Korea's President Kim Dae-jung in 1998 provided North Korea with unconditional aid from the South, the opening of Kaesong Industrial Complex, and the beginning of tourist trips to Mount Kumgang. While the United States, Japan, and South Korea maintained (sometimes severe) limits on the formal trade that could be done with North Korea, by and large the environment in which North Korea operated did not unduly constrain either its diplomatic or economic operations overseas. What this meant in effect was that the constraints on North Korea's foreign trade behavior during the 1990s were largely domestic.

This is not to say that North Korean state enterprises were entirely unconstrained as they operated overseas. To the extent that state enterprises engaged in trade considered to be illegal (or even just undesirable) in other countries, outside of North Korea they faced hostile regulatory environments that mirrored in many ways the environments faced by private illicit enterprises. Where the enterprises associated with bottom-up coping mechanisms during the Arduous March had to deal with hostility from the state within North Korea, and at best indifference in China, the state-directed foreign trade networks moved from licit status within the North Korea to ambiguous or even illicit status outside of the country, depending on the nature of their activities. Both bottom-up and top-down networks, in other words, passed in and out of legitimacy as they crossed international borders.

At the same time, state enterprises both benefited from and were handicapped by what might be called state prerogatives, which created an operating environment outside of North Korea that was at the same time more permissive and fraught with greater danger. As a sovereign state, North Korea had access to a range of privileges and resources unavailable to private actors, even very large and wealthy ones. North Korean diplomats enjoyed diplomatic immunity and the use of diplomatic pouches to move goods, allowing them to conduct activities with only the threat of interdiction and potentially expulsion hanging over their heads. North Korean state enterprises also benefited from a worldwide network of trading company offices and diplomatic outposts, although the association of the offices with the North Korean state could also serve as a magnet for hostile state attention (particularly once sanctions began to take effect). State-directed trading networks also had access to North Korean state transportation resources, notably shipping companies, the rail network (when it worked), and Air Koryo (though the actual routes flown in the 1990s were few in number). This allowed state enterprises to bypass shipping routes and forgo shipping methods that would force them to go through standard commercial routes and transit points. Yet these state assets faced heightened scrutiny when the political winds were against them, with North Korean–flagged ships taking the brunt of unwanted attention.

In 1999, for instance, I visited the North Korean mission to the United Nations in New York, located in an office tower near the UN, as part of a seminar given by one of the North Korean diplomats stationed there. While the UN mission itself was unlikely to be engaged in business, it does illustrate the tradeoffs North Korea faced in using state assets overseas. The diplomats were highly constrained in their movements—they were not allowed to venture more than twenty-five miles from New York City without prior permission from the US State Department, and, assuming competent and capable US intelligence services, the mission would no doubt have been bugged, and the North Korean personnel placed under routine surveillance. Yet for state enterprises (or even just diplomats making trade contacts), the existence of a diplomatic outpost (or, for that matter, an actual trading company outpost) provided them a preexisting territorial footprint in a country, often geographically quite far from Pyongyang, and enabled them to make local contacts and seek business opportunities, however circumscribed. North Korean state-directed foreign trade essentially already had one of the most basic organizational structures of multinational firms—branch offices—built in. Moreover, not all diplomatic outposts around the world would be as closely monitored as those in the United States, and would be freer in their movements.

Where the Networks Were and How They Were Run

The stage was thus set for how top-down trading networks would attempt to cope with the collapse of the North Korean economy. Where and how North Korean central state enterprises attempted to do business in a bid to survive tells us much about the nature of North Korean foreign trade during the Arduous March. The building blocks for trade that North Korea was left with at end of the Cold War, and the relatively benign foreign environment it faced, made some options for where and how it traded more

viable than others. At the heart of North Korea's dilemma were two con-
tradictory realities: the North Korean state's general trade strategy in the
1990s and into the early 2000s was to structure trade networks so as to retain as much control of the chains moving goods, labor, and profits as possible. In doing so, the North Korean central state could capture as much of
the value derived from the trade as possible.

At the same time, because of North Korea's long-standing economic
isolation, and its previous dependence on the Soviet Union and China
(both of which bordered North Korea), the logistical infrastructure un-
dergirding the supply chains stretching to and from North Korea was
undeveloped. Even when it had products to sell, or goods it wanted to
acquire, North Korea's supply chains often did not extend to distribution
to end users or sourcing from initial sellers. Such was the result of having
attempted to minimize contact with the outside world until 1991. For certain goods, the lack of an in-country distribution network may have been
irrelevant—selling missile components to Iran, or small arms to Yemen,
required only a government-to-government relationship. For consumer
goods, however, North Korean networks had to establish relationships (or
at least make contact with) external distributors in other countries.

These two realities shaped the geography and governance of North
Korean top-down trade networks during the Arduous March in a number of ways. First, relatively quickly after the end of Soviet aid, and the
normalization of Chinese aid (and, indeed, before the worst years of the
Arduous March itself), North Korea expanded into a variety of trade areas
where it had some semblance of an advantage. In an early demonstration of pragmatism, state enterprises showed a willingness to do business
with anyone who would do business with them. North Korea was producing heroin by 1992 and methamphetamines by 1995, with wrappers
for counterfeit cigarettes being imported into North Korea by 1995.[26] The
Pakistan–North Korea nuclear technology-for-missiles deal also apparently began in earnest in 1993.[27] The advantage that North Korea had in
these cases was a willingness to straddle and, often, cross the line between
licit and illicit as defined by other states.

The sponsorship of the state provided an environment in which the
enterprises involved had access both to state-owned production facilities
(and the coercive tools of the state to force people to work for them when
necessary) and to what little logistical infrastructure the North Korean

state owned. This allowed unhindered production within North Korea of whatever goods the state enterprises thought they could sell outside the country. In the case of drug production, for instance, the central state apparently ordered farmers to set aside a certain proportion of their land for poppy cultivation.[28] By 1998, an estimated three thousand to four thousand hectares of land were under cultivation.[29] North Korean heroin developed a reputation as being unusually pure, suggesting if nothing else an attention to detail lacking in many nonstate heroin producers. Methamphetamine (or "ice" in North Korea) production seems to have developed directly from hiccups with heroin production. In the mid-1990s, after the heavy rains that caused the flooding officially (if erroneously) blamed for the Arduous March itself,[30] the North Korean state added two pharmaceutical factories engaged in methamphetamine production in Hamhung, and in Ranam in Chongjin to make up for the loss of the poppies washed away in the floods.[31] Similarly, counterfeit cigarettes in the 1990s and early 2000s were produced at factories in Rajin, North Korea's seaport on its east coast, from which the cigarettes could then be shipped to other countries.[32]

Second, for dealings outside of North Korea, the central state continued to use diplomatic outposts and state trading company branches to do much of its business. The outposts continued to function as before (with even less funding from the state), with their state prerogatives and resources, although as the Communist Bloc countries either threw off communism (in the case of much of Eastern Europe) or simply ceased to exist (in the case of East Germany), North Korean enterprises were forced to operate in less friendly jurisdictions. While North Korean central state enterprises did have a number of business connections dating from the end of the Cold War, in practice many of these connections ceased to be useful (or exist at all) after 1991.

Third, the spread of state-centered trade networks largely followed paths already hewn out by North Korean representatives during the Cold War, although North Korea now needed to move goods out of the country to buyers abroad to make up for the lost income from the Soviet Union, and to pay for the goods it bought from China and Japan. In practice, this meant an uneven distribution of trade: North Korean business deals were concentrated in lands far from Pyongyang that nonetheless hosted North Korean state outposts, within North Korea itself, or in certain areas in Northeast Asia where the North Korean state already had trade ties.

Brokers   Given these initial limitations, state enterprises engaging in foreign trade used brokers with whom they maintained nonmarket relationships as their links to overseas buyers and suppliers. While this channeled
the trade through a few locations (and more specifically, a few people in
those locations), it allowed the enterprises to overcome their lack of distribution networks or access to international markets.

The state often kept its brokers in-house, maximizing the control it
could exercise over at least part of the networks, and territorially concentrating trade around outposts of the state. North Korean cadres working
for state trading enterprises or with diplomatic cover (or both) over a long
period of time acquired experience in dealing with foreigners, built up networks, and demonstrated surprising flexibility in making sure that deals
went through. It was these brokers who, given enough time, were able
to make market contacts (and thus minimize the need for cadres back in
North Korea to do so). In the case of drug trafficking, for example, North
Korean diplomats in Egypt, Moscow, and Berlin were implicated in a
number of trafficking plots between 1995 and 2004. In East Asia, the Chinese government stymied at least three North Korean trafficking incidents
in the period, the first out of the Beijing embassy in July 1994, the second
in Shanghai in January 1995, and the third in Shenyang in February 1999,
in which a consulate employee was attempting to sell several kilograms of
heroin.[33] All were activities that would have been useless unless the diplomats had buyers in mind (or at least thought they could find buyers). Nor
was trade, illicit or otherwise, limited to diplomats. In 2001, an employee
of Zokwang Trading Company gave an interview where he claimed that
the company was mainly involved in exporting ginseng to Asia and clothes
to France and Canada.[34] While these claims of strictly normal trading were
almost certainly false—the director of Zokwang had in 1994 been detained
on suspicion of passing off counterfeit US currency[35]—they do speak to
the role that the branch offices played during the Arduous March as the
brokers between North Korea and the world.

Likewise, North Korean Yun Ho-jin, who had gone to Vienna in 1985
as ambassador to the International Atomic Energy Agency, and who spoke
both German and English, used his time in Vienna not only to serve as the
representative of North Korea to the IAEA during the 1994 nuclear crisis,
but also to make contacts with European suppliers for North Korea's weapons programs.[36] By 2001, Yun was acting as a representative of North Korean

import-export firm Namchongang, and approached Hans Werner-Truppel, the owner of an electronics export firm in Germany, about exporting licit and otherwise unremarkable items such as vacuum pumps. The next year, after successful business dealings, Yun ordered special aluminum alloy tubes from Werner-Truppel, supposedly for use as gas tanks in airplanes built by the Shenyang Aircraft Company in China.[37] Other diplomatic outposts spawned diversified trading firms. In Bangkok, another city with a North Korean diplomatic presence, Kosun Import-Export traded in food, commodities, paper, and clothing, as well as small-scale real estate deals, while Wolmyongsan Progress Joint Venture worked a mine in Kanchanaburi in western Thailand.[38] North Korea attempted to link the nodes in its network itself when possible. Throughout the 1990s, an Air Koryo flight made a weekly trip between Bangkok, Macau, and Pyongyang, although by 2001, the frequency had decreased to monthly.[39]

The state enterprises also relied on private actors with whom they had nonmarket relationships. Chief among these were businesses associated with Chongryon, and more generally, Korean residents of Japan who shared ethnic ties, ideological sympathy, and often familial ties with the DPRK. State enterprises used Korean resident brokers in Japan as distributors for drugs produced in North Korea between the early 1990s and the early 2000s, as agents for the acquisition of dual-use technology and training for North Korea's proliferation programs, and for the acquisition of luxury goods, nearly all of which were bought in Japan before Japanese sanctions kicked in in 2006. A North Korean vessel sunk during a firefight with the Japanese coast guard off the coast of Kyushu in December 2001, for example, was found to have a cell phone that had made a number of calls to a Korean Japanese organized crime figure.[40] Similarly, middlemen who handled the cargo off the *Mangyongbong-92*, the vessel that carried people and goods between North Korea and Niigata until 2006, were ethnically Korean,[41] and members of Chongryon were implicated in a methamphetamine trafficking scheme in February 2000.[42]

Elsewhere, North Korean state agents set up joint ventures with local businessmen in a bid either to sell their wares or acquire goods for the North Korean state. Swiss citizen Jakob Steiger, for instance, was sanctioned by the United States, Japan, and Australia in 2006 for alleged long-standing ties to North Korea's Ryonbong General Trading Corporation (the sanctions reports claimed that his company, Kohas AG, was partly owned by

Ryonbong), although Steiger himself denied the claims, the Swiss government backed up his claims by stating there was no evidence of illegal dealings, and the United States presented no open source evidence of his dealings.[43]

In a move that built on its experience sourcing goods for its own proliferation networks, and took advantage of North Korea's burgeoning understanding of global dual-use supplier networks and the commercial shipping industry, North Korea also provided brokerage services, connecting suppliers and clients (or buyers). These services brought in hard currency, and took advantage of the business links that North Korean diplomats and state enterprise representatives were slowly building up in Asia, Europe, and the Middle East, while minimizing the strain on North Korea's own state-owned logistical networks. The brokerage services could become quite sophisticated. North Koreans Kim Kun-jin and his wife Sun Hui-ri moved to Bratislava in November 2000, registered the company New World Trading Services with the Slovakian government in March 2001, and began living a lavish lifestyle, which lasted until they fled in August 2002 ahead of a Slovakian government investigation. Once ensconced, they began ordering dual-use items suitable for a missile program, and had most of the items sent to Kader Factory for Developed Industries, a member of the Arab Organization for Industrialization, an Egyptian military-owned conglomerate that produces weapons systems. Between 1999 and 2001, according to Bertil Lintner and Steve Stecklow, "Kim ordered more than $10 million worth of products—including chemicals, trucks, pumps, measuring devices, a high-speed camera and heavy vehicle parts—and billed them to Kader. His sources were in China, Russia, Belarus and elsewhere."[44]

Kim and Sun used three North Korean companies—Crocus Group, New World Trading, and Golden Star Trading—registered to the same hotel address in Beijing to order the items (presumably the New World Trading Services in Bratislava was either a "branch" of Beijing-based New World Trading, or the North Koreans had limited imaginations in naming their front companies during this period). The Crocus Group shipped a chemical ingredient for rocket propellant, under a disguised name hidden among standard chemicals on the shipping manifest, to Kader in December 2000, and followed it up with eight tons of a binder chemical for propellants in 2001. Kim also attempted (unsuccessfully) to source chemicals from Singapore, but did successfully order truck chassis that could be used for mobile launch pads. The parts were shipped from the Ukraine to a Cairo construction company and billed to Kader.[45]

Interestingly, it is not clear that any of the parts sent to Egypt came from North Korea. Instead, Kim and Sun's competitive advantage seems to have come in finding suppliers in third countries, ordering goods on behalf of their customers, and obfuscating the route, the parts, or the buyers from investigating authorities. Kim may have been especially useful to Egypt as a broker because he may have already had preexisting social ties with his Egyptian customers—he had worked in the North Korean embassy in Cairo before moving to Bratislava.[46] North Korean state agents' ability to connect parties outside of North Korea would prove useful in dealing with the problems inherent in moving goods into and out of a country with decrepit domestic transportation and trade infrastructure.

Distribution   State enterprises attempted to solve the problem of distribution of goods in several ways. The most straightforward solution was for North Korea to keep the entire distribution network in-house, in the hands of the enterprises that produced and then transported the finished goods to end consumers. In reality, given North Korea's limited contacts with the outside world, the only goods that could be moved in this way were components for chemical, biological, and nuclear weapons, missiles, and small arms, which starkly limited the pool of potential buyers.

None of North Korea's state-to-state business dealings during the Arduous March are particularly well documented, but of those that are known at all, its dealings with Pakistan in the 1990s are probably the least poorly known. The original state-to-state network with Pakistan appears to have been built by exchanges of high-level diplomatic visits in 1993 and 1994.[47] Choe Kwang, the vice chairman of the National Defense Commission, visited Pakistan in November 1995, and finalized an agreement wherein North Korea provided missiles, missile components, and training in missile manufacture.[48] North Korea began delivering the missiles and components to Pakistan in 1996 through Changgwang Sinyong Corporation, a central state–owned company that was at least controlled by the Korean Mining and Development Corporation (KOMID).[49]

What the Pakistani government actually gave North Korea in exchange for the missile cooperation is murky: the government officials involved in the initial deal claimed that they paid cash only for what North Korea gave

them, while other analysts conclude that the Pakistani government provided North Korea with nuclear technology, or at the very least, that government officials knew about Abdul Qadeer Khan's shipments of nuclear
components and information to North Korea, such as when he transported
crates containing P-1 and P-2 centrifuges on a Shaheen Air International
flight to Pyongyang in 1998.[50] Whatever Pakistan's role, North Korea,
for its part, seems to have relied at least in part on state-owned shipping
companies that continued to follow standard commercial shipping routes,
thus (in theory) maximizing its control over the supply chain, minimizing
transport costs, and mitigating concerns about interdiction (although we
know that North Korea was using its own ships largely because of incidents where they *were* interdicted). In March 1996, the North Korean ship
Chon Sung was intercepted in Taiwan with fifteen tons of rocket propellant, apparently bound for Pakistan.[51] Three years later, in June 1999, the
North Korean ship *MV Ku Wol San* was intercepted by the Indian Navy
off Kandla on the way to (apparently) Karachi with 177 tons of missile
components and documents for missile manufacturing. The consignment
form claimed the ship was carrying sugar and water purification equipment bound for Malta.[52]

As with the brokerage services offered to other countries, not all of what
North Korea provided to Pakistan came directly from North Korea. Kang
Thae-yun was assigned to manage the Pakistan–North Korea logistical relationship as the Pakistan-based representative of Changgwang Sinyong,
from 1996 until at least 1998, when Kim Sa-nae, a woman identified as
Kang's wife, was murdered under mysterious circumstances in Pakistan.[53]
In support of the Pakistani program, Kang acted as a broker for Pakistan
to acquire components from third countries, thus minimizing the need to
transport anything to or from North Korea itself. In 1997, Kang apparently brokered two deals for maraging steel to be supplied to Pakistan (or
at least through Pakistan), the first from the United Kingdom (where the
shipment was intercepted by customs officials), and the second from the
All-Russian Institute of Light Alloys in Moscow.[54] The next year, Kang
was apparently involved in discussions with a Russian company to provide mass spectrometers to Tabani Corporation in Pakistan.[55] Likewise,
when the *Ku Wol San* was searched, it contained many components that
had originally been sourced from Japan.[56]

North Korea's shipments to Pakistan were not the only use of state transport resources. North Korea's drug trafficking networks also saw North Korean merchant vessels take drug shipments directly to neighboring countries along legitimate commercial shipping routes. The North Korean cargo ship *Mangyongbong-92*, for instance, reportedly carried drugs from Wonsan in North Korea on a regular basis in the late 1990s to Korean Japanese criminal syndicates.[57] There were also documented cases of drugs entering China and Russia by land across the North Korean border by putative employees of North Korean state entities. In February 1995, for instance, two employees of a North Korean state logging company were arrested in Vladivostok, Russia, near the North Korean border with eight kilograms of heroin.[58]

Inasmuch as they were operating in an environment (within North Korea) that was quite favorable, state enterprises also avoided many of the problems associated with moving goods through hostile territory by bringing their business partners to North Korea itself. State enterprises invited businessmen with experience in drug production and trafficking to North Korea to discuss potential business deals, as occurred with Taiwanese gangsters in 2003.[59] In the case of those from the Golden Triangle, experts were brought in as consultants to improve North Korea's heroin and opium production.[60] North Korea's proliferation networks also took advantage of the ability to have their buyers (and suppliers) come to them, minimizing their need to transport goods themselves outside of North Korea. At the height of Pakistan–North Korea military cooperation in the late 1990s and early 2000s, there were at least nine flights per month (by January 1998) on Pakistani Air Force C-130 planes. It is unclear what Pakistan brought to North Korea, but the planes coming back from North Korea were apparently at least sometimes stocked with missile parts, allowing North Korean enterprises to cut out the logistical middlemen.[61] It was also a (presumably chartered) Shaheen Air International (a company owned by high-ranking Pakistani officials) flight that brought the centrifuges sold by AQ Khan to North Korea in 1998.[62]

In a move that prefigured how state trading networks would later adapt to sanctions, state enterprises also solved the distribution problem by providing the first step, in moving goods from North Korea, or providing the last step in moving goods into the country, and letting their business partners handle the logistics associated with moving the goods past the vicinity of North Korean territory. The linkages outside of North Korea between the North Korean state entities and the onward nodes in the networks seem to have been built to a large extent on relational ties of various sorts, including ethnic connections, and proximity to long-standing branch offices. In the case of drugs, for instance, North Korean military, fishing, and cargo vessels would often leave port in North Korea (often from Nampo in the southwest or Rajin in the northeast), and meet with criminal middlemen in North Korean territorial waters or the territorial waters of neighboring states.[63] The middlemen were themselves members of crime syndicates in South Korea, Japan, and Taiwan who would take delivery of the drugs at sea in their own vessels, return to their home countries, and then distribute them to retailers. The result was a network with little territorial spread by the North Koreans themselves, but a fairly robust ability to transport and the distribute drugs within the destination countries. In June 2002, for instance, the Taiwanese fishing vessel *Shun Chi Fa* travelled to North Korean waters, where it received 174 pounds' worth of heroin bricks from sailors on a North Korean gunboat before returning to Taiwan.[64]

Yet North Korean enterprises did not neglect licit distribution networks when they were dealing in goods that were not per se illicit outside of North Korea. Indeed, it is in these networks (particularly those dedicated to proliferation) that we can see the initial movements of North Korean state enterprises into the formal global economy, even though the goods they were buying straddled the border between licit and illicit. After Yun Ho-jin made the 2002 deal for the special tubes with Werner-Truppel, the German ordered the tubes from a German gross steel provider, Jakob Bek Gmbh, which had in turn sourced them from the German subsidiary of British Aluminium Tubes, Ltd. While the initial shipment of 214 tubes arrived in Germany in September 2002, the German government refused Werner-Truppel permission to export them. Nevertheless, Werner-Truppel contracted with Delta-Trading Gmbh to ship the tubes from Hamburg to Dalian (and ostensibly Shenyang Aircraft Corporation) in April 2003 on the French ship *Ville de Virgo*. The ship was interdicted in the Suez Canal.[65] The North Koreans' role was thus confined to finding a European broker (which required time and some level of knowledge about European dual-use suppliers) and moving the goods from arrival in Dalian back to North Korea.

State enterprises also made use of suppliers and distributors in East Asia, contacting local brokers with which they maintained nonmarket relationships, and relying on those brokers to move the goods to North Korea through commercial shipping routes, or at least to a point where North Korean state-owned transportation could complete the supply chain. Meishin, a Japanese company owned by a North Korean resident of Japan (that is, a Chongryon member) initially attempted to ship specialized power supply devices in 2002 directly from Japan to North Korea. When they were unable to do so without documentation, they shipped the devices to Loxley Pacific, a Thai communications company, which would presumably have forwarded them on to Daesong General Trading Company, a central state entity, in North Korea. The devices were intercepted in Hong Kong, indicating the company used Hong Kong as a transshipment point.[66] In another incident in 2002, a North Korean trading company approached the North Korean Japanese resident Kim Young-gun, the president of Meisho Yoko, with an order for a dual-use freeze dryer (purportedly for use by Pyonghwa lab, a pharmaceutical lab in Pyongyang). The North Korean contact of Meisho Yoko was in turn placing the order for a subsidiary of an unnamed North Korean central state trading company.[67] Kim then contacted a Taiwanese trading firm, which ordered the dryer from Seishin Soiji, which in turn shipped the dryer from Yokohama to Taiwan (where it was interdicted).[68] In both incidents, North Korean state enterprises minimized their exposure to the complexities of international trade by relying on brokers, and used regular commercial networks centered around standard transshipment hubs to move the goods back to North Korea.

When North Korean state enterprises did have their own logistical capabilities, but lacked the distribution network necessary to move products to end-users, they linked up with trade networks that did have such ties. The April 2003 *Pong Su* case, in which Australian authorities captured a North Korean cargo ship named *Pong Su* (owned by the North Korean company Pong Su Shipping), presents an interesting example. The ship had delivered a large shipment of heroin to three waiting drug couriers on a beach west of Melbourne. The ship itself, in the run-up to dropping off the drugs, had stopped in Yantai, China, to pick up a large shipment of sand, and had then gone on to Nampo in North Korea before continuing on to other destinations, ending up in Jakarta and, from there, Australia. The trafficker who actually brought the heroin ashore (and survived—an

unidentified companion named "Chui" drowned in the attempt), Wong
Ta Song, claimed to be a Chinese citizen of Korean ethnicity from near
the border with North Korea, and had boarded the ship either in China or
on the intermediate stop in North Korea.[69] On a previous visit of the *Pong
Su* to Hong Kong in September 2002, Kwok Wah Biu, the owner of Yue
On Company, a Hong Kong shipping agent that apparently specialized
in supporting shipping companies operating between North Korea and
Hong Kong, had provided a mobile phone to the *Pong Su* crew, a phone
that was later used in the drug importation operation.[70]

The network coordinator for the operation was apparently from Macau,
and coordinated the operation from Kuala Lumpur.[71] KIMTO, the fictitious company set up in Kuala Lumpur to manage the operation, had two
known purported representatives in Australia. Lam Yau Kim, the (apparently) Chinese citizen who was one of the three conspirators supposed to
receive the drugs on the beach in Victoria, arrived in Australia on a fake
Malaysian passport, also as a representative of KIMTO. An Asian man
calling himself "John Thompson" contacted an Australian customs and
shipping agent before the *Pong Su* arrived and said that he wanted to arrange for the export of luxury cars from Australia to Malaysia, with Pong
Su Shipping Company providing the ship that would pick up the cars.
While the Australian agent never completed the deal, KIMTO did apparently contract with Pong Su Shipping to carry goods to Australia.[72] The
two other members of the syndicate receiving the drugs in Victoria—Teng
Kiam Fah and Tan Wee Quay—were Malaysian and Singaporean, respectively. Teng had been living in Malaysia immediately prior to the operation (and was attempting to pay off gambling debts), while Tan had been
living in Bangkok (and had been involved in several operations before, including one to Copenhagen). All three had flown from Beijing to Australia
immediately before the operation. After receiving the drugs, Lam, Teng,
and Tan were supposed to give the drugs to someone named "Charlie,"
who would handle onward distribution of the heroin.[73]

It is unclear where the heroin itself was from. Chemical tests indicated
similarities and differences with known Southeast Asian heroin,[74] meaning the heroin was likely either Southeast Asian heroin that North Koreans
were transporting, or was North Korean heroin produced with expertise
and supplies provided by Golden Triangle drug syndicates. While the
media attention at the time of the Pong Su trials of the drug traffickers and
the North Korean senior crew of the *Pong Su* was focused on allegations

of North Korean state participation in drug trafficking, an allegation that was never definitively proven in court, of greater interest here is the trade network in which North Korean state entities were enmeshed. There were actually two networks: in one—the "licit" network—the state-owned Pong Su Shipping Company operated ships that engaged in mundane trade between China and North Korea, contracted with a (fictitious) company in Malaysia to transport goods on a Tuvalu-flagged vessel between Jakarta and Melbourne, and used a commercial shipping agent in Hong Kong as one of a number of North Korean shipping companies operating in East Asia.

In the second—the "illicit" network—the traffickers operated out of Macau and Kuala Lumpur, and recruited conspirators with social ties to the network in Singapore, Bangkok, Kuala Lumpur, and Beijing. Where the North Korean enterprises actually established ties with the drug trafficking network is unclear, although the presence of the drug trafficking syndicate in Beijing and Macau, both of which had North Korean trading outposts, suggests that the trading outposts could have been used to make contact. While Zokwang Trading was not implicated in the incident,[75] coordination with a Macau-based trafficking syndicate that used ethnic Korean traffickers suggests that North Korean state entities such as Pong Su Shipping were comfortable engaging in business with actors with whom they had nonmarket relationships, and in locations where they had prior experience. Regardless of whether North Korea produced the heroin itself or loaded it in Jakarta (as Wong Ta Song claimed),[76] hooking up with the Southeast Asian drug syndicates also allowed North Korean enterprises to profit from drug trafficking without setting up a distribution network (or even any contacts at all) in either Southeast Asia or Australia. Instead, North Korean enterprises capitalized on their strengths—a safe institutional environment in North Korea itself, a limited but commercial transport capacity that could be used for illicit purposes, and the ability to establish ties with other actors who could provide the rest of what was necessary.

Bottom-up Coping Mechanisms

For their part, private citizens were left to face the horrors of the Arduous March entirely on their own. Unlike state enterprises, private citizens did not have access to state capital assets, transportation infrastructure (when it functioned), or, perhaps most importantly, state sanction, either within North Korea or without. The trade networks that evolved to support the economic survival of private citizens were forced to rely on both market and nonmarket relationships to spread within and beyond North Korea, and faced deep state ambivalence. Hybrid networks—private trade networks that took on some of the trappings of state enterprises, and state enterprises that took on some of the trappings of private traders—were themselves partly a mechanism for private citizens and some state officials to operate with greater access to state resources and greater certainty in the political risks they took on. As such, both private and hybrid trade networks demonstrated a flexibility that the state enterprises did not, even though the bottom-up networks were not as geographically dispersed as state enterprises, or as individually profitable, and presaged the forms private and semiprivate enterprise would take as they matured after 2006.

A Desperate Environment

For both private citizens and low-level state officials, the collapse of the North Korean economy by 1994, and the famines and droughts that followed, were the dominant events that shaped the environment in which they did business. From 1990, people in areas short of food were allowed to travel to look for food, with travel permits, or barring that, with food ration cards, or "assignment" by factories of workers to rural areas so that the workers could get food from their relatives. Approximately 70 percent of travel was for the purpose of buying food, with 15 percent for "peddling."[77] As the food situation worsened, the state relaxed enforcement and punishment for crimes related to obtaining food. Economic crimes (unrelated to finding food) were primarily the domain of economic bureaucrats, trading company officials, and cooperative staff members, but punishment could be avoided by bribes or connections. Interviews with defectors led South Korean researchers to conclude that the state had lost control over petty offenses (such as peddling) by 1992.[78]

Much of the North Korean state basically stopped functioning inside the borders of North Korea with the coming of the first famine in 1996. Industrial production in the state-owned factories broke down for lack of electricity, and work places ceased to be places of work. The Public

Distribution System stopped distributing food to the public in the face of a lack of both electricity and any food as the central state hoarded what little food there was for Pyongyang elites and certain parts of the military. The lack of electricity also led to the breakdown of the internal transportation infrastructure (complicating the distribution of food). Internal controls over movement and external controls over border crossing also either broke down completely or faced lax or corrupt enforcement. The travel permit system essentially collapsed by 1997, allowing North Koreans to move around the country to search for food (possibly with a small bribe, although they still could not enter Pyongyang). When a new system was introduced in 2002, the regulations were more relaxed, and permits could be issued relatively quickly, with an escalating schedule of bribes between two dollars and ten dollars depending on the destination of the traveler (whether it was somewhere else in the countryside or a restricted area).[79]

Few laws or regulations changed at all during the peak years of the Arduous March between 1996 and 1999. In one of the few exceptions, in 1996, the North Korean government reclassified crossing the border into China illegally as a minor offense. North Koreans who were captured and sent back to North Korea were subject to interrogation and imprisonment in labor camps for a few months, as long as they were not in contact with South Koreans, non-Chinese foreigners, or Christian groups.[80] The family responsibility principle was also de-emphasized, and applied selectively, meaning that the family members of criminals were no longer automatically punished for the sins of their relatives. In both cases, it is possible the North Korean state made these concessions precisely because it no longer had the resources to enforce the regulations.[81]

For the next six years, as the Arduous March reached its peak, and then very slowly receded, the state officially remained impassive in the face of rapidly changing facts on the ground. In 2002, the central state finally promulgated a series of regulations for the new-style private markets. The "July 1 Economic Management Improvement Measures" contained several provisions. First, they raised official commodity prices, wages, and currency exchange rates. Second, they "abolished the low-price distribution system." Third, they strengthened the "incentive system for farmers." Fourth, they expanded the "autonomy of corporate management." Within the next year, the state also legally created several new special economic zones, allowed privately run (but still publicly owned) service companies (such as restaurants), allowed state-run businesses to be managed by corporations, and integrated the agricultural market.[82] By formalizing the way in which privately run enterprise was (in theory) supposed to be run, the state was simultaneously recognizing the reality of the growth of the informal economy over the previous six years outside of the decreasingly long arms of the state, and attempting to reassert some modicum of control over private markets and their participants.

The result of the breakdown of state provision and control, and the seeming imperviousness of the state to formal change was that would-be traders, both those operating outside the confines of the states, and those state actors trading without the benefit of central state resources, moved about in an environment where the rules were not only informal but ad hoc and evolving very quickly, where their trade activities were technically illegal and could bring the selective, pernicious wrath of the state at any time.

The ad hoc environment for bottom-up coping mechanisms was thus characterized by several constraints. First, traders dealt with a decline (but not disappearance) in state coercion. The central state did not approve of private markets, but it lacked the capacity to crack down on market activity at all times and in all locations. Second, traders took advantage of the peculiarities of North Korea's social control system. The men in households continued to be required to report to their workplaces (even if they were unable to work), but the women, being seen as comparatively unimportant outside of the home, were allowed to abandon their workplaces or bribe their way out in order to search for food, and later to start their own private market stalls, beginning in 1995.[83] Third, as with guards at road checkpoints and on trains, sympathetic local officials sometimes allowed private traders to operate right under their noses, both because they realized that the population could no longer rely on the state if they wanted to survive, and because they themselves needed to survive. When the food ran out in the mid-1990s, low-level officials who did not take bribes and depended on the Public Distribution System (which was cut off for officials below a certain threshold) tended to die. Those who were bribed to allow illegal activities or other coping mechanisms to take place tended to live.[84] The upshot was that the Arduous March, at the local level, saw the beginnings of a market of sorts for tolerance of market activity—the proper bribe to the proper official, delivered at the right time, could pave the way for traders to operate.

Yet such an informal, ad hoc "regulatory" system limited the viability and growth of private trade networks. Market activities could effectively only be carried out by half of the household members, since husbands were stuck at the factories. Market activity itself was always potentially subject to shutdown, and traders themselves at risk of confiscation of their goods and money earned, as well as punishment if some enforcers within the state could not be bribed, changed their minds, or lost their own factional battles that resulted in their removal.

The state enterprises that turned to trade as a means of survival faced a slightly different environment. Since low-level officials (and certainly the workers in the state enterprises they managed) were too far down the pecking order to continue to receive food rations when the Public Distribution System broke down, enterprise managers and workers were both faced with the prospect of engaging in trade or starving. Unlike women in regular households, state enterprises were also faced with the requirement of providing income up the ladder to the central state, regardless of whether their factories were actually functioning. They were required to do this with only limited access to state prerogatives or resources—low-level enterprises did not use diplomatic outposts or state trading posts overseas, and unless they were military enterprises, they did not necessarily have easy access to the state-run transportation system. What they did have, however, was a labor force (although starving, and largely unproductive) and residual assets left over from the Cold War when the North Korean economy actually functioned.

Where the Networks Were and How They Were Run

Many ordinary North Korean citizens, totally unaccustomed to a life where the state did not provide sustenance, were at a loss as to how to survive, and simply died of disease or starved to death in the mid-1990s. Those who did survive often did so by trading. Lacking access to state resources or even a regulatory environment (informal or not) in which to operate, trading necessarily began as small acts of desperation that emerged almost ineluctably when absolutely nothing else worked. The first response of many private citizens, and even managers in state firms (as they all were) that had been abandoned by the central state, was to sell off or trade items they already had on hand that might have some value to others, or to begin producing basic goods and services for sale.[85] The second response of many people staring at starvation for themselves and their families, particularly if they lived anywhere near the border between North Korea and China, was to cross into China to forage for food or find work.[86] The two responses combined to create bottom-up trade networks that were wholly internal, and as such concentrated geographically within localities, and networks that stretched between North Korean border areas and northeastern China. These networks, ad hoc as they were (almost by necessity), served as the basis for the more extensive and regularized networks that would take root as North Korea exited the Arduous March.

Private Trading Networks   Private citizens in North Korea were not wholly without experience in trading or the concept of markets—the private markets, constrained as they were, existed even before the Arduous March. The idea of private markets, notably those that sold excess agricultural products, was not new to North Korea. Indeed, Kim Il-sung himself had (grudgingly) approved of farmers' markets when they were required, even going so far as to write an essay justifying them ideologically in 1969.[87]

The government issued regulations for private markets in 1984, although into the early 1990s, the markets were largely confined to out-of-the-way locations, kept hidden from view, and limited to selling excess food (except for rice and grains). In practice, perhaps two-thirds of the stalls sold consumer goods, often smuggled in from China (and indirectly from the West) or pilfered from state-owned factories, at exorbitant prices.[88] Trade in all forms brought in knowledge of South Korean (and other countries') prosperity in the late 1980s and early 1990s. Japanese visitors brought in South Korean–made goods. Used car-smuggling rings transported Hyundai, Daewoo, and Japanese cars between Japan and China via Chongjin harbor and Onsong county (the North Korean county facing Tumen in northeastern China), allowing North Koreans to see the quality of foreign cars. Chinese reform and opening up also led to higher quality consumer goods that were then smuggled into North Korea beginning in the mid-1980s.[89] This unofficial trade, use of foreigner shops, and cross-border smuggling were arguably used by the state as a means of deflecting pressure from the state, and keeping "socio-political disturbances" from building up.[90]

With the onset of the Arduous March, the markets expanded dramatically, cross-border smuggling shot up, and the private sector economy became extensive, according to defector interviews.[91] Widespread private markets began in the 1990s when women in low- and middle-income households began selling "excess" household items, and then homemade food, taking advantage of "easier" travel to buy and sell throughout the country.[92] Because the initial markets were local in scope, with women buying and selling what they had on hand, they were not part of international trade as such, but their rise and operation both prefigured and provided the impetus for private international trade.

The central state's 2002 reforms were the first formal acknowledgement of the rise of widespread private trade networks. The primary formal effects of the 2002 agricultural reforms were to move official prices closer to black market prices (at least for a time—black market prices quickly outpaced the official prices once again), to expand the amount of land that could cultivated by farmers for private use, and to lower the portion of production that had to be given to the state from 70–80 percent to 50–60 percent, allowing farmers to dispose of more production privately.[93] Farmers cultivating private plots (unofficially) sent the produce to the private markets, and were allowed to dispose of food produced in excess of their quota themselves.[94] Because the state raised the price at which it would purchase rice from farmers but kept the Public Distribution System in place, its clear intention was to move the official market more into line with the black market, and preserve state predominance on providing rice at some point in the future.[95] The July 1 measures could actually be interpreted as an attempt by the state to rein in the farmers' markets and move people back to the national (state-owned) retail system through rationalizing prices. In reality, while the national retail system did rationalize its prices (the ability to set prices was also devolved to regional authorities and state-owned corporation), it could not compete on price or quality of produce, and the breakdown of the official distribution system meant that the commercial retail networks' role was strengthened—one analyst estimated that by 2007, 50 percent of the food consumed even by city dwellers came from the commercial markets.[96]

The state also expanded the formal private economy by transforming farmers' markets into markets for both food and consumer goods in March 2003, legalizing the already occurring private sale of manufactured goods (and recognizing that those goods were no longer obtainable from the state). The goods themselves were both legally obtained and illegally smuggled, with little ability for the state to differentiate among them. By December 2003, there were an estimated three hundred to three-hundred fifty integrated markets across the country, with thirty-eight in Pyongyang alone. While the markets themselves were officially state-owned businesses, the individual stalls were allowed to be owned by individuals and (since the reforms) state companies and cooperatives, all of whom paid usage taxes to the market operator and the state. The Tongil Street Market in Pyongyang reportedly had fourteen hundred stalls, with the marketplace itself being managed by thirty-six employees.[97] The state thus put itself in the position of attempting to profit from and maintain some semblance of control over market activity that was largely going to happen anyway.

Almost by definition, these traders relied on market relationships, hawking their wares in open areas with relatively little cost for buyers to shift between sellers (and vice versa). Farmers began to farm on their own in order to survive, cultivating small fields on less arable land outside of the state-owned farms. Any excess produce could itself be sold on the private markets (although not legally).[98] The markets spread rapidly, to the point that, between 1998 and 2008, approximately 78 percent of national income came from participation in the informal markets.[99] By the early 2000s, North Koreans received 60 percent of their food, and 70 percent of their consumer goods (often goods smuggled in from South Korea and China), from the markets, which expanded to encompass all types of goods.[100]

During the Arduous March, private trade networks also gradually spread across the border into China. In North Koreans' desperation to get out of North Korea, even the least connected refugees needed to interact economically with others to move between North Korea and China. Border guards on the Yalu and Tumen rivers had to be bribed (and the means to bribe them often had to come from selling something to someone within North Korea). If North Korean refugees were doing anything beyond foraging for food in China (which was viable to the extent that North Koreans could steal from farms on the border, or find food left out by Chinese farmers), they needed to find work in Chinese firms or shelter offered by South Korean missionaries. The less savory aspects of population movement across the border required networks that took trade more explicitly into account. North Korean families in dire straits sold their daughters into arranged marriages with Chinese husbands (thus simultaneously alleviating them of a mouth to feed and garnering payment) or, alternatively, young North Korean women were lured into China with the promise of work and then forced into prostitution or arranged marriages. In both cases, brokers with network nodes in both North Korea and China arranged transport and "sales" of refugees.[101]

The more "benign" people smugglers who moved North Korean refugees into South Korea had their own networks. Since North Koreans who worked in northeastern China or who had successfully arrived in South Korea often wanted to send money back to their relatives in North Korea, either for sustenance or to buy the relatives' way to South Korea, an industry for transporting people across the border sprang up. For relatives of North Koreans living and working in China or South Korea, a certain amount of money would pay for a people smuggler to go into North Korea and bring the relative back across the border (up to ten thousand dollars for Pyongyang, lower for other areas). A higher amount would move the defector to Seoul (presumably through third countries). North Koreans could also send money back to North Korea through couriers.[102] There were thus the rudiments of networks that "traded" in the movement of people (and people themselves) with nodes in North Korea, northeastern China, South Korea, and often a third country (if the refugees transited through there on their way to South Korea).

Within several years of the expansion of private markets, the more successful early movers moved on to become wholesalers. Some wholesalers moved into other enterprises, particularly restaurants, transportation, and retail, some of which depended on international trade. From the late 1990s private entrepreneurs took advantage of familial ties with China to expand their business opportunities and to source goods. These connections in China were able to provide small amounts of capital (with high rates of return), goods, or advice.[103] Private trade networks thus relied on a combination of market and nonmarket relationships: market relationships were useful for distribution within North Korea, while nonmarket relationships were useful for connecting the nodes in North Korea with those in China and beyond.

Elite wives, for example, resold goods produced by their husbands' factories. Andrei Lankov recounts one story of a Ms. Hwang, who used her connections to China—in this case, she had immediate relatives living in northeastern China—to obtain a travel permit to go to China (presumably because she was going to visit her relatives). As a result, she was able to leverage her ability to cross the border and bring in goods. In 1997, Hwang obtained enough nylon socks for the entire population of Yongchon, her home county, thus winning the favor of local state officials. She also culti-vated relationships with North Pyongan state security officials in the for-eign affairs bureau, as well as with the party and the police, to make sure that her business was allowed to operate freely.[104]

Technological and legal changes also made cross-border private trade more viable. From 2003 onward, Chinese mobile companies set up mobile phone towers along the border with North Korea, allowing North Kore-ans with access to Chinese mobile phones (and service) along the border to call outside.[105] From approximately 2003, the state also began issuing per-mits for traveling abroad (specifically to China), subject to checks by the se-curity services for the right social background and political loyalty. Lankov claims that the process could take up to six months, but could be shortened (and the outcome guaranteed) by a bribe of fifty to one hundred dollars, which was well within the budget of cross-border shuttle traders.[106]

Hybrid Trading Networks   Not all trading networks that arose during the Arduous March, and matured in its aftermath, were entirely the creation of private North Korean citizens or efforts by the central state to bring in hard currency. The collapse of North Korea's formal economy in the early 1990s also saw the emergence of creative new means of building trade net-works, as private individuals and state officials, driven by the breakdown in the ability of the state to provide sustenance, and taking advantage of the breakdown in the state's ability to monitor and punish economic trans-gressions, worked together to create hybrid trading networks. These new networks combined the (relative) political and legal security and access to state assets and resources enjoyed by state officials with the relative flexibil-ity (and later, the capital) of certain private citizens

As would befit a coping mechanism that took bits and pieces from both the public and private sectors almost entirely without guidance or sanc-tion from above, hybrid trading networks took on a variety of different structures and geographical configurations. The people best placed to take advantage of both hybrid and private trader opportunities were those with access to networks outside of North Korea. State officials with foreign currency-earning licenses, Korean Japanese, those with relatives living in

China, and Chinese citizens resident in North Korea all used their connections (and in the case of the Chinese, their ability to leave North Korea easily) to bring in investment capital, receive assistance in how to do business, and import merchandise that they could sell in North Korea.[107] It was these people—a mishmash of public and private actors—who created the initial hybrid networks. First, officials in state enterprises began to go into business for themselves. Second, state enterprises set up some joint ventures with overseas private companies. Third, private individuals started and operated what were essentially private businesses legally registered as state enterprises, with the collusion of state enterprise officials.

All but the loftiest of the elites were forced to fend for themselves during the Arduous March. Unlike private citizens, state officials had immediate access to resources (in the equipment in their factories), labor (in the form of the workers who were otherwise reporting for duty and sitting around), and perhaps most importantly, legal imprimatur for at least some of what they were doing, given that the enterprises were often licensed foreign currency–earners, and had preexisting contact networks (largely in China) that came with their role in the North Korean economy.

As surveillance broke down and chaos increased in the early 1990s, what deterrents existed to keep state enterprise managers (and workers) from shirking their duties no longer applied. State factory managers sold their factory goods on the market, retail shop workers distributed their goods outside of the distribution system, and foreign currency-earning enterprise managers turned their enterprises to their own ends. Enterprises that had access to transportation equipment could make money by moving goods between different parts of the country with different prices in the markets.[108] State officials also ate into their enterprises' seed corn. Managers of state-owned factories began selling their equipment (which was idled and useless due to a lack of electricity) in China for scrap metal, in some cases clearing out the entire factory.[109] Finally, the lack of anything resembling private financial institutions in North Korea meant that private moneylenders became a source of capital, lending at a rate of 30–40 percent monthly interest to state officials who could use their positions to engage in private enterprise.[110]

It was not just foreign currency-earning state officials who sought to go into business for themselves—state officials of all stripes were on the lookout for moneymaking opportunities. One Western diplomat recounted his dealings with North Korean diplomats on a development project in North Korea in the late 1990s. At one point, an aide to a North Korean official tasked with dealing with the Western diplomat inquired as to whether he would be able to put the aide in contact with Anheuser-Busch, as he wanted to start a Budweiser distributorship in North Korea.[111]

In pushing past the legal or moral limits of their positions to make money for themselves, state officials acquired poor reputations among private citizens. To deflect responsibility for problems from the supreme leaders, the propaganda machine behind the personality cults of Kim Il-sung and later Kim Jong-il blamed local officials for "corruptions, illicit trafficking, bureaucratic mannerism, and abuses of power."[112] Yet state officials often lived down to their reputations—they went into business for themselves by preying on private traders. Much of the entrepreneurialism of state officials could best be described as creative corruption—unlike private citizens, they were immune from the practical limits on black market trade, and could order the requisition of resources (such as bags of rice) that they could then sell for private gain. They had also had access to supplies not available to the general public, and ran businesses at the same time as they took a percentage of private traders' profits to allow them to operate.[113] Defectors in the 1990s identified railway safety agents, mobile safety agents who policed the markets, and soldiers as the most corrupt state actors most likely to be encountered by private traders—the state officials with the greatest ability to engage in rent-seeking from small-time businesspeople were thus those who were stationed at the transportation nodes necessary for trades and the points where traders interacted with customers.[114]

North Koreans themselves also began filling in the gaps created by the collapse of many state-owned enterprises, not only through the totally private enterprises seen in the marketplaces around North Korea, but also through mechanisms that were less prone to political risk and capricious rent-seeking. During the Arduous March, North Korea had no process for privately owned enterprises that were not joint ventures to operate legally. As a result, entrepreneurs who had the right political connections and some amount of starting capital increasingly established partnerships with state organizations to obtain legal status for their business. The entrepreneurs would pay a fee to the state organization, as well as (in some cases) a percentage of profits. In return, the state organization would register the business officially as state-owned, with the entrepreneur as the hired manager. In practice, the businesses would be run completely privately. These North Korean hybrid enterprises—officially owned by the state, but operating as private businesses—were not dissimilar from some of the *red hat* enterprises that emerged during the early years of China's reform and opening up period, when large swathes of the economy were reserved for state-owned enterprises, and thus private entrepreneurs in those sectors found it useful to register their company as a department of a willing state entity to operate legally.[115] In North Korea, restaurants became perhaps the earliest and most widespread examples of these hybrid enterprises, as state-owned restaurants largely collapsed in 1996 and 1997 in the face of famine. Privately run restaurants sprang up to replace them.[116] The managers would hire employees and run the restaurant, and provide a kickback to local state officials, who officially owned the restaurant in exchange for a portion of the profits that would go to the state. The model was successful, and by 2009, perhaps 60 percent of restaurants were privately run.[117] Other sectors soon followed suit, leading to an explosion of creative business arrangements as the Arduous March receded into history.

The means by which both state officials and organizations, and private citizens survived the Arduous March had roots in the Cold War, when North Korea established outposts and trade networks around the world as a means of acquiring supplies and making money, and private citizens began selling goods in markets. Both state and nonstate trade adapted in their own ways with the onset of the Arduous March, and through a combination of trial and error and desperation, trade networks began to show many of the characteristics that would become obvious after the Arduous March: state trading networks made relatively clever use of state assets and integrated themselves in creative ways into the global economy. They were opportunistic, and exhibited a willingness to straddle the line between licit and illicit, and to operate both in markets and through close-knit networks at different times and in different situations. To a large extent, state trading networks attempted to maintain control of their trade as far down the chain as they could, but were willing to compromise control when necessary. They also made creative use of contacts they built up to serve as brokers for trade in goods that never entered North Korea, thus eliminating many of the logistical problems North Korea faced. Private traders also had to survive, and built up their own trade networks that sometimes bypassed the North Korean state completely, and sometimes co-opted it, at times acquiring formal state status so that their informal businesses could operate with minimal harassment. As time went on, despite the central state's wariness, ambivalence, and at times outright hostility, the private and hybrid traders established a new, increasingly "normal" modus operandi that shaped how private citizens and even elites frozen out of the central state interacted with the outside world. These changes would affect how private trade networks, state trading companies, and those business-people stuck somewhere in between, dealt with the political and economic realities that appeared from 2005 onward.

2

STATE TRADING NETWORKS
VERSUS THE WORLD

In the travails of the Arduous March, North Korean citizens, for their part, learned that they could no longer rely on the central state to sustain them: if they waited for help from above, they were likely to die. Whatever citizens' views of the far-off and still idolized Kim family and of socialism in the abstract, the local state they actually experienced became an impediment to overcome and business became something at which they needed to become proficient if they wanted to survive.

The North Korean central state also learned some valuable lessons from the Arduous March, although perhaps not the ones that outsiders intended. It learned how a nuclear program could be parlayed into economic aid, and how fear over North Korean instability and collapse could drive North Korea's regional interlocutors—both friends and foes—to make concessions. The regime also learned that it could survive, for a time at least, without providing the barest necessities of life for its citizens. Even though it (and the North Korean economy) adapted enough to survive the 1990s, within several years of the lessening of the horrendous conditions of the Arduous March, the North Korean central state faced another crisis (almost entirely of its own making) as it entered a cycle of nuclear, missile, and other provocations, and increasingly punitive United Nations, United States, and trade partner sanctions.

This darkening international environment may have had little effect on private and hybrid trading networks (as will be discussed in chapter 3), but it certainly forced state trading networks to adapt as they fought to survive. Unlike with other North Korean business, international sanctions explicitly targeted central state trading companies (often even by name). The sanctions also proscribed trade in the items—nuclear, chemical, biological, and conventional weapons technology and luxury goods—that state trading networks monopolized and were tasked with both importing and exporting. At the same time, unlike private (and to a certain extent hybrid) networks, state trading networks had access to state-owned transportation infrastructure, diplomatic outposts and passports, and significantly greater financial resources than smaller companies.

North Korean state companies attempted to adapt in part by shifting their product offerings to nonsanctioned exports and goods that did not require much North Korean involvement in the supply chain. For goods that were unquestionably sanctioned, however, state companies were forced to use more creative methods. As they had been during the Arduous March, state prerogatives and resources proved both a blessing and a curse. While North Korean planes and ships continued to transport goods when the networks wanted to avoid routing goods through transshipment hubs and maintain control of the goods along entire chains, in an increasingly hostile world, North Korean state assets were subject to greater scrutiny. Because of the limited number of buyers for much of what they were exporting (notably weapons), North Korean exporters could not simply shift the destinations of their goods. Instead, they adopted a strategy in which the governance of the networks was geographically separated from the logistical structure. Put bluntly, North Korean state operators adapted by managing to be located nowhere near their sanctioned goods. Diplomats largely recoiled from transporting goods themselves. Instead, they took on a greater role in state trading networks as brokers, and diplomatic outposts served as the geographic loci for negotiations and deals that increasingly took on the forms and behaviors typical of international commercial business. The sanctioned goods themselves left North Korean state companies' control either in North Korea itself or through nearby foreign logistics brokers (often in China) and entered (and thus followed the spatial distribution of) the global commercial shipping hub-and-spoke network as regular commercial goods. State companies thus lost control of the supply chain and captured less value up and down the chain but also avoided scrutiny of their activities and became more integrated into the global economy.

The increasing reliance on foreign commercial brokers (often with fairly long-standing relationships with North Korean state companies) also became apparent as North Korean state companies went about their other main task: importing sanctioned goods. With the collapse of Chongryon companies (and Japan more generally) as suppliers and brokers, North Korean companies began to arbitrage jurisdictions themselves, moving on to brokers in Taiwan and especially China, which possessed the right combination of North Korean personal connections, access to industrial and luxury markets, and transshipment points that were both connected to the global economy and insufficiently mindful of North Korean trade activities. Perhaps just as importantly, the North Korean companies let these brokers handle much of the logistics associated with moving the goods into North Korea, thus alleviating the pressure associated with being a North Korean state entity. In practice, because these strategies relied on geographically proximate foreign brokers operating out of areas with governments that were indifferent to North Korean trade, North Korea became increasingly dependent on brokers in China for logistical support, and on Chinese companies for investment. China subsequently emerged as North Korea's primary trading partner (as discussed in chapter 4). The chapter closes with case studies, of Taiwan's rise as a broker for goods imported into North Korea and of a Dandong import-export company that obtains goods for North Korean clients through China, that illustrate North Korean state trading networks' strategic use of foreign brokers and brokerage locations, and the creative methods the brokers themselves use to acquire and transport goods for North Korea.

The Darkening Foreign Environment

All this adaptation took place in the context of clouds that gathered around North Korean business activities outside North Korea. Several years before

North Korea's 2006 nuclear test, the United States had begun eyeing North Korean–crewed and North Korean–flagged ships more closely. On 9 December 2002, on a tip from the United States, Spanish naval forces boarded the North Korean–crewed *So San* after it refused to stop in the Arabian Sea. They discovered fifteen Scud missiles and their conventional warheads, as well as quantities of high explosives, fuel, and chemicals. As North Korea was not at the time under sanctions prohibiting the export of missiles (let alone chemicals), the Yemeni government publicly stated it was the buyer, and the ship was allowed to continue to Yemen.[1] But the United States was not mollified, and in May 2003 announced the Proliferation Security Initiative (PSI), a US-led international effort to stop proliferation through a combination of new national laws, joint military and law enforcement exercises and, most importantly from North Korea's perspective, ship and aircraft interdictions. While North Korea was not facing significant sanctions in 2003, the PSI did lead to greater scrutiny of North Korean ships, scrutiny that would increase in intensity once sanctions began to be implemented in 2006.

In September 2005, the United States also triggered a bank run at Banco Delta Asia (BDA) in Macau by posting a notice to US banks to avoid BDA because of its laundering of North Korean money and passing of counterfeit US currency (presumably produced by North Korea). The Macau government subsequently took over the bank's board, and fifty-two North Korean accounts (not all of them connected to the central state or engaged in illicit activities) in Banco Delta Asia were frozen.[2] Banco Delta Asia was not the only bank doing business with North Korea—in fact, nearly all banks in Macau were—but it was the bank judged by the United States to be small enough that a bank run would not bring down the Macau banking system. Banco Delta Asia was intended to scare other banks in Macau (and other parts of the world) away from doing business with North Korean enterprises, which it did.[3] In March 2007, the United States formally issued a report ordering US banks to stay away from Banco Delta Asia. Although Banco Delta Asia was never charged, and the Macau government returned control of the bank to the owner in September 2007, it remained on the US blacklist as a warning to others.[4] North Korea subsequently moved its finances out of Macau and into mainland China.[5]

The US sanctioning of Banco Delta Asia was *pour encourager les autres* partly because there was not yet consensus among UN Security Council permanent members about the need for sanctions against North Korea. Luckily for the United States and Japan, North Korea itself provided the consensus, and formal UN-backed sanctions came in the second half of 2006. In June 2006, North Korea conducted a ballistic missile test despite warnings from the United States, Japan, and other countries. The next month, the UN Security Council passed UNSCR 1695, which prohibited UN member states from dealing with North Korea when buying or selling material or technology related to missiles or chemical, biological, radiological, or nuclear (CBRN) weapons.[6]

Of perhaps greater relevance for North Korean trade, Japan imposed its own sanctions soon after the missile test, virtually banning all imports from North Korea, and prohibiting the *Mangyongbong-92* from berthing at Niigata, thus cutting the main legal logistical link between North Korean Japanese companies and North Korea.[7] This was followed by a 2009 ban on virtually all exports to North Korea. As the economy was collapsing in the early 1990s, the North Korean government had leaned even more heavily on Chongryon,[8] to the point where remittances from Japan to North Korea hit between $650 million and $850 million annually immediately after the end of the Cold War.[9] South Korean sources estimated that Chongryon members alone accounted for 30–40 percent of Japan–North Korea trade in the early 1990s.[10] But Chongryon members' enthusiasm and monetary donations dropped off markedly after Kim Il-sung's death in 1994 and the first nuclear crisis in 1993 and 1994.[11]

Even as Chongryon members' support for North Korea waned, the Japanese government turned a critical eye toward the activities of Chongryon itself. For decades, because Chongryon had served as the unofficial diplomatic representation of North Korea in Japan, the Japanese government had largely ignored the involvement of Chongryon members in money laundering, organized crime, smuggling, and the like. With the coming of sanctions, Chongryon's activities came under scrutiny, and Japanese law enforcement began staging a series of raids and investigations that resulted in the arrest of a number of Chongryon members. By 2012, Chongryon was in sufficiently dire straits that it was forced to put its headquarters up for sale.[12] With the sanctions and revelations of North Korea's involvement in kidnapping Japanese citizens in the 1970s and 1980s (which was at odds with the North Korean government's statements to Chongryon itself), Chongryon's membership and fundraising abilities crashed. Within a few years, Chongryon had ceased to be a major force in Japan–North Korea trade. The remnant left was geriatric and obviously out of touch with the new reality, with younger Koreans living in Japan either integrating more readily into Japanese society or affiliating with Mindan, the South Korean equivalent of Chongryon.[13]

North Korea continued to show defiance, and on 9 October 2006 conducted an underground nuclear test. The UN Security Council responded five days later with UNSCR 1718. The resolution banned trading with North Korea in large-scale weapons systems (such as tanks, aircraft, and large-caliber artillery) as well as the export to North Korea of luxury goods (although this was not defined). The resolution also encouraged, but did not require, UN members to stop and inspect cargo moving to or from North Korea to make sure the cargo did not contain weapons of mass destruction or related items. Finally, the resolution froze the accounts of individuals and companies involved, directly or indirectly, in prohibited weapons programs, and placed travel bans on them and their families. There were, crucially, a number of loopholes built into the sanctions—luxury goods were not defined, countries were not obligated to stop or inspect North Korean shipments, and the sanctions against individuals and companies directly or indirectly involved in weapons programs could be read expansively or very narrowly, particularly since North Korean state enterprises used front companies as a matter of course.[14] Nonetheless, North Korea began 2007 with an international business environment that was at least theoretically hostile to the country's firms trading in what had been cash cows—missile and nuclear technology, and chemicals—and that wanted to make those same firms go through contortions to move money around the world.

North Korea and the UN Security Council soon settled into a comfortable tit-for-tat, with repetitive cycles of North Korean provocations and refining and deepening of Security Council sanctions. On 25 May 2009, North Korea again tested a nuclear device, and the Security Council responded (again) with increasingly tightened sanctions the next month. All arms trade (including both transfer and financing) to and from North Korea, with the exception of small arms and light weapons, was banned. This time, member states were authorized (but not required) to search North Korean cargo being shipped on land, by sea, or by air to make sure that goods related to North Korea's nuclear or military programs were not being transported. If they found such goods, they were authorized

to destroy them. The resolution also required member states not to provide supplies to North Korean vessels suspected to be involved in prohibited activities, although it made explicit exceptions for humanitarian
and "legal economic activities." Finally, the resolution called upon states
not to engage in financial transactions with North Korean institutions or
persons that could conceivably contribute to the North Korea's CBRN
programs, and to freeze any North Korean assets that could be used for
WMD development. States were further called upon not to provide loans
or financial assistance to North Korea, except for "humanitarian and de-
velopmental purposes directly addressing the needs of the civilian population," and not to provide financial support for any trade with North
Korea where that financial support could contribute to CBRN or missile
programs.[15]

On 12 December 2012, North Korea launched a satellite into space
using a modified ballistic missile, a feat that was met with UNSCR 2087 on
22 January 2013. The resolution was strongly worded and added some individuals, institutions, and items to the sanctions list, but otherwise instituted
no new measures.[16] In response, North Korea conducted a third nuclear
test on 12 February 2013. The Security Council then passed UNSCR 2094
on 7 March. The resolution expanded sanctions to include intermediate
services related to banned trade, and extended travel and trade freezes to
a new list of North Korean institutions and individuals suspected of being
involved in the nuclear, missile, or arms trade (as well as institutions and
individuals acting on their behalf). Financial sanctions were expanded to include bulk cash transfers that could aid the sanctioned programs, and made
mandatory for states to enforce. Interestingly, the resolution did not require
states to close down existing North Korean bank accounts, but called upon
states to prohibit new accounts, branches, joint ventures, or subsidiaries of
North Korean banks from being opened in their territory if they may be
connected to sanctioned programs, and to prohibit their own banks from
doing business in the DPRK. States were asked to watch North Korean
diplomats more carefully, and were instructed to carry out inspections of
vessels carrying DPRK-related sanctioned goods, and to ban DPRK-related
ships and airplanes from their ports if they refused to be inspected. The resolution furthermore defined what exactly luxury goods were (in response
to the perceived undue vagueness of previous sanctions), and listed specific
individuals and institutions to be added to the sanctions list.[17]

The 2013 nuclear test was just one part of a slew of measures North Korea took to ratchet up the pressure on China, South Korea, Japan, and the United States between the passing of UNSCR 2087 on 22 January and a ramping down of North Korean rhetoric at the beginning of June. Aside from declaring the 1953 armistice agreement null and void, fueling missiles, and warning foreign personnel to leave Pyongyang in preparation for hostilities, North Korea also shut down the Kaesong Industrial Region, closing entry on 3 April and banning North Korean workers from reporting to work on 8 April. Kaesong would not be reopened until 16 September, thus denying not only South Korea business but also North Korea hard income for over five months.[18]

The end of the 2013 crisis was followed by relative stability in North Korea's international behavior, and even included a tentative (if temporary) rapprochement with Japan in 2014 and 2015, in which North Korea agreed to conduct an investigation into the fate of Japanese abductees in return for a partial lifting of Japanese sanctions.[19] Yet this relative calm was not to last. North Korea and the international community returned to a tit-for-tat once again when North Korea conducted a fourth nuclear test (of what it claimed was a hydrogen bomb) on 6 January 2016, and the United Nations Security Council responded with UNSCR 2270 on 2 March. The new round of sanctions required all cargo entering or leaving North Korea to be inspected for sanctions violations, banned aircrafts and ships potentially connected to sanctions activities from member states' ports, generally prohibited the provision of aviation fuel to North Korea, and further banned North Korea from chartering foreign planes or ships, and other nations from operating North Korean-flagged vessels. In addition to the usual travel bans and asset freezes, the resolution also banned the small arms trade with North Korea, virtually prohibited foreign financial institutions from dealing with North Korea, prohibited training of North Koreans in fields relevant to nuclear weapons or missile development, and required the expulsion of North Koreans connected to sanctioned organizations. Of greatest relevance to North Korea's income streams, the resolution also banned the export of North Korean natural resources (coal, iron ore, and rare earth metals in particular) if the revenue would be used to fund sanctioned programs.[20]

The overall environment for overseas North Korean business activities thus became markedly more hostile from 2005 onward. Whether the sanctions were intended to change North Korea's behavior for the better, serve as a signal to demonstrate other powers' resolve in their antinuclear stance, or actually prevent North Korea from building (more) weapons of mass destruction or profiting from military transfer, in concrete terms, the sanctions were designed to force changes in where North Korean companies could do business, who they could do business with, what they could do business in, and how they could transfer goods or money into or out of North Korea.

The sanctions identified brokers (and end users) by name and placed travel and asset freezes on them, thus (theoretically) taking many experienced North Korean operators out of action. Individual banks and companies were also identified and sanctioned by name (although, given that North Korean banks and firms change names, registration, and ostensible ownership frequently, it is unclear how relevant these particular sanctions were). Certain financial transactions with North Korean firms were made significantly more difficult, or banned altogether. Given the difficulty of proving that the provenance or even ownership of North Korean assets were not under WMD-related sanctions, many banks that were not already subject to blanket sanctions requirements (such as US banks) chose not to do business with North Korean banks at all. In the case of the North Korean money in Banco Delta Asia, for example, when the United States tried to have it returned to North Korea during subsequent negotiations, the transfers were delayed because Chinese banks that could have done the transfers were reluctant even to touch the money.[21]

North Korean firms and accounts were also forced out of certain areas. Many companies no doubt decided it was easier simply not to do business with North Korean companies than navigate the sanctions regime's increasingly onerous regulations. Macau was closed off as a financial destination. The second most convenient trading partner of North Korea, Japan, was essentially cut off, and the primary brokers in Japan were neutered. Europe and Australia became significantly harsher environments for North Korean businesses. The North Korean state was thus faced with an external environment where it was no longer just a backward, neglected country struggling to survive, but now had the full attention of many countries' trade and finance regulators, and faced private companies and banks that were reluctant to do business (openly) with its representatives abroad. How state trading companies reacted is the focus of this chapter.

Adaptation in State-Centered Trade: Exports

Adaptation of Product Offerings

The simplest response that state trading networks could have to the darkening foreign environment would be to cease doing business in sanctioned activities, and to make a play for legitimacy. There does appear to have been a shift out of central state companies directly trading non-weapons-related illicit goods since about 2005. There are a number of problems with illicit income that may have led the central state to move out of at least certain sectors of illicit trade, including drugs and possibly counterfeit cigarettes. First, illicit goods are often not a reliable source of income. Profit, if it comes at all, tends to come in clumps as deals pay off, which is not a satisfactory situation for central state budgets. This profit must also be sufficiently high to overcome the inevitable losses associated with losing the cargo or seeing it interdicted by hostile governments.

Second, up until about 2005, while North Korean diplomats were not infrequently found to be serving as middlemen for minor drug shipments that North Korea had not (apparently) initiated, by and large the North Korean central state trading networks seem to have attempted to make money from illicit goods (particularly drugs) by controlling the supply chain from production through transportation to as close to street distribution as possible. This allowed it to pocket much of the profit to be had from drug production and distribution. As surrounding, hostile countries turned their attention to North Korea's state trafficking networks, it became increasingly difficult for central state enterprises to dominate the supply chain. This may have made it less lucrative for state enterprises to be involved directly in illicit trade. In sufficiently small amounts, drugs may have been worth the effort for private enterprises, but not for state enterprises seeking enough hard currency to keep the government afloat.

Perhaps most importantly, the changing structure of the North Korean economy may have rendered much of the state-run illicit trade networks obsolete. Out of the Arduous March evolved a system where state enterprises up and down the North Korean state hierarchy were forced both to fend for themselves financially and to provide income for the central state. Private enterprises also sprang up, and often, by paying off state enterprises, became hybrid firms that both provided state officials with some income and allowed private business to operate in a country that officially has none. As will be seen in chapter 3, increasingly the central state had little reason to trade directly in illicit consumer goods: if private and hybrid firms were going to operate in any case, and if they had to pay bribes, taxes, and other fees up the food chain in order to operate freely, then the central state could collect money from private and hybrid business, regardless of the source of that income. The central state could thus benefit from drug production and distribution, for example, without having to endure the stigma of state-sponsored drug trafficking, set up and maintain its own distribution networks outside of North Korea, or even approve of drugs or other illicit trade themselves. While the proportion of drug profits going to the central state no doubt would decline relative to the period when the state controlled much of the supply chain, the state received income nonetheless.

North Korean state enterprises also moved into businesses that, as will be discussed in chapter 3, required little to no logistical support (by North Koreans, at least). Aside from collecting rents from loaning out their official imprimaturs, state companies also used their trading permits to set up deals with foreign companies to export natural resources, particularly minerals, timber, fisheries products, and specialized agricultural goods. From 2006, North Korean mining exports skyrocketed as North Korean state companies built partnerships, mostly with Chinese mining firms, to extract minerals and export them abroad.[22] Both iron and coal exports, among others, increased dramatically, although both had been increasing since 2004 (see figure 2.1). The income from mining was ready-made, nearly guaranteed, and best of all, involved outside investors making infrastructure investments (if nowhere else than at the mines themselves and for the roads from the mines to the border) that could be nationalized if desired (as we will see in chapter 4). As the mining industry has grown in North Korea, state companies, particularly those from the military, have become so dependent on the income it provides that North Korea has in many respects become a resource export–dependent rentier state.[23]

This is not to say, however, that the North Korean central state abandoned illicit or sanctioned trade entirely. Indeed, sanctioned trade continued apace when the central state found a way to make money, or in areas where the central state was loath to subcontract out the trade itself, notably in the sale of weapons to other states. How North Korea continued to attempt to

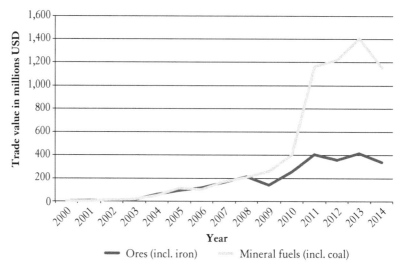

Figure 2.1. Reported North Korea mineral exports to China (2000 to 2014)
Source: UN Comtrade mirror data.

sell weapons after the imposition of sanctions sheds light on how state trading networks adapted their structure and location in the face of increasing international hostility. In short, North Korean companies adapted by blurring the lines between state and nonstate actions, and by integrating themselves even more deeply than before into the flows of the global economy.

Adaptation in the Weapons Export Network

While sanctioned nuclear, biological, chemical, and other weapons trade is not the only trading done by North Korean state companies, or even necessarily the majority of trading, it is useful to focus on the weapons trade for several reasons.

First, weapons are one of the few areas of North Korean business where the central state clearly is controlling or at least knowingly permitting trade.[24] Other more prosaic types of trade may be through private entities, or through privately managed entities that are formally registered as state-owned companies. Indeed, while Haggard and Noland find in their survey of Chinese businesses that the vast majority of Chinese–North Korean trade appears to be with North Korean state-owned firms, there is no way to know (as they acknowledge) whether these firms are actually traditional state trading companies or are hybrid entities.[25]

Second, given that nearly all weapons North Korea sells are sold to other states, state-to-state trade is the sector of North Korea's involvement with the global economy most likely to involve the use of state prerogatives, allowing us to see how state prerogatives shape the structure and geography of North Korea's trade networks. In addition, given that the buyers span the globe, the weapons trade is also the sector of North Korea's foreign trade that is the most likely to involve high-level elites with extensive international knowledge. This allows us to see whether North Korean elites engage in international business differently from lower-level elites or common people, or whether their practices share key commonalities.

Third, it is true that as sanctioned goods, weapons are unlikely to be traded in the same manner as legitimate goods, and as such, the weapons trade may not be representative of all North Korean state trade. Yet there are still reasons to think the weapons trade can tell us at least something about how North Korean state trading networks operate in general. Even in legitimate business transactions, either because of the international stigma associated with dealing with North Korea at all or because of how North Koreans are used to dealing with each other inside the country, North Korean state companies tend to act conspiratorial and engage in shady practices.[26] The United Nations has also observed that North Korean firms "make unquestionably legitimate transactions in roundabout ways," perhaps for the purposes of testing financial systems for future illicit transactions.[27] In 2012, for instance, Air Koryo set up a contract to purchase new aircraft (an unsanctioned transaction). It apparently acquired the funds to pay the supplier through eight shell companies registered in Hong Kong, all of whom claimed to owe significant debts to Air Koryo, and all of whom seem to have been connected to gold trading.[28] For this particular transaction, there was no need to engage in such subterfuge, and yet they did. Weapons trading may involve similar amounts of subterfuge, possibly even using the same methods. In the case of the weapons networks, adaptation came in the form of changes in the use of state prerogatives and assets, increased use of commercial forms and infrastructures, and a shift in the network structure away from North Korea into the broader region and the world.

Changing Use of State Prerogatives   Even before the onset of international sanctions in 2006, North Korean state entities were under close surveillance by other states: the beginning of the Proliferation Security Initiative, much of which was aimed at North Korea, and the *Pong Su* incident, predated the second North Korean nuclear crisis by several years. Rather than totally abandoning the use of state resources after coming under greater scrutiny, however, North Korea shifted the means by which it used them. Before, diplomats were called upon to traffic in drugs and other illicit goods themselves. After, diplomats, or at least personnel carrying diplomatic passports, became brokers, making deals with private foreign brokers and other state companies, and overseeing the paperwork and logistics associated with trade deals. In practice, this meant that the geographical distribution of the command and control networks associated with state trade became distinct from the logistical networks. State trade networks were directed from Pyongyang, and the negotiations often done over email or conducted in cities with a North Korean official presence, but the goods themselves often came nowhere near those outposts when being transported (unlike, for example, the regular Air Koryo flights to Macau in the 1990s). In a failed attempt to sell light arms, GPS systems, and man-portable rocket launchers to Azerbaijan in 2008, for example, North Korean representatives of Hesong Trading, a subsidiary of the Korean Mining Development Trading Corporation (KOMID), met with the British broker in public places in cities in Nepal and Malaysia, both countries with North Korean embassies. The plan would have been to charter a Russian-made cargo or passenger aircraft to fly the weapons out of North Korea.[29]

That same year, in another deal, a contract to sell maintenance services, weapons and weapons parts (including spare parts for T-54/T-55 tanks) to the Republic of Congo was negotiated by Song Chang-sik, a locally posted diplomat, on behalf of the Korean People's Army's General Department of Military Cooperation. A senior colonel traveling on a diplomatic passport, Kim Kwang-nam, oversaw the project's operation and the nearly forty North Korean technicians in Congo. State outposts themselves also served as loci for the finances associated with deals. In the case of the Congo deal, initially the North Koreans attempted to receive payment from the Bank of Congo to the North Korean embassy's commercial attaché in Beijing, although this was unsuccessful. Later they opened an account at the Bank of Congo itself in the name of the military attaché of the DPRK mission in the Congo.[30]

Use of Commercial Shipping Methods and Companies   State trading networks also adapted to the increasingly onerous sanctions by ceasing by some measures to be state trading networks as they relied more frequently on the use of commercial shipping methods and international companies for nearly all aspects of the supply chain. Because they relied on the global commercial shipping network, North Korea's own networks became constrained in several respects.

First, North Korean shipping conformed to the hub-and-spoke geographical distribution of the global shipping network. In practice, with the closing of Japan in 2006, North Korean companies shipped goods via their own vessels or chartered (and therefore expensive) ships to nearby Chinese cities, where they were loaded into regular shipping streams by Chinese freight forwarders and consigners. There is little evidence that the shippers beyond the Chinese cities knew what the containers actually held (regardless of what the bills of lading said), but that is true for most containers shipping companies move around the world. Once they entered the regular shipping stream, the goods were essentially out of the control of North Korean state companies.

In October 2009, for example, in the aforementioned Congo deal, the Machinery Export and Import Corporation in North Korea shipped spare parts for the Soviet-era tanks to the Republic of Congo. The cargo, listed as "spare parts of bulldozers," was shipped to Dalian, where it was loaded on to the *CGM Musca*, which in turn delivered the cargo to the *Westerhever* in Port Klang, Malaysia (one of the largest transshipment ports in the world). Both ships were owned by the French company CGM CGA. It was at least the fourth shipment of weapons and weapon parts meant to be delivered to the Republic of Congo, with two going by sea and one going by air in 2009.[31] In the case of the 2008 sea shipments to Congo, CGA CGM also handled the shipments, picking up one from Guangzhou Surfine Shipping Service Company Limited in Huangpu (near Shanghai), and the other in Dalian from Complant International Transportation.[32] Similarly, in the case of an air shipment (of tank and armored vehicle engines, among other things) to the Republic of Congo in 2008, Seajet Company Limited, a company based in Beijing and affiliated (in some way) with Air Koryo, contracted

with Ethiopian Airlines to fly the shipment from Beijing through Addis
Ababa to Brazzaville on its regularly scheduled flights. Presumably the
shipment started in Pyongyang.[33] In these cases, North Korea contracted
with commercial shippers for a state-to-state transaction, and the shippers
themselves used standard routes that passed through transshipment hubs.

Using commercial shipping companies and routes had both downsides
and upsides for the companies. By shedding state prerogatives in the logistics of trade, North Korea was able to avoid some amount of scrutiny, and
to take advantage of the efficiency of the global commercial shipping system. With no control over the shipping chain, obviously North Korea had
no means to obfuscate or otherwise hide the goods besides false customs
declarations and fake end users. As the goods themselves moved through
the global shipping system, they also moved through the transshipment
hubs created by the hub-and-spoke system of containerized shipping,
opening them up to scrutiny at the hubs.

North Korean companies made extensive use of Chinese brokers as
consignors and freight forwarders to arrange the shipments from Chinese
ports. These brokers had connections to both global shipping and (apparently) to North Korean state companies that persisted over multiple
transactions. The original consignor in a shipment of graphite cylinders
found in Busan, Dalian Liaosin Trading Company, was a Chinese company based in Dalian with a representative office in Pyongyang and a molybdenum ore processing plant in Hamhung. It was acting on behalf of
Korea Tangun Trading Corporation, a sanctioned North Korean military
company.[34] In the case of the *MV San Francisco* incident in 2010 (discussed
below), the shipper was Dandong-based Jing Huan Trading Company,
acting on behalf of Korea Ryongbong General Corporation, a sanctioned
state-owned company. Dalian-based COSCO Logistics, a company known
to be involved in trading with North Korea, served as a freight forwarder.[35]

Yet the use of commercial shipping (and Chinese forwarders) also imposed certain risks on North Korean state trade. Integration into global
trade was not costless: the sanctioned goods inevitably passed through
countries, both proximate to North Korea and further afield, that had
strong incentives to enforce sanctions. In May 2012, for example, South
Korean officials in Busan seized a shipment of graphite cylinders useful for
constructing ballistic missiles from the container ship *Xin Yan Tai* (owned
by a Chinese shipping company). The shipment was bound for Latakia,

Syria, where it was supposed to be delivered to Electric Parts Com, which was apparently a front company for the Syrian Scientific Studies and Research Center.[36] Using Busan as a stop after the initial on-loading in Dalian was not unusual. Several years earlier, a North Korean company shipped four containers of protective clothes for potential use in chemical weapons development from Nampo to Dalian in September 2009. In Dalian, the Panamanian-flagged *MSC Rachele*, owned by the Switzerland-based Mediterranean Shipping Company, took on the containers and moved on to Busan in South Korea, where the container were seized by the South Korean government. The intended recipient was the Environmental Studies Center in Syria.[37]

Elsewhere, in August 2012, Japanese authorities seized five aluminum alloy rods from the cargo ship *Wan Hai 313*, which had taken on cargo in Dalian from a company known as Korea Kumpyo Trading. The shipment was apparently bound for Myanmar.[38] Likewise, the container ship *MV San Francisco Bridge* was stopped in France in November 2010, when the French authorities determined that the items labeled as copper bars and plates were actually "brass discs and copper rods used to manufacture artillery munitions (pellets and rods for crimping cartridges and driving bands) and aluminum alloy tubes usable for making rockets."[39] The designated recipient in Latakia was the Company of Metallic Constructions and Mechanical Industries, a front company for the Syrian Scientific Studies and Research Center.[40]

Shift in Network Structure Away from North Korea   Finally, North Korean state companies sought to solve the logistical and security problems associated with shipping goods from North Korea by integrating themselves into the shipping networks such that the structure of the logistical network minimized the involvement of North Koreans (or the territory of North Korea). While the use of commercial shipping networks and brokers certainly was part of this strategy, state companies took even more radical steps to both integrate themselves into the global economy and deflect evidence of North Korean involvement.

In situations where the foreign broker was located in North Korea itself, North Korean state companies were able to remove North Korean state assets from the supply chain entirely. In July 2009, the United Arab Emirates seized rocket fuses from the DPRK that were labeled as "oil boring machine (spare parts)" from the *ANL Australia* while it was docked in Khor Fakkan in Fujairah. Except for the original North Korean company, none of the companies involved were North Korean, even within North Korea: the original shipper was in fact the Pyongyang office of an Italian company, OTIM SPA, which was not allowed to inspect or ask questions about the pre-customs sealed containers it was given to load onto a ship in Nampo. The *ANL Australia* was a Bahamian-flagged vessel owned by an Australian company, and had an intended destination of Bandar Abbas, Iran.[41]

As during the Arduous March, North Korean state companies also continued to serve as brokers for transactions that never entered North Korean soil. Aside from solving the problem of involving North Korean state assets in the transaction, such transactions demonstrate North Korean state companies' continued ability to operate in a number of different countries, and perhaps more importantly, to have sufficiently good connections with both buyers and suppliers that their brokerage services are worth paying for. According to Japanese authorities, in 2008 and 2009, the Beijing office of New East International Trading, Ltd., a North Korean front company based in Hong Kong (with a sanctioned Pyongyang office) approached an ethnic Korean resident in Japan (almost certainly a Chongryon sympathizer) to source and then ship via Malaysia sanctioned machinery and tools that could be used to make missile gyroscopes, as well as other equipment, to the Directorate of Myanmar Industrial Planning in the Ministry of Industry II (in actuality the Directorate of Defence Industries). Shinfung Trading Company and Korea Paekho Trading were involved in separate sales of air conditioning units to Myanmar.[42] In this case, North Korean state companies used state assets in multiple countries to broker the transaction, but the logistical network itself was put together by a foreign broker with ethnic, nonmarket ties back to North Korea, and used commercial shipping networks to source and move the goods from Japan to Myanmar.

The Chong Chon Gang *Incident*   The *Chong Chon Gang* incident in July 2013, when Panamanian authorities discovered MiG-21 aircraft and aircraft parts, and surface-to-air missile components hidden underneath thousands of bags of sugar as the *Chong Chon Gang* passed through the Panama Canal, illustrates the complexity of North Korean state trading networks in a postsanctions world, and the advantages and disadvantages of using state assets to move goods around the world in a bid to make money. The *Chong Chon Gang* had left Chongjin on 11 April 2013, refueled in

Vostochny (a port in Russia east of Nakhodka) and apparently sailed directly to Cuba, arriving in Havana on 4 June. Over the next month, the ship moved from Havana to Mariel to Puerto Padre before leaving Cuba on 5 July and arriving in Colon, Panama, on 11 July. The intent was to drop off the cargo in Nampo upon returning to North Korea.[43]

There are several interesting points to consider about the incident. First, the *Chong Chon Gang* had always been North Korean–flagged and operated, so in this sense it was not disguised particularly well, or at least North Korea's primary means of concealment on this particular trip did not involve concealing the fact that it was a North Korean ship. The *Chong Chon Gang* did, however, make efforts to conceal its physical movements by, for example, turning off its automatic identification system and falsifying the specific ports at which it called.[44] Overall, the concealment came through minimizing contact with the commercial shipping grid. The *Chong Chon Gang*'s behavior, and the routes that it followed, are indicative of what North Korean state trading networks look like when they actually do make full use of state prerogatives and assets outside of North Korea.

Second, the ship actually did deliver export goods—specifically rolled steel plates and locomotive wheels—to Havana before picking up the weapons for refurbishment in Mariel and picking up sugar in Puerto Padre.[45] North Korean state companies sometimes make money refurbishing other developing countries' Soviet-era weapons, either in the client country (with North Korean technicians, as in the Republic of Congo) if the demands of the job are not too great, or back in North Korea for more complex tasks. However, this entails shipping the weapons back to North Korea, potentially putting both the job and the client country at risk for sanctions violations.[46] In this case, the movement of weapons from Cuba to North Korea was part of more general trade between Cuba and North Korea. The ship was itself part of a larger trading network that may have included smuggling at other times and places as well. The *Chong Chon Gang* had been involved in a previous incident in January 2010, when Ukrainian officials in a port in the Mykolaiv region seized small quantities of undeclared alcohol, cigarettes, drugs, and small arms ammunition from the ship, although the small quantities led the Ukrainian government to conclude there was no organized state effort behind it.[47]

Third, the state trading companies made extensive use of state prerogatives in the trade. In doing so, they were able to shape the geography of the transportation chain at least somewhat and bypass commercial transshipments hubs—the *Chong Chon Gang* seems to have sailed directly from Vostochny to Cuba without stopping, and the crew retained full control over the cargo throughout the voyage. The captain of the *Chong Chon Gang* also communicated with DPRK embassy personnel in Havana, who apparently arranged the contracts and payment for shipping both the weapons and the sugar (which was ostensibly being shipped from Cubazucar to Korea Central Marketing & Trading Corporation).[48] As with other postsanctions deals, diplomats and diplomatic outposts functioned more as brokerage and command and control centers than as logistical waypoints.

At the same time, the state assets themselves—the shipping companies and the diplomats—found it useful to adopt the forms and processes of international commercial enterprises. The geographic distribution of these commercialized assets, which handled the paperwork associated with the deal, was spread throughout East Asia and concentrated in cities where North Korean state outposts had a presence. The *Chong Chon Gang* itself was owned by what was almost certainly a state company, the Chongchongang Shipping Company, which contracted for management and operation of the ship with Ocean Maritime Management Company, Ltd. (OMM), a Pyongyang-based company with branch offices in Vladivostok and Dalian. Ocean Maritime Management in turn used Chinpo Shipping Company, a Singaporean company co-located with the DPRK embassy in Singapore, as the shipping agent. All three—OMM Dalian, OMM Vladivostok, and Chinpo—provided money or information to the local shipping agent in Panama to attempt to move the ship through the Panama Canal.[49] Even when North Korean state companies were sufficiently concerned about concealing a transaction (as they were in this case) that they accepted the risks (and, to be fair, benefits) associated with maintaining control of the shipping chain, using state prerogatives in a postsanctions world still involved becoming part of the global economy even as they sought to undermine it (or at least avoid outside scrutiny).

Adaptation in State-Based Trade: Imports

Adaptation in Import Broker Networks

The trading networks North Korea set up to import goods, sanctioned or otherwise, as it encountered a more hostile foreign environment were somewhat different from state companies' export networks, although there was nonetheless a great deal of overlap, in no small part because the same companies were often involved in both: state companies increasingly took themselves out of the supply chain for goods they desired, and turned to foreign brokers, commercial shipping routes, and commercial suppliers.

Compared to export networks, state import networks appear to have been more flexible in shifting the geographical distribution of the nodes within the supply chain, and thus were better able to adapt to encroaching foreign hostility. In part this is likely because there was greater substitutability in the firms and states with which North Korea needed to deal for import networks than for export networks. For state export networks, there were a limited number of governments that needed (let alone wanted) North Korean technology, weapons and weapons-related services. The primary logistical and financial considerations in selling weapons were figuring out how to move the goods from North Korea to the same target country without being interdicted, and how to receive payment despite financial sanctions. The demands from different countries were not necessarily easily substitutable—Iran's demand for missile components was not substitutable with Congo's demand for battle tank components and maintenance contracts. The nonstate suppliers that ultimately produced North Korean imports, however, could come from many different countries, with a number of different suppliers able to produce equivalent goods if one was unwilling or unable to.

This was in part because many of the goods North Korean state companies imported were either not sanctioned at all, were of unclear status relative to sanctions (in the case of luxury goods, which are classified differently in every country), or were standard commercial goods that were only sanctioned if it was known that North Korean companies were the ultimate buyers. In effect, this meant that there was either little need to hide North Korean involvement, or that a relatively simple camouflaging process (through nonsanctioned brokers) was sufficient.

The logistics of the supply chain—whether to use commercial shipping, how to avoid being interdicted—presented fewer issues. After North Korea tested an Unha-3 missile in December 2012, for example, South Korea salvaged parts of the rocket from the ocean floor, and the UN Panel of Experts attempted to ascertain the origin of the parts. The parts, almost all of which were "off-the-shelf," appeared to come from the former Soviet Union, the United Kingdom, China, the United States, Switzerland, and

South Korea. None of the companies that could be contacted remembered having sold parts to North Korea when sanctions were in effect, suggesting that North Korea had used foreign brokers to buy the goods.[50] The pressure transmitters for the missiles, for instance, were sold in 2006 and 2010 by a British company to a Taiwanese company.[51] The parts imported by North Korean companies thus came from a variety of countries, most of which had some form of sanctions against North Korea. If one country (or firm) presented problems as a supplier, North Korea could shift to another.

State import networks used a variety of foreign brokers to ease the acquisition process. As with the export networks, these brokers were largely either territorially proximate to North Korea, or in North Korea itself. As seen from the luxury goods brokers below, they also seem to have maintained relationships with North Korean companies across multiple transactions. North Korea's use of brokers may have integrated it more tightly into the global economy. As North Korean state companies have built up relationships with foreign brokers to mask end users and handle logistics, sanctions may have actually in some ways strengthened North Korea's procurement abilities.

In 2013, for example, to determine how sanctions had influenced the North Korean state procurement process, John Park conducted interviews with North Korean defectors in South Korea who had been involved in positions of responsibility with state trading companies. Whereas in the past North Korean state companies had procured goods directly from Eastern Europe and the Middle East, with the onset of sanctions, they were forced to turn to Chinese broker companies, who procured and transported the goods, handled the financial arrangements, and otherwise camouflaged North Korea as the final destination for the goods. According to Park, as Chinese companies have become adept at operating within the global economy, increasingly sophisticated middlemen have jockeyed for North Korean brokerage contracts. While sanctions have led brokerage fees to increase, they have also led to more opportunities for North Korean state trading companies to procure goods. Han Chinese who are resident in North Korea (hwa-gyo) are especially valued as brokers (and command a premium in their fees), since they are already in North Korea, speak Korean fluently and appear (to suppliers) to be regular Chinese companies.[52] Absent sanctions, in other words, North Korean state companies would not have cultivated relationships with foreign import-export or shipping companies. Once sanctions forced them to do so, both the foreign companies and the North Korean firms learned through experience how to operate in a hostile business environment.

North Korea's search for luxury items, which the central state distributes to elites as rewards for loyalty, and which those with money can buy in some stores in Pyongyang, is especially illustrative of import networks, inasmuch as North Korean companies faked end users and documentation, and hired foreign brokers. The foreign brokers were not only used multiple times, but also used for different types of goods, and for moving goods both toward and away from North Korea. The UN sanctions committee found, for instance, that the same firms in Japan that procured luxury items for North Korea also shipped the sanctioned items mentioned above to Myanmar.[53] Between 2008 and 2010, according to the Japanese government, North Korean companies illegally imported tobacco, high-quality sake, a number of Mercedes-Benz and Lexus sedans, thousands of notebook computers, used pianos, and cosmetics from Japan.[54] Nearly all of the transactions went through Chinese brokers, who received the goods from the Japanese suppliers and sent payments via cash deliveries or wire transfer so that no money came directly from North Korea. Many of the items were funneled through the Chinese company Dalian Global Unity Shipping Agency (presumably a shipping agency in Dalian), which reached out to the Japanese suppliers, and gave instructions for how to handle the goods after the North Korean companies (Korea Rungrado General Trading Company, Shinfung Trading Corporation, and Sang Myong 2, all based in Pyongyang) placed orders. According to the Chinese government, the majority of items were not illegal to export to North Korea, so once North Koreans had successfully exported the goods from Japan, they faced a simple task in moving them into North Korea.[55]

The Rise of Taiwan

Aside from China itself, nowhere was North Korean state companies' post-2006 shift to foreign suppliers and brokers for importing goods more evident than in Taiwan. With Japan declining as a useful source of goods, with the onset of sanctions in the middle of 2006, North Korea turned to other countries as suppliers and brokers. For goods that could potentially be sanctioned, along with Hong Kong, Taiwan emerged as a partial replacement trading partner for the loss of Japan, in both imports and exports. Although (recorded) Taiwanese trade with North Korea never reached anywhere near the levels of trade with Japan at its heights, Taiwanese imports from North Korea began picking up almost as soon as Japanese imports cratered in 2007 (see figure 2.2). Meanwhile, North Korean imports from Taiwan reached a plateau as imports from Japan fell (indeed, trade with Japan was falling precipitously even before sanctions), hit a high in 2006, and stayed relatively high through 2011 (although it was still only a fraction of what Japanese trade had been) (see figure 2.3).[56] Interestingly, trade with Hong Kong followed similar patterns, with North Korean imports from Hong Kong increasing on and off from 2007. This suggests that Hong Kong may have also served as a partial replacement for Japan, although nearly all of Hong Kong's exports to North Korea were reexports, implying that Hong Kong functioned as a transshipment point rather than as a supplier for North Korea.

Here it is useful to dwell for some time on Taiwan's role as a broker for North Korean import networks. Taiwan was an ideal location for both suppliers and brokers for several reasons. First, as a developed country with

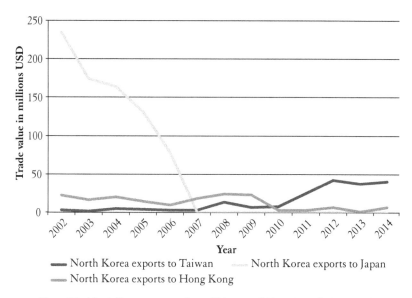

Figure 2.2. North Korea exports to Japan, Taiwan, and Hong Kong (2002 to 2014)
Source: UN Comtrade mirror data. The Taiwan figures are actually UN Comtrade's figures for all countries in Asia that are not otherwise listed, which in practice are almost entirely Taiwan.

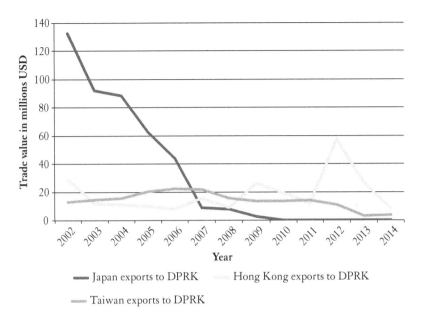

— Japan exports to DPRK   Hong Kong exports to DPRK

— Taiwan exports to DPRK

Figure 2.3. Japan, Taiwan, and Hong Kong exports to North Korea (2002 to 2014)
Source: UN Comtrade mirror data.

an extensive high-tech industrial sector, Taiwanese companies were able to source locally many of the goods that North Korea demanded. Second, Taiwan's traditionally strong economic relationship with Japan meant that brokers in Taiwan had experience working with Japanese companies, and shipping goods from Japan through Taiwan to North Korea was relatively straightforward. Third, Taiwan's proximity to Japan, China, and North Korea minimized the transportation time and costs for North Korean ships, thus limiting the opportunities for interdiction by counterproliferators. Fourth, Taiwan's developed economy and close relationship with the United States allowed companies operating out of Taiwan to avoid the scrutiny that companies operating out of mainland China (to say nothing of North Korea) would have received.

This is not to say that Taiwan was lackadaisical in its approach to trade relations with North Korea. In fact, at the same time that the United Nations and Japan were limiting trade with North Korea, Taiwan was also expanding its export control regime. Taiwan enacted relatively strict trade controls on dual-use exports to North Korea (and China) in May 2006, and did so again in December 2006, in line with UN sanctions. In both cases, Taiwan increased the number of different dual-use items that were subject to export licenses for countries of concern, which since 2003 had included both China and North Korea, among others.[57] Yet Taiwan's unique status in the international community played in North Korea's favor. As a de facto independent state that was nonetheless not recognized by most other states in the world, Taiwan was (and is) not a party to any nonproliferation treaties, conventions, or agreements. Nor was it formally bound by whatever sanctions were placed on North Korea by the United Nations Security Council, given its lack of membership in the United Nations. To be sure, successive Taiwanese administrative have been eager to adopt and enforce regulations to prevent proliferation of dual-use and nuclear materials and components. Yet because of Taiwan's exclusion from many bodies requiring state status (including the Nuclear Suppliers Group), its regulations and enforcement activities necessarily mimic those of other countries rather than being integrated in a formal way. In areas where state-to-state cooperation and information sharing are necessary, Taiwan may be substantially hampered from thoroughly implementing policies designed to address problems. This was most evident in 2003 when Taiwan's lack of membership in the World Health Organization arguably inhibited its ability to fight SARS.[58] Yet this disconnect also made it difficult to deal with transnational crime or gray market trading.

This was especially true of goods and people moving between Taiwan and mainland China. From 2006 until 2008, during the latter half of Republic of China President Chen Shui-bian's administration, China-Taiwan relations were chilly and essentially frozen in place, with China content to wait out the end of a Democratic Progressive Party administration, and hope for a more pliant Kuomintang administration in 2008. While political relations stagnated, economic ties actually continued to grow throughout the Chen administration.[59] The result was increasingly dense trade networks stretching between Taiwan and mainland China that were largely free of formal cross-strait regulation. While Taiwanese law enforcement officials built informal ties with their mainland counterparts, often quite successfully, and could call upon these ties when they needed to coordinate, without formal agreements, their relationships were put on hold during downturns in cross-strait relations.[60] This provided political space for organized criminals and companies seeking to evade import and export regulations as they piggybacked on burgeoning legitimate trade, while counting on the inability of the Taiwanese and Chinese governments to coordinate effectively against them.[61]

Even before 2006, Taiwan had already proven useful to state trading networks in North Korea that sought to import dual-use goods. In 2002, Kim Yong Gun, the CEO of the Japanese trading company Meisho Yoko, ordered a freeze dryer from Seishin Soiji (a company that also supplied dual-use goods to companies in Iran) and shipped it through a Taiwanese trading company to a North Korean state trading company. The transaction came to light during Japan's crackdown on North Korean business activities beginning in February 2006.[62]

As other countries began exercising more scrutiny over North Korean activities in the early 2000s, and particularly once North Korea faced a new, more hostile international environment in 2006, it appears to have leaned heavily on Taiwanese brokers and suppliers, something reflected in the plateau in Taiwanese exports to North Korea from 2005 to 2007 at the same time that Japanese trade cratered (see figure 2.3). In 2006 and 2007, Royal Team Corporation, a trading company in Taiwan, in fourteen separate transactions sourced and then shipped precision machine tools, computers, refrigerators, and other industrial equipment to North Korea. In some cases, the goods were flown to North Korea directly by air. In other cases, they were shipped to mainland China (presumably to Dalian), from where they were forwarded to North Korea.[63] Likewise, in the same time frame, the Taiwanese Yi-Cheng Corporation exported a dual-use industrial filtering device to what was apparently a North Korean front company in Dalian.[64]

With the election of the Kuomintang's Ma Ying-jeou as President of the Republic of China in May 2008, China-Taiwan relations improved dramatically. Within the first several years of Ma's first term, China and Taiwan had concluded a number of agreements to formalize trade and cooperation. Regularly scheduled direct shipping and air routes were opened up between Taiwan and mainland cities, and a judicial cooperation agreement provided a formal means for law enforcement officials on both sides of the strait to share information, institutionalize cooperation, and improve coordination on joint anticrime efforts. Most momentous of all, the Economic Cooperation Framework Agreement (ECFA), which came into effect in September 2010, decreased tariffs and opened up markets in both

Taiwan and China, allowing for a blossoming of formal trade across the strait. Closer China-Taiwan ties had the potential to push North Korea's ability to use Taiwan as a broker location in two countervailing directions: denser direct economic ties between Taiwan and the mainland presented many more opportunities for North Korean companies to hide their goods within the overall cross-strait trade flow, and meant that more Taiwanese brokers were used to dealing with shipping to and from China. At the same time, closer Chinese and Taiwanese cooperation on law enforcement issues may have impinged on North Korea's ability to engage in jurisdictional arbitrage, moving between two mutually hostile jurisdictions that neither cared about nor coordinated with each other, and taking advantages of loopholes or blind spots in each.[65]

Improving China-Taiwan relations may have thus paradoxically made it both more difficult for North Korea to arbitrage law enforcement and customs authorities and easier for Taiwanese brokers to set up supply chains that funneled goods into North Korea through China. In May 2013, Taiwanese resident Alex Tsai was arrested in Estonia, while his son Gary Tsai was arrested in Chicago on charges relating to violating US sanctions.[66] The Tsais, in connection with their associate Chang Wen-fu, allegedly set up a number of companies, among them Global Interface Company Inc., Trans Merits Co. Ltd., and Trans Multi Mechanics Co. Ltd., to buy precision machine tools and components in the United States, ship them to Taiwan, and then on to KOMID or its subsidiaries.[67] In 2008, Alex Tsai had been convicted in Taiwan of forging invoices and shipping controlled goods to North Korea, and had been designated, along with Global Interface and Trans Merits, as a sanctions violator by the US government in 2009. The general modus operandi for the Tsais, according to the US criminal complaint, was to use the names Global Interface and Trans Merits interchangeably, and after the US designation, to use the name Trans Multi Mechanics as the front company (given that it was not designated as a sanctions violator).[68] Gary Tsai, from his position in the United States, would negotiate with midwestern US suppliers to buy precision machinery (either new or used), and arrange for it to be sent to Taiwan, either by air (through Air Tiger Express) or by cargo ship. Subsequently, in September 2009, Gary Tsai set up a company called Factory Direct Machine Tools that both imported and exported precision machine tools between the United States and other countries. Income from the company's business was paid to a Hong Kong bank account in the name of Alex Tsai.[69]

Although no evidence was presented in the US criminal complaint that the goods bought in the United States were shipped to North Korea, the 2009 US Treasury press release designating Alex Tsai as a sanctioned individual alleged that the Tsais had been doing business with KOMID since the 1990s.[70] The Tsais' activities do have some implications for how to think about post-2006 North Korean state trade. While an ethnic Korean broker in Japan would have likely have been preferable, North Korean central state companies were apparently happy to maintain a long-term trading relationship with a non-Korean broker in another nearby country. By using Taiwanese brokers, North Korea could tap into a country that was directly integrated into the global economy (specifically the aspects of the global economy that could provide the high-tech components North Korea wanted) and enjoyed good trade relations with the United States. At the same time, the North Korean aspect of the network was entirely contained within North Korea, its contacts with the broker in Taiwan, and possibly a receiver of the goods in mainland China, thus limiting its risk of failure and exposure to counterproliferators. The North Korean recipients were also spared from having to worry about sourcing or logistics until the goods arrived in China or at least Taiwan. Through the strategic use of Taiwanese brokers, North Korean state companies were able to straddle the boundaries between state and nonstate, between licit and illicit. All nodes and links within the networks but the final leg and recipient were nonstate (non–North Korean) firms, and the goods themselves, generally prosaic machinery, tools, and chemicals, remained technically licit until the moment they passed into North Korean hands, reducing the need for subterfuge.

Case Study: A Dandong Trading Company

A conversation in November 2013 with a representative of one trading company in Dandong that (as of 2013) does hundreds of thousands of dollars of business with North Korea every year sheds light on the ways in which (what are most likely) state trading companies use foreign brokers to import what they need, with or without complying with the sanctions regime. Not surprisingly, North Korean state trading companies first and foremost appear to value brokers with ethnic connections (or at least Korean-speaking ability) and personal relationships that have persisted over a relatively long period of time. The director of the trading company speaks Korean, as do two of the employees (both Korean Chinese from Yanbian). The company's business is based on the connections that the boss has built up over the past twenty years with North Korean import companies, through meeting and drinking with them. The trading company's business depends on the director's connections: the company is successful only in two-fifths of its orders, but use of its connections allows it to get successful bids at higher pricing points. With the difference in bids, the trading company is sometimes able to share the profit (read: kickbacks) with its North Korean partners. The long-term connections are also valuable because they establish a certain amount of trust. According to the trader, North Koreans who come to China to do business are terrified of being cheated by Chinese businessmen, who they view as cheaters. In 2012 a North Korean in the building next to the trading company (presumably the building housing the North Korean trading company) came to China, and was cheated out of his money. He committed suicide by jumping out of a high floor on the building and smashing on the pavement below.

The state companies importing goods have a spatial distribution that is similar to those exporting goods (and presumably are often the same companies). The Chinese trading company has more than ten North Korean partners, most of whom are based in Pyongyang. Those partners in turn have representatives around China (notably Hong Kong, Macau, Shanghai, Beijing, and Shenyang) as well as other countries (particularly Singapore and Indonesia). For a given desired good, multiple representatives from different branch offices of the same North Korean import company will ask for quotes for goods the company wants. This has several desirable effects: first, it masks and confuses the origin of the import company (as is true of export companies); second, uniquely to import companies, it allows the company to get lower prices, as suppliers attempt to underbid each other; and third, it creates the impression of more widespread demand for the suppliers' business. North Korean companies essentially attempt to create a competitive market for their own imports.

Besides obfuscating the origin of import orders and creating artificial demand, one of the other functions of the Southeast Asian North Korean representatives is to source goods that are cheaper in Southeast Asia than in China (such as semimanufactured goods and electronics). Singapore in particular has cheaper electronic goods than China. In fact, according to the trading company representatives, it can sometimes be cheaper to have the components made in China, ship them over to Southeast Asia for final manufacturing, and then ship them to North Korea than simply to source them from China. Through a spatial distribution that stretches across East and Southeast Asia, North Korean firms can thus build and take advantage of knowledge of regional production chains and international variation in the price of goods.

As with many of the Chinese brokers doing business with North Korean state companies, the trading company is a general import-export company, moving a range of products. The North Korean partners themselves also appear to be generalists, acting on behalf of companies with a variety of operations in different sectors. The business of importing and export is itself their specialty, which may explain why North Korean state companies appear to be so good at sourcing goods. There is no specific limit to what the trading company exports to North Korea, although the North Koreans themselves have a predilection for scientific instruments, power tools (particularly Bosch tools from Germany), Chinese glass (which is stronger and less breakable than North Korean glass), cornmeal, chemical reagents, urea-based fertilizer (in 2012 alone, the company exported 164 tons of fertilizer to North Korea), and semimanufactured goods (specifically components for electronic goods that the North Koreans can then put together themselves). Most of the goods the trading company sources are directly from factories in southern China (Fujian, Zhejiang, Guangdong), with some specialty products made in northeastern China. With that said, North Koreans prefer US, German, and Japanese goods because they do not have the reliability problems or terrible service of Chinese products. Such goods are great for the trading company's profit margins (since it can charge more for sourcing them), but the equipment often comes with instruction manuals that are complex and difficult for the company to decipher (no doubt because of both language issues and the more complex nature of the equipment being bought).

Some of these items, particularly the scientific instruments, power tools, and electronic components, are almost certainly either sanctioned or at least would attract scrutiny for potential sanctions violations. The company solves this problem in several ways. In some cases, it buys goods that are theoretically banned by the originating country from being sold to North Korea from another country: the trading company once bought a US-made diesel engine from Singapore, and exported it to North Korea. The company also uses its own set of intermediaries separate from the brokers used by the North Koreans. For example, the trading company once received an order for very accurate bioinstrumentation equipment that the Japanese supplier refused to ship to North Korea. The trading company had it shipped to a university laboratory in China, which in turn shipped it to the trading company in Dandong, which then sent it into North Korea.

The trading company also faces the challenge of moving goods through Chinese customs and into North Korea (where customs officials obviously do not care about sanctions, but do care about the nature of the goods entering the country). On the Chinese side, the trading company is embedded in a network of import-export companies that complement each other's connections and resources to move goods into North Korea. The trading company might have good connections with North Koreans, but another company with no connections in North Korea nonetheless knows how to smuggle goods out of China. One company might have exceeded its quota for a certain good in a given year, while the other has not, so the goods are shifted around until every company is theoretically under quota.

The trading company also uses its own network of ghost companies to evade tax. If it is worried about being taxed, or being scrutinized by Chinese customs (whose hackles might be raised if the goods are destined for North Korea) and losing its business license, it has goods shipped to the ghost company instead of itself. In combination, it can use a network of agents who have relationships with Chinese customs officials, and who can pay the officials (high monetary bribes) to look the other way when possibly untaxed or sanctioned goods come through. This is not particularly unusual. Indeed, the informant estimates that 70 percent of the trade between North Korea and China going through Dandong is smuggled. Figure 2.4 illustrates the complex networks that facilitate the movement of goods into North Korea, and the movement of orders and money out of the country.

Once the goods cross into North Korea, North Korean customs officials inspect everything closely (even to the point of uncapping pens), but give greater leniency to "business materials" (such as USB drives for business). North Korean customs officials refuse to allow in goods with labels that say "Made in Korea" so the trading company has the suppliers scratch

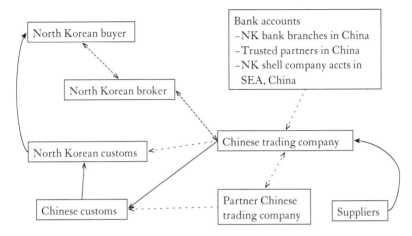

Figure 2.4. Notional schematic of a North Korean acquisition network in China
Note: Solid lines indicate the physical movement of goods, while dashed lines indicate
a relationship, and dotted lines indicate the transfer of money.

them off. The North Koreans are fine with (in fact, they actively desire) South Korean goods made in China (and for that matter goods that say "Made in Japan" or "Made in USA"); when North Koreans visit China, they actively seek out Samsung phones.

When crossing between China and North Korea, it is the partners' choice as to which drivers they use for delivery of their goods. Chinese drivers are cheap, while North Korean drivers are expensive. The drivers of the trucks that pass between China and North Korea are themselves petty smugglers (hiding smuggled goods underneath their seats in the cab, as well as on their persons). Chinese drivers take beer and Chinese cigarettes into North Korea to bribe the North Korean customs officials and workers offloading the goods. North Korean drivers take North Korean cigarettes, which they sell to the Chinese North Korean souvenir sellers in the area near the Broken Bridge (the bridge across the Yalu River in Dandong that was bombed by the US Air Force during the Korean War and has become a tourist attraction on the Chinese side).

In terms of making payments, once again North Korea's methods include a combination of foreign brokers around the globe and nonmarket relationships where necessary, and state organizations operating discreetly outside of North Korea where possible. According to the trading company,

North Koreans have ghost companies throughout Southeast Asia, Hong Kong, Macau, and China with bank accounts in those countries that they use to make payments to the trading company. The money for those accounts is often physically carried in suitcases from North Korea to those other countries. The North Koreans also use real accounts in extremely trusted, nonsanctioned individuals' names. To make a payment, the North Koreans might transfer (physical cash) to trusted Person A, who then pays the trading company (Person B) via normal means. North Korean banks also have their own branches in Dandong that can pay out to traders. The offices themselves are unsigned, heavily guarded anonymous places with cameras and security systems. The traders all know where the offices are, however.

The existence of the trading company's business at all is a testament to the North Korean importers' use of brokers and subterfuge to access the global economy. Yet North Korean importers have a high learning curve, and are increasingly extruding themselves into China to interface directly with suppliers. The informant found that the current trend is for North Koreans to come into China themselves to buy goods. They come officially as individuals rather than as officially licensed businesses, which can make it somewhat more difficult for them to do business by themselves. As a result, even though they source the goods themselves, they will still need help.

And yet, the North Koreans are getting better and better even at the import-export side, although they are now concentrating on sourcing the goods themselves in China, and then having the trading companies export the goods back to North Korea. North Koreans are becoming more comfortable with buying small, everyday goods and exporting them on their own. They still rely on the trading company to source and export complicated, large equipment because they do not want to be cheated by Chinese suppliers. The informant foresees that within five years, and ten years at the outside limit, there will no longer be any need for Chinese import-export companies in Dandong. He anticipates there will continue to be money for Chinese merchants to sell goods directly to North Korean import-export companies in China. But as North Korea figures out ways to navigate regional production networks, his company has no future in its present business.[71]

In response to a tightening noose from 2006 as the North Korean central state and the international community ricocheted between provocations and sanctions, state trading firms adapted: even as the idea of doing business with North Korean state firms was being stigmatized, the same state firms moved more forcefully into the global economy, although in a manner and in forms that would not have been recognizable to many observers.

The goods North Korean state firms traded often straddled the boundary between licit and illicit—they were goods, often quite prosaic ones, that were legal and otherwise unremarkable in almost any context. The one exception—when the goods passed into or out of North Korean hands—could be sidestepped by North Korean firms masking the origin or destinations of the goods and enmeshing themselves in commercial trading networks that officially began just outside of North Korean territory. North Korea could resolve the problem of illicit goods by removing itself from the chain until the goods themselves became licit.

As they traded these licit/illicit goods, state firms jumped strategically between state and nonstate status and behavior. Although they had access to state prerogatives and assets, state trading networks shed them in many respects, and deployed them strategically in others. As seen in the case of the *Chong Chon Gang*, the North Korean state was still willing to use state assets for transportation under certain circumstances. But even as they moved away from using the resources of the state for transporting goods, state firms made judicious use of them to negotiate and oversee deals, and otherwise govern the relationships among the nodes of their networks. A hostile environment also led North Korean state firms to build often long-term relationships with a range of brokers (brokers who themselves built up networks to move through or around hostile governments) to move goods in and out of North Korea. Clearly the firms preferred to work with brokers who were ethnically Korean or at least sympathetic to North Korea, and they did so when presented with the opportunity (as was the case with the Dandong trading company). Yet they were willing and able to do business with nearly anyone. In building up brokerage relationships, the state firms took on commercial forms, engaged in standard commercial behavior (often with the support of state assets), and made extensive use of commercial shipping companies, hubs, and routes. While dependence on the commercial world made North Korean trade more vulnerable to interdiction, it also gave state firms experience in dealing with that world.

It was not just state firms that adapted to the new world spawned by the Arduous March and, later, sanctions. Other trading networks within North Korea and stretching between North Korea and the rest of the world also matured in an environment that both encouraged and required diverse forms of entrepreneurialism to survive. They will be the subject of the next chapter.

3

ENTREPRENEURIALISM, NORTH KOREA–STYLE

While North Korean state trading networks, under pressure from sanctions and general hostility from other countries, survived, adapted, and even managed to thrive through creativity, flexibility, and, ironically, greater integration into a global economy that reviled them, they were not the only actors in North Korean society that demonstrated an ability to survive in harsh conditions. Indeed, the private sector, and an emerging hybrid sector within North Korea stretching to the outside world, also demonstrated surprising flexibility and adaptability in a tough environment (one created by the North Korean state itself).

This emergent entrepreneurialism has not necessarily been looked upon with approval by the state. In the wake of the Arduous March, the North Korean central state became deeply ambivalent about the existence of markets in a nominally command economy, and the loss of control over the population they entailed. It tried to pull them back, with a number of measures wreaking havoc on the markets and private enterprise, but after every retrenchment the new status quo settled back into something resembling what had emerged during the Arduous March. While the state has in fact lost control of much of the economy, it also has become dependent on gray market activities by increasingly active private and hybrid entrepreneurs for much of the money that helps it survive. In essence, the North Korean state is stuck with a system its own disastrous policies helped create.

In this chapter, in necessarily broad strokes, I look at the emerging political economy of private and hybrid entrepreneurialism in North Korea since 2005, particularly as it relates to trading networks. North Korean society has evolved to encourage (and in some ways require) entrepreneurialism by both state and nonstate actors as a means of their survival. Both state and nonstate actors have to interact with each other and, just as importantly, become more like each other in this new environment, in which their activities are technically illegal but unstoppable on a large scale because the state depends on activity it has banned for its survival. Private actors take on formal trappings through informal agreements with state actors, and state actors often behave like (predatory) businesspeople in their own drive to make money. In certain respects, entrepreneurialism has become pervasive in North Korea. A food chain provides a de facto governance structure for the trade networks, in which the state at all levels has adopted new, creative ways to extract rents from the population and make money abroad. While entrepreneurialism as a low-level means of survival has become pervasive throughout North Korea, the networks that connect North Korea and the rest of the world, particularly China, are concentrated territorially in Pyongyang and the border regions, with the ability to extend further outside of North Korea dependent on their relationship with the North Korean state. These networks function best, and North Korean entrepreneurialism is most prominent, when both state and nonstate actors find ways around the roadblocks put in place by the North Korean central state. Aside from paying rents to the state, private and hybrid entrepreneurs have found creative ways to sell their own wares abroad and at home, and to serve as logistical, social, and financial brokers to connect the parts of the formal and informal economy disconnected by the terribleness of the regime.

I conclude the chapter with an in-depth look at two different types of hybrid and private North Korean entrepreneurialism in the postsanctions world: North Korean restaurants abroad, and drug trafficking networks.

One is totally legitimate from the central state's perspective, and one is illicit. One requires people and goods to be moved across international borders, while another only sends money (and occasionally people) back to North Korea. Neither is a particularly happy story: drug traffickers obviously bring products that harm many people, and, as will be seen, it is clear that the benefit to average North Koreans is not particularly high in North Korean restaurants outside of North Korea. Yet, whatever the social value (or lack thereof) of their trade, both are examples of creativity, flexibility, adaptation to difficult circumstances, and a mix of public and private, formal and informal interaction, both within and outside of North Korea.

The State's Deep Ambivalence about the Market

The environment that North Korean trade networks faced at the beginning of 2007 was very different, and significantly more hostile, than the one they faced at the beginning of 2005, both inside and outside of North Korea. Inside North Korea, the end of the most "liberal" period in North Korea's sad history began when the central state decided it no longer needed to rely so heavily on foreign aid or on its citizens fending for themselves. Beginning in August 2005, the central state issued regulations designed to bring the private markets to heel, discourage cross-border (private) trade, and return ordinary citizens to at least partial dependence on the Public Distribution System (PDS), despite the continuing inability of the PDS to provide enough calories to keep the average North Korean alive. In November of the same year, perhaps in a bid to move the PDS back to the center of North Koreans' lives, North Korea told the World Food Program it no longer needed food shipments, cutting off one of its major external food suppliers (and the monitoring that went with it). It is an open question as to the effect these measures had on the operation of the markets (or cross-border trade, for that matter). Surveys of defectors after 2005 suggested that the vast majority continued to depend on markets and private enterprise for both food and income after retrenchment, with the PDS failing to restart in any substantial way and state enterprises failing to provide income, despite the state's proclamations.[1]

The ineffectiveness of the state's pushback against private enterprise in 2005 could be seen in its continued efforts to limit participation in the markets through 2009 (measures that would not have been necessary if the 2005 retrenchment had had a satisfactory effect).[2] In 2007, the government issued regulations allowing only women over the age of fifty to sell goods in the private markets. The next year, state authorities imposed restrictions on the foreign goods that could be sold in the markets (which were theoretically going to return to being farmers' markets), and stepped up enforcement inspections. State authorities increased their attention on enterprises operating in border areas (particularly Sinuiju), and also issued an order that allowed the markets only to open every ten days.[3]

The 2009 currency redenomination was the crowning blow in the central state's bungled offensive against the private *won* economy. On 30 November, the government suddenly announced that the old *won* would be replaced with newly denominated *won* that had a face value of one one-hundredth of the old currency. In theory, this amounted to chopping off two zeros from the face value of the currency, and would not necessarily have been a problem if the announcement had been made months in advance to give the population time to prepare, if the two currencies were given time to circulate side by side to allow for a smooth conversion process, if there was no limit on the amount of currency that could be converted, and if relative prices of goods remained the same. None of these happened. Instead, the government initiated the currency "reform" without any advance warning, gave the population one week to exchange their currency, limited the amount of *won* that could be converted to approximately thirty dollars at black market exchange rates, and put restrictions on commercial transactions for the duration of the conversion period. The conversion limit effectively wiped out many households' life savings, caused the value of the North Korean *won* to collapse on the black market, and shot up commodity prices as North Koreans rushed to convert their *won* to harder currency or physical goods while they could.[4] Unusually in North Korea, the currency reform was so unpopular it actually led to public protests by angry citizens. In response, the government executed a senior economic official, Pak Nam-gi, purportedly for planning and executing the currency reform,[5] but the damage was done: with their faith in the currency smashed, even the lowest businesspeople made strenuous attempts to minimize their use of North Korean *won* and trade in foreign currencies. The net effect was that a large volume of *yuan* (and to a lesser extent US dollars) disappeared into North Korea as North Koreans began storing foreign currency as a hedge against further *won* depreciation or other damaging antimarket shocks.[6]

Yet even if the retrenchment from 2005 to 2010 was ineffective in ultimately stopping private trade or returning North Koreans to the nutritional embrace of the state, it did signal a shift in the thinking of the central state: while private trade in North Korea before 2005 took place in an ambiguous political environment, where activities that were nominally illegal could be allowed for the right price and the right connections, after 2005, the central state underlined its unhappiness with the gray market. This unhappiness did not, however, necessarily lead to any slackening in the gray market or end the state's dependence on it.

Kim Jong-il's death in December 2011 catapulted his son Kim Jong-un to the top of the North Korean state. While Kim Jong-un was already Kim Jong-il's designated successor, the accelerated manner in which the torch was passed left uncertainty about what Kim Jong-un would do, and even whether he would survive in power. What followed over the next two years was a series of high-level purges. In December 2013, Kim Jong-un's uncle Jang Song-thaek was very publicly purged, excoriated in an unprecedented twenty-seven hundred–word official statement, and then executed. While Jang Song-thaek may have fallen from Kim Jong-un's favor (to the extent he was ever in it at all) as early as November 2012, when he was appointed as the head of a relatively minor sports body, or January 2013, when he failed to be invited to a meeting of top national security and foreign affairs officials to discuss North Korea's situation in the wake of a new round of sanctions, his days were numbered indeed after an alleged flare-up between forces loyal to himself and the military left several people dead in the second half of 2013.[7] According to newspaper sources, several crab and clam fisheries had been taken over by Jang's organization from the military. On a visit to a military outpost, Kim Jong-un supposedly noticed that the soldiers were malnourished, and ordered the fisheries returned to the military. When a military force came to reclaim the facilities, Jang's forces refused to hand them over without personal authorization from Jang, and proceeded to engage in a firefight. Several soldiers were killed, and the military contingent withdrew. While a bigger military force came back later and did repossess the fisheries, the damage was done, and Kim Jong-un ordered a purge.[8]

One possible subtext for Jang's purge was not simply his own self-aggrandizement to the point that he threatened Kim Jong-un's power, but a larger conflict among North Korean elites over control over trading rights, the opportunities for graft that arose from controlling those rights, the firms that exercised those rights, and the income that flowed to those who had all three. Kim Jong-il had lavished support on the military through his military-first policy, including granting it extensive trading rights, especially for mining concessions. With Kim Jong-il's death, the military was left vulnerable to encroachment from the party and the cabinet. The trading permits became a source of conflict within the North Korean state, as factions vied for control over access to foreign income. The new mainstream faction of party civilians now needed their own sources of hard currency, and had other priorities for both exports and spending.[9]

Given their value, organizations with trading permits were reluctant to give them up, even under duress. Before Jang's purge, for instance, on 16 July 2012, North Korean media reported that Ri Yong-ho, the chief of the General Staff of the Korean People's Army, was relieved from all of his positions in the military and the party.[10] One theory surrounding the purge of Ri suggests that upon his own ascension to power, Kim Jong-un wanted to take back some of the trading rights that had been lavished on the military under Kim Jong-il. Ri Yong-ho balked, and as a result was forcibly removed from office.[11] Kim Jong-un appears to have been attempting to rein in the military and redistribute foreign income opportunities to other interest groups in the state, notably the party and the cabinet.[12] At least for a time, Jang Song-thaek, as a civilian within the party organization (despite his military commission late in life), benefited from this shift away from the military.

Jang was known for being close with the Chinese government; his trip to China in August 2012 was intended to drum up investment, and closer economic ties were likely a by-product of his influence. Following Jang's visit to Shenyang during his China trip, for instance, foreign diplomats noticed that the North Korean diplomats in Shenyang were more willing to talk to other diplomats. The North Koreans also made more of an effort to come to trade fairs put on for them by the Chinese government. Interestingly, one of the Jang's listed crimes was selling North Korea's "coal and other precious underground reserves at random" and then selling off land in Rajin-Sonbong "to a foreign country" to pay off the debts of his associates who lost money on the deals.[13] While one interpretation of this charge is that the faction of the government that opposed selling natural resources (or, more specifically, the faction that was uneasy about selling land and minerals to China) triumphed relative to Jang's supposedly more export-friendly approach, the charge could also be seen as what was possibly a deeper criticism: if Jang was going to sell off state assets to foreigners, he could have at least made a profit. It was Jang's business incompetence, not just his corruption and lust for power, that was worthy of opprobrium.

For North Korea's trade networks—and certainly for low-level traders—it is not clear that the game playing out in the towering reaches of the state had much of an effect. In interviews, Chinese traders doing business with North Korea cited little to no impact on their businesses of the transition to Kim Jong-un or the purges of Ri Yong-ho and Jang Song-thaek other than greater attention at customs and the removal of some low-level officials,[14] something backed up by newspaper accounts, which had North Korean officials proclaiming that North Korea was still open for business after Jang's execution.[15] While Kim Jong-il's death had some impact, this was largely because North Korea closed its borders, canceled business deals, and cut off communications with most outsiders in the months after his death, making it difficult for Chinese traders to conduct business.[16] The currency reform in 2009 did cause problems, although again this was because of the inability of North Korean partners to do business during the transition process (at least some Chinese traders had insulated themselves by refusing to do business in North Korean *won* even before the reform).[17] Aside from the currency reform itself, the traders did not notice any significant changes in the North Korean state's attitudes toward trade or investment, at least through 2014.[18]

There are some signs that, after the crackdowns of 2005 to 2010, the state began to reverse its official policies, even if the facts on the ground had long since failed to reflect official dicta, and the implementation of the new policies was nonexistent, highly flawed, and potentially reversible. In 2012, for instance, North Korea announced the June 28 measures, which would allow farmers to organize themselves into production teams that were in practice made up of their household members, and keep 30 percent of the food produced for themselves (rather than having to work for a daily grain ration). There is some controversy about whether the June 28 measures actually were introduced, but in 2013, North Korea almost fed itself. In 2014, the Central Committee of the Workers Party released the May 30 measures, which raised the proportion of the harvest that households could retain to 60 percent and apparently moved the managers of state-owned factories to a system in which they had greater autonomy in hiring and firing, pay decisions, supply chain management and procurement, and to whom they could sell their wares.[19]

While the central state did attempt to reassert control over the economy after 2005, it became impossible to roll back the changes that had allowed North Koreans to survive the Arduous March, and it is not clear that attempts to do so were more than sporadic after 2009. This uneasy peace seems to have persisted not only across the reigns of both Kim Jong-il and Kim Jong-un, but also through the purges and high-level turmoil that marked the first several years of Kim Jong-un's rule. Perhaps the state has finally relented, as from 2012, there seems to have been some grudging official acceptance of private and hybrid economic activity. As we will see, this may be because the state at all levels profits from the existence of economic activity that takes place in a legal gray area, at least partially outside state control.

The Political Economy of North Korean Entrepreneurialism

When the central state began pulling back the excesses of the Arduous March from 2005, it faced a fundamental problem: while the central state no doubt would have liked to return to the status quo ante of near total control over the population, it could no longer guarantee the security and welfare of the vast majority of the population, the prerequisite for near total control. It was also unable to totally stamp out the practices and markets that had arisen during the Arduous March as a means for the population to survive. At the same time, the central state wanted the money (often hard currency) that the (formally illegal) economic activity produced.

The result was perhaps inadvertent pressure from three directions to create something approaching a culture of entrepreneurialism. From the bottom, private citizens must find ways to support themselves financially without much help from the state, as the contradictions of the formal economy have become too great to ignore. Haggard and Noland found, for instance, that nearly half of North Korean refugees in South Korea surveyed had derived all of their income from private enterprise in the retrenchment era, and only 4 percent were not involved in the market at all.[20]

In this they were not unlike the citizens of other socialist and postsocialist countries. The USSR's informal economy, for example, was the source of 23 percent of households' expenditure on average in the last twenty years of the Soviet Union's existence.[21]

From the top, in a departure from most socialist countries, the central state demanded income from all levels of officials and state organizations, and was largely indifferent as to where this income came from. In the middle, officials with the legal ability to engage in either trade or enforcement (or both) moved to find ways to make money both for themselves and the central state through an often creative combination of rent seeking and going into business for themselves. This has become particularly important for midlevel officials as their formal incomes are insufficient for survival, so either they or someone in their families need to engage in entrepreneurial activity.[22]

While the central state has the means to crack down on specific individuals or specific activities at specific times, it no longer can crack down everywhere at all times, and has settled into a deeply ambivalent relationship with entrepreneurialism. The North Korean state still has coercive mechanisms at its disposal when it wants to crack down. The regime allows officials to seek rents, for instance, but then punishes them if they get out of line (or need to be made an example of).[23] Loyalty to the state, however, may no longer be based on unquestioning support of the paramount leader (although there no doubt remains residual support for the Kim family), but on a combination of the fear of the consequences of stepping out of line, and the opportunities the state provides (or at least allows to exist) to make money on one's own. In broad strokes, the state survives because it no longer presents insurmountable obstacles to the population's survival.

The Food Chain

One South Korean analyst describes North Korea's new modus vivendi as similar to a food chain, in which the apex predators feed on the predators below, who in turn feed on the predators below. Because both citizens and officials at all levels are expected to bring in income for the state, it is not unimportant for officials and citizens alike to seek relatively stable relationships, in which the bribed higher-up protects the subordinate in exchange for a cut. The food chain is thus effectively a mutually reinforcing ladder of patron-client networks.[24] At the bottom of the food chain are the politically unconnected citizens who earn income from the informal markets and basic trade, and who pay bribes to low-level officials in order to operate at all (inasmuch as the informal markets themselves are in a legal gray area), either by entering the market themselves, or by working on the side after paying their employers to release them.[25]

The low-level officials in turn pay higher-level officials for positions, protection, and business opportunities. While the state still officially assigns workers to their positions, there is some room for flexibility and discretion, both of which can be obtained at a price.[26] These arrangements are not unlike those found in other communist countries in transition (willingly or not). In China, for example, in the early stages of the rise of the private sector in the early 1980s, it was not uncommon for small-time entrepreneurs to develop relationships with local state officials in the formal hierarchy in order to improve the viability of their businesses and mitigate political risk, leading to a web of informal ties between the state and society in an area of economic activity that was still (at the time) often pushing the limits of what was legally allowed.[27]

At the higher levels, the formally recognized trading companies (and their officials) often bring lower-level market actors into their orbit.[28] Opportunities to make money, either through rent seeking or actual trade, are part of the incentive package for elites to maintain loyalty to the Kim family. As with many aspects of the new North Korea, the central state does not have the ability or the desire to monitor the activities of companies, and remains largely indifferent as to where the income the companies provide come from, resulting in a large degree of autonomy for state trading companies and state officials.[29] There are opportunities for bureaucrats within the state organizations, and for the state organizations themselves, to make money coming and going, both in terms providing political protection and connections for those selling imported goods, and in renting out the ability to export.

It is not clear that this state of affairs is actually the best of all worlds for the central state, but paradoxically, attempts by the central state to reassert control have actually solidified corruption and patron-client networks within the food chain. Within North Korea and at the international borders, during crackdowns the central state has at times attempted to reassert its control over population movement by establishing checkpoints to check for travel and identification documents. This has had the (perhaps unintended) effect of increasing opportunistic (but not necessarily long-term) rent seeking by low-level state officials, as they are able to solicit bribes from travelling traders they happen to catch.[30] The existence of markets in North Korea on the edge of legality more generally provides opportunities for state officials, who can demand bribes for protection from punishment for violating the frequently changing state rules and attitudes regarding market activity.[31] In this way, the informality and borderline illegality of much of the new economy works to aggrandize government officials even as they do not regulate it.[32]

State officials can also establish longer-term, more intensive relationships with traders, and give them political cover.[33] Aside from direct trading (either on their own or through central state trading enterprises) and rent seeking, high-level officials can also let their relatives import goods. The relatives pay a promised cut to the government, and can sometimes bring luxury goods into North Korea to sell to other elites.[34] For lower-level markets, inspection teams, ostensibly meant to crack down on private trade and often consisting of State Security Department, Ministry of People's Security, and prosecutor's office workers, are susceptible to bribery (through the provision of expensive foreign goods) in exchange for ignoring transgressions by smugglers, and issuing "permits" for future cross-border trading.[35] Smugglers moving goods between China and North Korea can also establish longer-term relationships with border guards themselves, who tell smugglers when and where to go to avoid being captured. One analyst of North Korea estimated in 2012 that for bulk goods, three hundred dollars in bribes would allow a boatload of goods to cross the Tumen or Yalu rivers.[36]

Within the food chain, North Korea's business community can be divided into broad groups: businesspeople who use *won*, businesspeople who do business in hard currency (who are both heavily connected to state officials, and state officials themselves), and the top leadership.[37] In practice, only the lowest rung of the food chain has traditionally done business only in *won*—the hybrid enterprises and state trading companies do as much of their business as possible in foreign currencies. In the 2009 currency reform, the main victims were petty capitalists who did all of their business in North Korean *won*. In practice, these were the small private businessmen (or, more realistically, businesswomen) operating in informal domestic markets. While they are ultimately the source of income upon which much of the state depends, they are also politically dangerous to the regime, inasmuch as their success (such as it is) does not depend on any opportunities for rent seeking as it does with officials. The central state faces a quandary where the bottom of the food chain is also the least politically dependent on the state. Although the currency reform was a policy "failure," it was a political signaling success, inasmuch as it had the effect of knocking back politically unconnected *won* businessmen and keeping them from joining the ranks of the hard-currency businessmen.[38]

How these businesspeople and enterprises make money within the food chain is a matter of resourcefulness, flexibility, and no small amount of creative corruption. Much of North Korea's culture of entrepreneurialism, such as it is, springs from the interaction between the economic geography of the country and the need for people and institutions at all levels to provide for their own survival and enrich those above them in North Korean society. North Korea is politically centralized but economically decentralized, leading state agencies down to the local level to be viewed as profit centers by the central state, with units at all levels tasked with raising money and funneling it up the hierarchy to the center.[39] North Korea's economic landscape is divided into several hundred city- and district-level units that are each theoretically economically self-sufficient as a means of defending against external attack. In practice, the units must find their own way to raise hard currency for their sustenance and that of their superiors. With some exceptions, the central state is largely indifferent as to where this money comes from.[40] This leads to many small, state-supported businesses run by units stretching from the local level up to the central state, all vying to sell whatever goods and services are at hand, and to do deals with foreign companies.[41]

State enterprises up and down the food chain are permitted to engage in foreign trade by the central state through possession of a foreign trading permit. The foreign trading permit system originated during the Cold War, when Office 5 was established to purchase domestic products and sell them for foreign currency, as well as to import goods that would be sold in official foreign goods stores. In the 1980s, other state organizations, particularly the security services and the military, started their own trading companies, with over two hundred in existence after the end of the Cold War, all mobilized to sell goods to raise foreign currency.[42] The permits themselves are ultimately doled out by the supreme leader (previously Kim Jong-il and now Kim Jong-un) as a way of privileging favored elements of the state—whether the military, the cabinet, or the party—depending on the specific balance that the supreme leader is attempting to maintain.[43] By managing the distribution of trade permits (and thus the distribution of rents that come from trade), the supreme leader can maintain control over the system, and keep elites in competition with each other.[44] Indeed, the competition for foreign currency–earning permits and, more generally, for control over the resources that allow the different central trading companies to have anything to trade is apparently quite intense, and which faction of the state is on top has varied considerably since 2006, with the military brought to heel in the years immediately before and after Kim Jong-il's death.[45]

Aside from the support of the supreme leader, the requirements for obtaining a permit are not particularly surprising: a company applying for a permit must demonstrate that it has foreign business partners, sufficient capital, a viable business plan, and access to facilities (factories, farms, and research institutes) and resources that actually allow production and export, although the informal intervention and support of the relevant bureaucrats and cadres is no doubt important. While the central trading company receives the permit, the permit can be used by a local branch of the company.[46] The permit structure for foreign trade is largely based on specific types of goods from specific areas in set quantities (for example, a permit holder might have the right to sell a certain quantity of squid from a particular province), but the number of permits is limited and only state enterprises can hold them.[47]

The state trading companies that have been granted permits have the ability to export primary commodities or manufactured goods, and then import goods to sell in markets within North Korea. State trading companies and the bureaucrats associated with them and their constituent organizations can use the trading permits to enter and sustain hybrid trade networks. While companies cannot buy or sell the licenses themselves, once granted the ability to export a certain quantity of goods from a certain area, a trading company can rent out any unused quota to other countries and entrepreneurs.[48] The fee cited by some sources is around 10 percent of the value of the exports.[49] This allows the officially permitted company to charge a fee for the quota's use, while it allows the company actually doing the exporting to operate with some measure of political protection.[50] For further political protection, agency bureaucrats can even take bribes from entrepreneurs to give them formal state positions (such as military commissions).[51] When the trading companies do not themselves have access to foreign buyers for their products, they take advantage of trade agents in border area company branches or private entrepreneurs who can serve as brokers, introducing trade companies to foreign buyers and sellers.[52] This can be a lucrative business, with perhaps eighty North Korean foreign currency earning companies operating in Dandong in 2012, in large part as consultancies.[53]

While the involvement by state officials in hybrid trade networks might be seen as merely monopolistic rent seeking, and indeed the money earned by renting out trade permits and political protection does not appear to funneled back into production,[54] the public-private partnership system can result in efficiencies otherwise unobtainable by the formal state enterprises. In coal mining, for example, private operators "purchase" the extraction and export rights from the state enterprises, and then start their own coal mining, arranging not only for equipment and workers, but also processing (when possible) and transportation. Workers at moribund state mines, in turn, pay bribes to state officials to get out of their obligations and move over to the private mines, which are generally far more productive, in terms of both production and export to China, than the state mines. With hundreds of these private mines in coal-producing regions, workers are able to move relatively easily among different employers. In 2011, one observer estimated there to be two hundred private mines and one thousand private laborers producing tons of coal per day in Cheongsung alone.[55] North Korea's new hybrid business networks are not only taking advantage of ambiguity within the system, in some cases they are producing more than the formal economy.

The Economic Geography of Entrepreneurialism

Within North Korea, entrepreneurs with foreign links appear to be concentrated in areas defined by a combination of political influence, infrastructure connections (such as they are), and natural resources. Thus it is that Pyongyang—the center of North Korea's transportation network, the locus of political power, the area with the highest concentration of foreign trading licenses, and the nexus of the food chains—is also the home of many (perhaps even most) entrepreneurs seeking outside investment and business ties.[56] Enterprises in areas bordering China (and to a much lesser extent Russia), while not necessarily politically favored, can take advantage of their proximity to countries with functioning economies and transportation networks and their relatively low (compared to areas further inside North Korea) dependence on North Korea's terrible transportation infrastructure.[57] Enterprises with access to North Korea's natural resources, especially mines, can also contract with foreign companies, although, even here, minimizing the exposure of the operation to North Korea's economic infrastructure is also a benefit. It is not an accident that North Hamgyong province's Musan Iron Mine, the largest mine in North Korea and the recipient of large investments from Chinese firms, is less than ten kilometers from the Chinese border.

Of course, the North Korean central state has also established special economic zones—Rajin-Sonbong, at the corner of North Korea's border with China and Russia, and Hwanggumpyong-Wihwa, near Dandong (as well as Kaesong Special Industrial Region, which is more specifically a joint North Korean–South Korean project)—and has made provision for local economic zones as loci for development. In practice they appear to be designed to bring in foreign infrastructure investment and companies that have use for North Korean labor rather than build up North Korean private and hybrid trade networks, although in the next chapter, we will see that the special economic zones (specifically Rason) are where some Chinese companies in need of labor do in fact link up with North Korean hybrid entrepreneurs willing to provide that labor.[58]

A territorial dynamic is also at work outside North Korea, as enterprises higher up the food chain of North Korean society are frequently capable of maintaining business networks further from North Korea. While the central state enterprises that conduct North Korea's most sophisticated trading have frequently engaged in trade with businesses (and governments) around the world, the higher-level enterprises within Northeast Asia can operate as far away as Beijing, and lower-level units seeking income within China run businesses in Shenyang, Dandong, Hunchun, and Yanji.[59] Outside of North Korea, usually in China, representatives of state trading companies are usually given an annual foreign currency quota they must meet (often in US dollars). Once they meet that quota, however, they are free to keep any additional income.[60]

Around 2010, there appears to have been an increase in the number of North Koreans who went overseas on official permits, and were often employed in joint ventures in China, particularly Liaoning and Jilin provinces. For the North Korean government, this was a win-win situation. If they went as part of an officially sanctioned group, they could be monitored and segregated from outsiders, even in China. The state (and the overseeing state company) can also get a cut of their salary, and develop business connections in China.[61] It is also possible, however, to invent "relatives" to visit on social passes. Once in China, North Korean visitors can then look for work or business opportunities.[62] North Korean units that are unable to trade can also send politically trustworthy individuals into China to make money. The units take a set fee (one analyst estimated this fee as around three hundred dollars) for a specific number of months away; the individual then tries to make as much money as possible in China, and keeps the rest.[63]

Within the territory in which they are capable of operating, the areas of commerce that enterprises are willing to enter, and the ways in which they attempt to make money, are nearly unlimited. State enterprises often do not stick to their official industrial categories—they will expand into whichever industry presents opportunities for making money.[64] In Yanji, for example, one visiting South Korean academic saw small Oriental medicine clinics (with one doctor and one nurse) as well as small restaurants run by small North Korean unit entities.[65]

The opportunities for state officials to make money through inserting themselves into trade networks varies not only with status but also by geographic location. A 2010 report, for example, claimed that police had to pay up to one million *won* for the opportunity to be transferred to Hyesan on the border with China so as to profit from the bribes and opportunities associated with trading.[66] Different locations can produce different opportunities for state officials to profit from business. A 2011 report, for instance, described a minor gold rush in Nokbong-san, where private small-time miners paid off local soldiers and bureaucrats for the "right" to dig for gold in the area.[67]

Entrepreneurialism and the Operation of Trade Networks

The changes in North Korea led to the creation of a culture of entrepreneurialism that is formally illegal but also necessary for state survival; informal, with shifting rules, but also one with an increasingly regularized way for the state to exploit corruption and entrepreneurial activity. One foreign visitor noted that, since perhaps 2010, the idea of making money has become acceptable, and described being at a presentation in Pyongyang where a female entrepreneur from Rason was lauded as an example to follow. Many, even most, officials have a sideline way to make money.[68] Yet there is still ambiguity and confusion built into the system. One non-governmental organization that teaches entrepreneurship to North Koreans encountered this even among its students. While the NGO's contact in North Korea was technically a party organization, the relationship between the organization and the party was unclear, even for the people who actually worked there. Most of the students, who were in their 20s, 30, and early 40s, apparently came from government ministries, although some came from hybrid companies (it was difficult to tell whether they were founders or staff). The youngest people did not appear to know how to navigate their own system, such as where to get permissions to start or do business.[69]

North Korea is an environment where essentially everything is for sale, and both private individuals and public officials barely hide their ambitions and their actual efforts to get rich.[70] The creativity that blossomed from both the public and the "private" sectors was remarkable. In December 2008, students in Hyesan were reported to be bottling water from the Yalu River and transporting it on handcarts for sale to other parts of the country as water supplies became more erratic.[71] In 2008, South Korean–produced goods such as rice cookers, imported through China from South Korea by ethnic-Korean Chinese brokers, had become popular in the markets (*jangmadang*).[72] By 2011, South Korean clothes and DVDs were being imported into the markets.[73] When the real clothes were unavailable, seamstresses would take patterns or pictures of South Korean and Chinese clothes from smuggled fashion magazines, and make them to order for North Korean men and women who could afford to pay. The seamstresses were often trained in the state-owned clothing factories, and as such represented a similar leak of talent and resources from the public to the private sector as meth producers did.[74] By 2012, one analyst estimated that 80 percent of the consumer goods sold in the markets had been imported from China.[75]

While the ventures may not always pan out, and North Korean potential entrepreneurs may not necessarily always know how to work the system, the trend is clear: a culture of entrepreneurialism has sprung up that is at once creative, in that entrepreneurs actively look for goods and services that are ripe for exploitation, and flexible, in that entrepreneurs appear to be generalists who are willing to move into any market to make money. This dynamism can be seen especially in entrepreneurs who have become logistical and financial brokers, often starting out as small operators and scaling up, who connect nodes within trade networks, both within North Korea, and between North Korea and the rest of the world. North Korea's terrible infrastructure means that brokerage opportunities exist for transport within the country, while North Korea's formal financial isolation means that opportunities exist without.

Transport Brokers   There is profit to be made in serving as the physical link between different nodes in North Korean trade networks, both domestic and transnational. The high cost of moving around North Korea, and between North Korea and the rest of the world, allows middlemen to engage in price arbitrage, so long as they are able to move goods between local areas. One report in 2010 describes a "runner" who bought fabric in Chongjin in North Hamgyong province from traders there, transported it to Pyongsong in South Pyongan province, where he sold it to retailers, who in turn sold the fabric at a 20–30 percent premium relative to its initial price. The runner then used the profits to buy goods to sell in Sinuiju on the border with China.[76]

In addition, North Korea's atrocious transport infrastructure imposes severe time and monetary costs on businesses that need to acquire or sell physical goods anywhere beyond their local area. As a result, one of the first industries to become semiprivatized during the Arduous March was transportation. Despite periodic inspection crackdowns, transportation services (or *servi-cha*) sprang up out of two sources during and then after the Arduous March.

First, state enterprises that own buses or trucks can transport people and goods themselves, taking on long-distance fares as way to raise extra money. Second, enterprise officials can enter into "red hat" hybrid arrangements with private owners. The private owners buy the bus or truck from China or Japan (presumably through China), and the state enterprise cadres register the vehicle as owned by the enterprise, and "hire" a salaried driver to operate the vehicle. The driver then goes looking for passengers and cargo. The profits are split between the vehicle owner and state enterprise cadre, who takes his own cut, and imputes the rest to state enterprise profit (which is eventually partially paid up the food chain).[77] By 2011, *servi-cha* companies had begun to become professionalized and more organized as state enterprises licensed operations encompassing several vehicles running specific routes. The 116 Task Force Team, for example, was affiliated with the Ministry of People's Security, and ran services between Sinuiju and Pyongyang.[78]

Interestingly, according to reports in both 2010 and 2014, the state enterprise officials and the owners enter into a complementary relationship, where the owners obtain transportation permits for clients' goods and pay bribes to senior security officials to ensure quick passage through checkpoints set up along all major roads in North Korea. State enterprises in turn provide their status within state hierarchy, with the monetary value of that status approximating a sliding scale. Higher state enterprise status (for example, a public security branch office as opposed to an agricultural collective), as indicated by the license plate number, is associated with a lower cost of bribes (apparently with both security officials and checkpoint guards). As a result, the owner has an incentive to maximize the status of the state enterprise he or she affiliates with (presumably the higher status enterprises are also able to demand higher fees for registration or a proportionally higher cut of the profits), and the passengers are willing to pay higher transportation fees in exchange for fewer demands for bribes, fewer problems at checkpoints (particularly if they do not have individual travel permits), and the resulting faster transportation times.[79] The *servi-cha* services are not only linked into political economic structures that allow them to operate, they are also linked into trade networks, both through facilitating the trade itself, and through the goods the owners buy to maintain the vehicles: vehicle repair services, tires, and North Korean fuel, which as of 2014 was sold by fuel traders along major thoroughfares. The *servi-cha* reportedly take only US dollars or Chinese *yuan*, although it is unclear if this reflected merely one source, or is reflective of a larger pattern of transport services attempting to do business in harder currencies.[80]

Financing   The currency redenomination not only shattered what little trust existed in the North Korean financial system, it also served as the catalyst for the (continued) rise and scaling up of finance services that bypassed or suborned state-controlled institutions. While loan sharking was already in evidence during the Arduous March, the state cracked down immediately before the currency redenomination, and loan sharks did not reemerge until several months later (when the private traders also reemerged). According to reports, individuals borrow capital for trading from those within their social network at relatively low rates (5 percent), and from loan sharks at higher rates (10 percent). For smugglers, lenders are willing to provide capital at even higher rates (15–20 percent) with extremely short repayment windows measured in days, presumably because successful smugglers are likely to realize their windfall profits very quickly. The moneylenders also provide other financial services to traders, including handling their financial transfers, in effect acting as informal banks.[81]

The remittance system for transferring money from South Korea (and China) to North Korea also functions with a series of informal brokers. A 2012 *Washington Post* article describes the system as one in which a North Korean defector might receive a call from his contact in North Korea (using a mobile phone within range of a Chinese mobile phone tower) asking for money. The defector then transfers the money to a broker with a South Korean bank account, who in turn transfers the money to a Chinese bank account (of a different broker). This broker (or his own contact) does business in North Korea frequently, and has currency already stashed in North Korea itself. When he goes to North Korea, he gives cash to the North Korean defector's contact, who in turn distributes the money to the ultimate end user. In this way, no actual currency needs to physically cross the border, and the financial sanctions facing North Korean financial institutions and citizens are rendered irrelevant. The various brokers generally take between 20 and 30 percent commission, all told.[82] Tudor and Pearson provide a similar description, with the senders transferring money to a broker, who wires the money to a Chinese account. A broker in North Korea then uses a Chinese mobile phone in the border region of North Korea to check that the money is there, and then hands the pre-positioned cash to the recipient (or hands the cash to a North Korean transporter for delivery elsewhere in the country).[83]

The success of the remittance system thus depends on several factors. First, the system is built on a series of relationships stretching from South Korea to China to North Korea that, if they are more permanent than market relationships with low transition costs and high substitutability, are not dependent on trust throughout the entire chain. Each node in the chain needs to trust the next onward node sufficiently to transfer money, but no one either knows about or controls the entire chain. While the emergence of North Korea's semiprivate entrepreneurial economy in some sense means markets in everything, with the exception of *jangmadang* themselves, the networks rely on more intimate and reliable relationships, partially for security, partially for assurance in the face of a lack of institutions to enforce contracts, than would be typical for a market in a more open economy. Second, and perhaps most interestingly, the remittance system requires the existence of businesspeople who move relatively easily between China and North Korea, and who have bank accounts in China, and some way of storing physical currency securely inside North Korea itself. While the informal remittance system is required because North Korea is cut off from international financial institutions, and North Koreans would not trust them even if they were not, it works precisely because North Korea is *not* in actuality cut off from either communications networks or international business networks. North Korea's peculiar integration into the regional economy is what allows the remittance system to function.

Drug Traffickers as Entrepreneurs in the New North Korea

Entrepreneurialism in everything, and the willingness and ability of North Korean trade networks to serve as logistical and financial brokers connecting North Korea and the rest of the world do not always have beneficial effects for North Koreans or their economy. The evolution of the drug trafficking networks emanating from North Korea since 2005 is a particularly illuminating example of the creativity and flexibility exhibited by North Korean entrepreneurs in the face of an ambiguous and confusing business environment. Where the central state receded from engaging in drug trafficking itself, and replaced its involvement with official hostility, private and hybrid trading network rose up to take its place. Post-crackdown drug trafficking networks provide a useful case study of the food chain at work, as the low-level drug production and trafficking networks appear to have operated and scaled up with the involvement of officials and organizations at different levels of the state who were acting for both private gain and the need to bring in income for the central state. The private and hybrid networks proved adept at navigating the spaces and opportunities created by the North Korean central state's reliance on gray market activities and the entrepreneurial, rent-seeking food chain for income. They also illustrate the territorial effects of the withdrawal of state resources for producing and distribution of drugs. While the new North Korean networks did not have the territorial reach outside of North Korea that the central state had had, they made up for this by establishing connections with outside networks closer to North Korea, in effect integrating North Korea's drug trade even more heavily into the regional economy.

Whether due to international pressure or concern over spreading drug addiction within North Korea itself, the North Korean central state apparently abandoned large-scale drug production as a matter of formal policy sometime between 2004 and 2007. The central state's turn against drug use and trafficking seems to have begun in earnest in North Korea at least by August 2005, with crackdowns in Sinuiju, Hamhung, and Pyongyang. Where drug users used to be sent to labor camps for detoxification, they were now sent for longer sentences at prison camps.[84] The state was actively cracking down on drug production and drug addicts by 2007,[85] and the annual US presidential report on countries of concern in drug trafficking stopped mentioning North Korea after 2007. The last verified drug trafficking incidents with official North Korean state involvement were in 2004, and the scholarly and analytical literature devoted to North Korean drug trafficking dried up around the same time.[86]

Within North Korea, since the central state crackdown began in 2005, the two state-run production centers from the North Korea state's experiment with state-led drug trafficking, Chongjin and Hamhung, have continued to be the center of the two main territorial agglomerations for ice production and distribution within the country. Evidence suggests that production has spread within those areas outside of the factories and into private factories. By 2008, unofficial production had spread to Pyongsong, Tanchon, and Nampo. There were allegations that state-run production in Hamhung continued to function as of 2011,[87] when it was reported that the Chinese government requested (strongly) that North Korea shut down remaining drug production factories. According to a South Korean newspaper, the central state did respond by shutting down a portion of the production in Hungnam (a suburb of Hamhung). It is unclear whether this production was from a state-run factory, or what "state-run" even means in a country where private firms operate under state imprimatur.[88]

Interestingly, none of the production centers, either before or after the crackdowns began, were anywhere near the North Korean border with China. The routes taken in transporting the drug from production to the river crossing into China are unclear, although the crossing points themselves, such as Hyesan and Hoeryong, have a number of traits that make them attractive as drug trafficking points. First, certain areas such as Hoeryong were exit points for North Korean refugees during the Arduous March; illicit movement continued after the famine eased.[89] Second, parts of the Tumen River dividing China and North Korea are shallow in summer and covered by ice in the winter, allowing relatively easy crossing year-round.[90] Third, the border cities have inhabitants who are comparatively knowledgeable about the logistics of crossing the border, and who may be disproportionately addicted to drugs (and are thus available to serve as drug mules), as indicated by the North Korean state's focus on border cities in many of its crackdowns.[91] The availability of drugs and addicts in border cities is of course endogenous, but it does suggest that drugs move from North Korea to China in ways that are related to the social environment around them. Both the production and border-crossing points have developed networks of people involved in the "industry" that have made it difficult for the central state to destroy, largely because there is no longer simply one route or network operating to smuggle drugs.

The actual crossing into China is done by drug mules who swim, wade, boat, or walk across the river, and deliver the drug shipment to Chinese partners, who receive the package at the river bank and then move it further into China. For distribution, in most cases, drugs are moved by land until they reach a hub for transportation out of China. Drug shipments enter China across the Yalu River or the Tumen River from North Korea. With the exception of Dandong, these transshipment points are often small border crossings in relatively isolated sections of the border. One Taiwanese source cites Dandong in Liaoning province, Sanhe and Kaishantun in Longjing county, and Changbai village in Changbai county (across from

Hyesan in North Korea), all in Jilin province, as primary entry points for drugs, although there are other transshipment points as well.[92] Spatially, the entry points share one of two characteristics: they are either major entry points for legitimate commercial goods (in the case of Dandong), or they are the border cities closest to the primary North Korean drug production centers and within heavily ethnic Korean areas of Jilin. In the case of the "5.20" drug trafficking incident in 2010, for instance, the drugs entered China through Dandong,[93] while in the 2010 "9.20" incident the smugglers brought in ice through Nanping village in Helong along the Tumen River (across from Musan),[94] and in the 2009 "2.11" incident, the smugglers moved through Longjing.[95]

For the known cases between 2006 and 2011, once the drugs entered China, they were moved to intermediate points within Liaoning or Jilin before being distributed to other areas outside northeastern China. In the case of the "5.20" incident, the main broker moved the drugs from Dandong to Yanji, Shulan, and Jilin city within Jilin, and to Qingdao in Shandong. In the "9.20" case, the coordinator Jin Xiangyun would pick up the drugs from his North Korean contact "President Chang" at Helong, take them to Yanji, and then check them as baggage on a long-distance bus to Qingdao. In the 2008 "4.01" incident, the mules were arrested in Dunhua, on the way from Yanji to Qingdao.[96]

Within China, then, the spatial distribution of meth trafficking is concentrated in the northeast, and in terms of transport and secondary distribution is even more concentrated within certain cities with good road links to the rest of China, such as Yanji, Dandong, and Changchun. The primary distribution cities to points outside the country are then Qingdao and Dalian, given their convenient connections to South Korea and Japan, and in fact, most of the trafficking major incidents since 2006 seem to have ended up in those two cities.

As the main drug shipments move from the North Korean border to international departure points, smaller quantities are stripped and diffused through local networks to other parts of China, or to networks in China that would not otherwise be connected to North Korea. In the "9.20" incident, the coordinator, Jin Xiangyun, and his accomplice, Jin Longzhu (both likely ethnic Koreans), sold a portion of the drugs Jin Xiangyun had picked up from "President Chang."[97] Likewise, in the "5.20" incident, quantities of drugs were sold off in Shulan and Jilin before the main shipment reached Qingdao.[98]

In the international departure points, the drugs are then handed off to foreign buyers, who use mules to fly the shipments back to their home countries, where presumably the drugs enter the local distribution networks. The image painted through analysis of the major drug trafficking incidents in China since 2006 is one in which the involvement of the traffickers who had to deal with various levels of the North Korean state ended essentially just on the other side of the Yalu and Tumen Rivers, with North Korean émigrés or refugees (or both), Chinese citizens of Korean ethnicity, Han Chinese citizens, and Japanese and South Koreans moving the goods beyond until they reached their destination in China or elsewhere in Northeast Asia. Compared to the state-encouraged drug trafficking networks of the Arduous March, contemporary networks occupy the middle range—with much of the network outside of North Korea, but few to no network nodes further afield than Northeast Asia.

How do these networks operate without central state direction? For obvious reasons, the Chinese media does not report on the North Korean side of drug trafficking operations. However, other sources give some idea as to the governance of post-famine networks with North Korea. Within North Korea, during the "official" period of drug production, private trader networks began as a result of theft by the workers at the plants in Hamhung and Ranam,[99] in much the same way that manufacturing facilities provided much of the equipment sold off in the 1990s in China. Other state workers also started using their positions and knowledge to produce meth outside the confines of the state entities, such as a professor at Hamhung University who was apparently manufacturing meth by himself.[100]

What little information exists suggests that governance actually moved up the ladder of state involvement from private traders to local state entities, even as the central state was cracking down. Although the first "producers" were theoretically private traders using their official positions for profit, within a few years, meth production seems to have spread up the ladder. Hamhung Chemical Engineering University and Hamhung Academy of Sciences came under suspicion of production, and thirty members of Hamhung's Defense Security Command were punished for drug trafficking in February 2008.[101]

Transportation and distribution have also moved up the food chain. The original private traders seem to have had something approaching a market relationship with onward nodes in the chain for transport and distribution (sacrificing sophisticated means of evading capture), but soon smugglers were moving toward interactions with state officials that allowed them to operate relatively freely.[102]

North Korean state entities also engage in the drug trade as a means of surviving and doing their duties as sources of income within the food chain. The drug trade is attractive to local branches of state entities because the high per-unit profits of meth trafficking (relative to trading of more mundane goods such as natural resources and low value-added manufactured goods) allow a relatively small number of individuals to support the entire work unit's quota of income and gifts for the central state. By one estimate, the average branch office sees half of its workers engaged in drug trafficking, although the distribution across the country and types of units no doubt varies widely. As with private traders, State Security Department and Ministry of People's Security officials can be bribed to look the other way at state entities' business, or even raise their own quotas for hard currency income through drug trade.[103]

The actors that cross the border into China are invariably North Korean, but interestingly many of the coordinators and other nodes on the other side of the border are as well. The coordinator of the "5.20" operation, Park, was a "foreigner" who entered China illegally in 2007,[104] as was the coordinator in the "2.11" incident, Fang.[105] It is unclear how these coordinators established and maintained business relationships with the North Korean smugglers coming from North Korea, but these relationships seemed to last over multiple smuggling incidents, suggesting costs to finding new suppliers. In the "9.20" incident, for instance, Jin Xiangyun retrieved drugs from "President Chang" by the riverside six times over four months,[106] while in the "4.01" incident in 2008, the main perpetrators, Fang and Cai, took four deliveries over the course of four months.[107]

Familial ties and prior social ties are also important in solidifying the links in the chain, and in ensuring optimal operating conditions (such as the availability of safe houses). In the "5.20" incident, Park originally worked with her cousin Li in Dandong selling cosmetics, and when she smuggled meth into China, used Li to distribute the drugs to buyers in Liaoning and Jilin. She also used her prior network of associates from her days working as a housekeeper and cook for factory workers in Shandong to distribute drugs in Qingdao.[108] Likewise, Jin Xiangyun, the coordinator of the "9.20" trafficking network, had another North Korean associate, Jin Longzhu, who used his relative Jin Hailian's rented house in Qingdao as a meeting place for the Chinese side of the network to pass the drugs to the South Korean side, which would physically smuggle the drugs out of the country.[109]

Interestingly, the coordinators with direct ties to the smugglers from North Korea (essentially playing brokerage roles) are also often not the nodes in the network that engage in much of the retail (or onward trafficking), suggesting a certain level of specialization, and further diffusing the locations where value is captured as the drugs move from production to retail. In the "5.20" incident, while Park did have direct retail buyers, she also gave drugs to her cousin, and an associate named Zheng in Qingdao, to sell to street users.[110] Similarly, in the "9.20" incident it was Jin Longzhu, not the coordinator Jin Xiangyun, who served as the broker for the onward trafficking to the South Korean smugglers in Qingdao.[111] Likewise, Fang of the "2.11" incident was able to coordinate the entry of the drug shipment into China, but ultimately it was her associate Park who found a suitable buyer through a friend of his in Yanji, resulting in four degrees of separation between Fang's supplier ("Little Brother") and the ultimate buyer.[112]

Although it is an open question as to whether the North Korean central state still engages in drug production and trafficking, networks that operate seemingly without access to the resources of the central state do exist inside and outside North Korea. While these networks include private traders, they also include actors with considerably more complex relationships with various levels of the state. Navigating such a complex institutional environment results not only in more private and hybrid actors within the chain, but considerable diffusion of the value derived from production and trafficking, to include not only those directly integrated into the chain, but also those, such as border guards and security officials, who capture rents by providing secure conditions for operations. As with other forms of trade, the central state benefits, albeit indirectly, by collecting "taxes" up and down the food chain on the income that officials and private businesspeople, and people in between, generate to support themselves. Unlike the central state networks, the new networks are horizontally integrated. Relationships between the actors within the chain run the range from market-based, fairly modular and hands-off, to deeply dependent on long-term experience and nonmarket ties, with relatively dense networks outside of North Korea relative to the Arduous March–era networks.

Drug trafficking networks have emerged since 2005 as the epitome of North Korean entrepreneurialism: they take advantage of the food chain in North Korea's economy to become a mixture of private and public activity, they operate in a hostile environment without seemingly being too encumbered, they provide connections between disparate organizations and individuals stretching across North Korea and China, and they have, in their own way, become well integrated into the trade networks of East Asia.

The Shadiest Restaurateurs

Compare drug trafficking networks with their legitimate cousins and exemplars of North Korean entrepreneurialism: restaurants. North Korean restaurants usefully illustrate how North Korean trade networks are able to tie in with non–North Korean companies and consumers outside of North Korea in creative ways, and solve many of the problems that North Korean trade networks have traditionally faced: a lack of ability to market their goods directly to foreign consumers, a complicated (or downright hostile) relationship with both North Korean and foreign governments, and terrible transportation and financial infrastructure and inefficient supply chains within North Korea, and between North Korea and the rest of the world. Unlike drug trafficking, the trade networks needed to support restaurants are not particularly complicated. There is little need for logistical nodes, given that only labor and money (and sometimes specialty food products) cross between North Korea and the rest of the world. Instead, the creativity, adaptability, and flexibility come in the form of a variety of joint venture and ownership agreements with foreign investors and firms, an appreciation of what makes North Korean food and restaurants marketable to different types of customers, and the back end within North Korea that is able to respond to demand and supply the ecosystem of North Korean restaurants around the world.

The initial evidence for creativity is the existence of the restaurants themselves. North Korea may be the only country in the world with its own international restaurant chain. The existence of North Korean restaurants is the object of much fascination to many journalists,[113] as is the possibility that the restaurants are serving as outposts of potentially more nefarious activities than attractive young women serving extortionately priced food and alcohol.[114] Among the claims about the Pyongyang Restaurant chain in particular is that the restaurants are partially owned by (or at least connected to) Office 39 or its front companies.[115] It would not be surprising if central state entities were connected to North Korean restaurants, particularly those far from Pyongyang, but the positive evidence is slim. In principle this could make the restaurants subject to sanctions, as Office 39 and its known subsidiaries are on sanctions lists, although in practice this has not happened.

While restaurants are considered a risky investment in much of the developed world, restaurants as a source of revenue make sense from a North Korean perspective. Restaurants are a good way for North Korean entities to make money quickly, without having to negotiate with other states. The aid from China (and particularly from others) needs to be negotiated, takes time, and can get complicated—the draw of the restaurant industry is quick cash.[116] They are also often the primary business outposts of North Korean organizations in a given location. For example, in northeastern China, while Dandong and to a lesser extent Yanbian have a number of North Korean trading companies, with the exception of the hotel and the Air Koryo office, most North Korean businesses in Shenyang are restaurants.[117]

North Korean restaurants are not without proven risks: the joint venture restaurant in Amsterdam apparently closed down in acrimonious circumstances a few months after opening in 2012 (before reopening in 2013 under new management).[118] The restaurants can also serve as loci of scrutiny by foreign governments: following the imposition of new sanctions after North Korea's second nuclear test in February 2013, for example, the Chinese government apparently inspected North Korean restaurants for work permits and other regulatory compliance as a way of pressuring North Korea.[119]

But North Korean businesses in general are risk-acceptant, and compared to many other North Korean trade activities (such as the drug trade or arms trafficking), restaurants may actually be fairly low risk. A stationary, legitimate business that does not need to move goods across borders has less of a chance of being interdicted or shut down by hostile governments, and North Korean restaurants have never been subjected to any of the sanctions regimes instituted since 2006. The restaurants themselves may largely do business in untraceable cash, and the supplies for the restaurants may largely be sourced locally, such that the only connections back to North Korea that are required are the occasional North Korean–origin foodstuff (notably North Korean alcohol, seafood, and possibly ginseng), the movement of the North Korean staff, and some way to repatriate the profits back to North Korea itself (which is a problem faced by all North Korean businesses overseas). The restaurants may also be used as loci for other business: Pyongyang Restaurants, for example, also run side businesses such as art and ginseng selling.[120] The network needed, in other words, is small and cheap, requiring few nodes and links and even fewer risks.

The appeal of the restaurants to patrons, both in China and further afield, comes in playing on the mystique of North Korea as an isolated, mysterious country, offering customers a chance to see North Korean dancing and culture, eat (expensive) North Korean food, and meet real North Koreans—the hostesses at many North Korean restaurants in China are actually North Korean, not just ethnic-Korean Chinese. The North Korean hostesses are willing to talk and joke with guests (although not about politics), and build up relationships over time.[121] North Korean enterprises are taking advantage of the country's seeming isolation from the global economy to seek out and exploit a niche market in that very same global economy.

The exoticism of North Korea is especially apparent far from Northeast Asia, which is arguably why the restaurants in Southeast Asia and Europe have attracted the lion's share of international media attention. Yet even outside Northeast Asia, North Korea's restaurants' locations may be both opportunistic and following a logical pattern that stretches back to Northeast Asia. It may the case that restaurants are targeted toward a broader Korean diaspora, and follow the spatial distribution of that diaspora (within reason—North Korean restaurants are unlikely to open in the United States). That the targeted market for North Korean restaurants would be South Koreans makes a certain amount of sense. There is little culture shock and few language problems between South Koreans and North Koreans, and South Koreans are used to spending lavishly on food and alcohol. South Koreans may also be prone to talking about matters they should not. During one dinner with a trader at a Dandong North Korean restaurant, the trader told me that it was best if we discussed North Korean trade in his office after dinner, as the waitresses rarely talked, but were always listening. Customers at other North Korean restaurants around the world have reported being the target of eavesdropping by hostesses as well.[122]

A trip in June 2013 to the Pyongyang Restaurant in Jakarta was illuminating. The restaurant itself was located in the same general area of the city as Jakarta's South Korean expatriate community (and far from the North Korean embassy), but was situated some way off from the primary cluster of South Korean restaurants to differentiate it from those restaurants. The restaurant itself contained fairly standard (if slightly faded) décor similar to most South Korean restaurants, with the exception of an overhead flat screen TV that played North Korean patriotic music videos on a nonstop loop. It was empty on a weeknight except for our party and a party of several South Korean businessmen. It quickly became obvious that the primary expected clientele of the establishment were increasingly drunk and generous South Korean businessmen, of the sort who were seated across the restaurant from us. At 7:30 p.m., the waitresses, all clad in *hanbok*, climbed a small stage, took up drums, guitars, and bass, and belted out incredibly loud Korean folk songs and pop song covers for half an hour, all the while looking directly at the Korean businessmen. This was especially apparent once we realized that the waitresses were unable to communicate adequately in either English or Indonesian.

In northeastern China, the market for North Korean cuisine is larger and attracts more than just patrons looking for an oddity. While the North Korean aspects of the restaurants in Xita, the Korean neighborhood in Shenyang, are not downplayed—the façades of several of the restaurants are festooned with giant North Korean flags—in general, the North Korean restaurants in northeastern China are not significantly different from a typical Chinese or other type of Korean restaurant: they do not have the aura of otherness that Pyongyang Restaurant in Jakarta does. This larger market is associated with four kinds of Korean restaurants in China, as distinguished by their ownership structures. The first are those owned by South Koreans (and ethnic-Korean Chinese) and serve Korean food, but not necessarily specifically North Korean food. The second type is owned directly by North Korean enterprises. The third are joint ventures between North Korean businesses and Chinese partners (often ethnic-Korean Chinese), and the fourth are fully Chinese-owned, with North Korean staff.[123] As elsewhere, the North Korean theme is a draw for customers. In one Shenyang Military District–owned restaurant, the waitresses in particular, who were first brought to the restaurant in 2009, turned out to be a huge draw for business. They performed two hours per day, and were so popular for their beauty, and polite and attentive service, that by 2014 the restaurant was often booked out a month in advance.[124]

Which restaurants are owned by which enterprise is opaque at best. According to one ethnic-Korean Chinese businessman, in 2013 there were sixteen North Korean restaurants in Xita, Shenyang. Two were joint ventures between North Korean enterprises and Liaoning businessmen. At least one restaurant was owned by a local businessman and merely hired waitresses from a North Korean partner.[125] Although the Pyongyang Restaurant chain outposts are often joint ventures between foreign partners and (apparently) fronts for Office 39, with little or no local market competition, North Korea restaurants in China compete with each other, particularly if they are owned by different organizations (such as the party versus the army), and the employees spy on each other.[126] In Beijing, for example, one restaurant is owned by a party organization, while one analyst in 2012 described going to another restaurant that was owned by the North Korean Taekwondo Association.[127] The ownership of the restaurants may also be more prosaic, and simply another example of the food chain in action: Tudor and Pearson describe many North Korean restaurants overseas as being financed by groups of female relatives of senior officials, who pay the central state for permission to start the restaurants. The costs include the "franchise fee," the costs of the restaurant itself, and the loyalty taxes of 20–30 percent of profits.[128]

Many North Korean restaurants in China are actually owned by Chinese companies that only contract with North Korean companies for labor. The provision of labor is a relatively easy way for North Korean enterprises to enter the restaurant business without taking on the financial risk of opening a restaurant in a foreign country. One Chinese businessman in 2014 described hiring North Korean workers to serve food and perform in a northeastern China restaurant, owned by the Shenyang Military District, as well as clean the rooms in the affiliated hotel. In concert with running the restaurant, through Hunchun, he also imported North Korean seafood and wild vegetables, which were obtained through a Chinese import-export company specializing in North Korean goods.[129] The arrangement was similar to that of many other restaurants in China: the company sent its requirements for workers to its military superiors, who in turn contracted with local government entities in North Korea and, with North Korean central government approval, delivered the workers as a group to a port of entry into China. The workers, suitably vetted by the North Korean security services, were usually dropped off in Dandong or Hunchun (or less frequently other entry points) in groups of twenty or thirty, with two to three North Korean government minders. The waitresses were replaced every year, while the other service staff and room cleaners were replaced every two years. As with other such arrangements, while the businessman was responsible for room and board, the workers were not paid during their tenure in China, and received their back pay upon returning to North Korea.[130] In this way, the company can minimize its contact with North Korean companies, and stay out of North Korea itself entirely.

It is the provision of labor that allows many North Korean enterprises to participate in a simplified and semi-institutionalized trade network, in which they export a good (trained hostesses) that is relatively straightforward to produce within North Korea. At a North Korean restaurant in China in November 2013, one waitress had trained for several years at a university dedicated to hospitality management in North Korea (learning to speak Chinese, sing, dance, and play musical instruments), and had then been assigned to the restaurant in Shenyang. New waitresses are given a contract of several years, and can specify their preferences for the cities where they are to work, but they are not guaranteed their top choices. According to a trader in Dandong, southern Chinese cities (Macau, Hong Kong, Shanghai, Guangzhou) are not preferred by the waitresses because, while the customers have more money, they are also disrespectful and freer with their hands. Northeastern Chinese cities have less money, but the customers are more polite and respectful.[131]

The waitresses are watched closely to prevent defection, necessitating close proximity of restaurants and living quarters, particularly since the North Korean workers are not allowed to move far from their workplaces under Chinese law.[132] One Chinese trader described an office building in Dandong that contained several North Korean restaurants. The hostesses who worked at the restaurants lived in dormitory rooms in the building next door, which was not dissimilar from the waitresses at Pyongyang Restaurant in Phnom Penh, who lived above the restaurant.[133] Aside from ideological indoctrination and making sure the waitresses did not defect, the minders enforced service and performance standards. The manager of the Chinese military-owned restaurant once saw a dancer accidentally drop a fan onto the floor during a performance; later that evening, the minder was seen beating her about the face with a belt as punishment.[134] In Dandong, there were spies assigned to watch over each small group of the waitresses, and keep tabs on their contact with customers and other outsiders. The waitresses listened to customers' conversations for information, and kept their hair jet black (unlike, the trader intimated, Chinese and South Korean women).[135] This does not stop all attempts at defection, particularly once the women see the standard of living in China. Speaking to the minders' attempts to keep control of the workers, the Chinese manager of the military-owned restaurant described how, in 2013, one waitress did in fact attempt to defect from his restaurant into China proper. North Korea's security service contacted China's local Public Security Bureau, and the waitress was found and recaptured that same afternoon, then sent back to North Korea.[136] At times, groups of waitresses have attempted to escape *en masse*. On 7 April 2016, for instance, thirteen waitresses from Ryugyong Restaurant in Ninbgo, Zhejiang province in China defected to South Korea using legal North Korean passports.[137]

The chance of defection is also minimized by recruiting the hostesses from certain politically safe social classes in North Korea, maintaining their links back to North Korea when they are working abroad, and minimizing their ability to make new social connections. Any woman allowed to work in a North Korean restaurant outside of North Korea is already in a trusted position in North Korean society—their families will be arrested or placed under suspicion if they defect or do something otherwise untoward. The Ryugyong Restaurant defectors' group, for example, originally had twenty people, but seven waitresses refused to go at the last minute due to their fears about what would happen to their families back in North Korea.[138] The hostesses are forbidden from entering into relationships with foreigners, *especially* ethnic-Korean Chinese, who have more money than them, speak their language, and live nearby (so can take them away fairly easily).[139] Food can also serve as a disincentive to defection, even for members of the broader elite. One waitress noted that the pay was not high, but as long as she was working in China, she was guaranteed enough to eat, and just as importantly, her family would not have to worry about feeding her. This view was corroborated by another Chinese employer of North Korean waitresses, who told him in private that the three simple daily meals they received in China were more than what they received in North Korea, where they ate whenever food was available.[140]

North Korean waitresses themselves can also be seen as exportable "commodities," even when the restaurants are not specifically North Korean or serve Korean food. In December 2011, Longxi International Hotel, one of the tallest hotels in the world (at seventy-four stories and 328 meters), and the most prominent eyesore/landmark in Jiangsu province's Huaxi village (the so-called richest village in China), brought in thirty North Korean waitresses to serve at one of its restaurants, apparently to boost flagging patronage. Chinese customers flocked not only to see the waitresses, but also, according to customers, because the North Koreans' service standards were twice as high as Chinese servers, they stood up straight and comported themselves well, and they acted together with sense of solidarity (again, apparently unlike Chinese servers).

The waitresses, all from high-level families in North Korea, were sent by the North Korean government for three-year "internships" after studying "business" for four years at a university in Pyongyang. The monthly salary paid by the hotel to the North Korean entity contracted to provide the waitresses was apparently between five thousand and six thousand *yuan* per waitress (a massive sum even by the standards of China's richest village). The waitresses themselves saw only 150 *yuan* of this money, with some Chinese observers suspecting that at least some of the salary was retained for the waitresses back in North Korea if and when they returned at the end of their "internship."

Every morning the waitresses, who lived together in a dormitory two hundred meters from the hotel, would walk to the hotel in three rows, singing songs in praise of socialism. After starting work at 9 a.m., they would work until midnight, with a break in the afternoon and the standard fifteen-minute music performance during dinner. While the hotel offered meals for the waitresses, their supervisors insisted on eating only their own Korean food, including kimchi. Outside of work, the waitresses practiced their Chinese, but were apparently not permitted to use computers or the Internet. While the waitresses spoke a little Chinese when they arrived, they were not allowed to develop relationships with local Chinese men (despite the men's unrequited desires), and would spend their once-monthly excursion into the village getting their hair done, and shopping on the nearby market street for cosmetics, cheap goods, and food.[141]

The Longxi waitresses were clearly treated better than the average waitresses sent out of North Korea—they received at least some of their pay while they were in China, and they were able to venture outside occasionally to go shopping—suggesting that there is not a standard package for waitresses, but at least some flexibility in contractual and employment conditions from both the North Korean and Chinese sides. While all the waitresses are watched by North Korean minders, and appear to come from politically safe families, not all are equal: the training for waitresses appear to vary substantially (both in foreign language ability and the abilities of the waitresses), some are clearly provided with more autonomy than others, both in how they spend their time and how and when they receive their income, and the length of the contract also appears to vary by foreign partner.

All of this points to the surprising variety in North Korean restaurant enterprises around the world, and particularly in China. Multiple types of organizations in North Korea, at both the central and local levels, own restaurants outside of North Korea, and perhaps even more enter into contractual relationships with foreign investors, either to provide labor or to take an ownership stake in the restaurants themselves. The existence of multiple North Korean restaurants in the same locales in China suggests that, while the Pyongyang Restaurant chain exercises something of a monopoly in the areas where it operates, other North Korean restaurants are subject to competition with each other, and jockey for opportunities to make money. As with other types of international North Korea joint ventures and partnerships, the North Korean suppliers tend to hold on to the same foreign partners across multiple transactions if they can, and appear to deal with brokers who serve as go-betweens to their Chinese partners.

For both business within North Korea and trade with the outside world, it is not only state firms that have been able to adapt to a more complex environment. Since 2005, even as its state trading networks have adapted to sanctions and international stigma, the North Korean state has attempted to rein in private and hybrid trading networks within North Korea itself. Instead, despite its deep ambivalence, the state has been unable to get rid of private enterprise, and in some ways has become dependent on the existence of actors who are making money outside of the command economy (and in some cases against the wishes of the central state). Indeed, the imperatives of survival have led to the deepening of a culture of entrepreneurialism among nearly all sectors in North Korean society, one in which North Korean entrepreneurs are quick to respond to the needs created by international isolation, and the decrepit state of the North Korea's economy and infrastructure. These new entrepreneurs surely lack many of the characteristics necessary to be successful in developed countries (as will be seen in the next chapter), but are adaptable, flexible, and creative in how they make money.

As with the state trading networks, these private and hybrid networks flourish by blurring the boundaries between state and nonstate, formal and informal, and licit and illicit. Private traders pay off state officials for informal sanction of their activities, or establish informal contractual relationships that formally turn their enterprises into state companies and give them access to some state resources, even as they continue to be privately managed. State officials go into business for themselves, or extract rents from private and hybrid traders by virtue of their positions. All of this takes place within an environment where private enterprise and initiative remain illegal even while they are informally encouraged because they are among the few ways to make money in the country. Many of the goods and labor traded within North Korea and across borders are mundane and unremarkable, but even the goods that are outright illegal everywhere they are moved, such as methamphetamines, skirt the line between licit and illicit, as drug producers appear to occasionally have local official sanction, and make use of the same resources that other traders do.

Despite going without access to substantial state resources, and at times in the face of official opposition from the North Korean state, these networks have found ways to integrate economically with the outside world. If anything, the withdrawal of state resources from private and trade networks has increased their tendency to integrate with non–North Korean trade networks. Private networks find ways to transfer money back to North Korea even as the formal banks are sanctioned. State hostility to drug trafficking has meant that North Korean producers and brokers have been driven to build longstanding and apparently robust relationships with non–North Korean brokers and traffickers in China. North Korean restaurants have experimented with a variety of ownership structures, labor conditions, and contractual relationships with foreign firms.

At the same time, the very success of these entrepreneurs is enabled to a large extent by how they have adapted to suit North Korean conditions and by the extent to which they have figured out how to operate in indifferent, or even hostile, environments. When the tables are turned—when North Korea needs to attract foreign investment into North Korea and the state is unconstrained within its own borders—North Korean business networks fare less well. This apparent paradox will be the subject of the next chapter.

4

A Terrible, Horrible, No Good, Very Bad Investment Environment

There is a strong objection to the idea that North Korea is a particularly enterprising country: if North Koreans are so good at business, why is North Korea still so poor? North Korea is not as poor or destitute as it was during the Arduous March—the reported trade surplus in 2012,[1] the decrease in the percentage of malnourished children since the Arduous March, and the apparent narrowing of North Korea's food deficit thanks to increased production,[2] stand as evidence of this. Yet the country is still an economic, political, and demographic disaster. This task of this chapter is to address why North Korean trade networks can be so effective while North Korea itself remains so far behind economically, and so feckless in its contacts with foreigners inside its borders.

North Korea's problems as a place to do business are legion. A survey in 2007 of Chinese businesses dealing with North Korea, for example, found that the companies' biggest complaints about North Korea were the atrocious quality of basic infrastructure; infuriating regulations, which could be changed on a whim by the North Korean government after investments were made; and fear of property expropriation.[3] Communication with and within North Korea is difficult. Until relatively recently, the country was without mobile phones, and only specially appointed gatekeepers were allowed to access email that could reach the outside world. Even now, with the advent of the Egyptian company Orascom's domestic mobile phone network, phones are legally prohibited from being able to call the outside world.[4] The transportation infrastructure is crumbling or nonexistent, with trains often taking up to a week to travel from Sinuiju to Pyongyang, roads in dilapidated condition, and the national airline not flying domestic routes for years at a time. The workforce is of poor quality, encumbered by low levels of nutrition and health and a socialist work ethic. The state-owned industrial sector is massive but insolvent and nonfunctional. Levels of corruption are astronomical.[5]

Even if all of these problems were resolved, political and economic institutions are incapable of giving investors credible assurances about their investments. Political risk is high: even if companies latch onto powerful officials, no North Korean official aside from members of the Kim family is ever safe from the possibility of being purged. North Korean institutions are unable to enforce contracts, engage in reliable regulation or conflict resolution, or give formal laws any teeth. North Korea also has a terrible international reputation. While most countries outside of the United States, the European Union, Australia, South Korea, and Japan do not have their own sanctions against North Korea, United Nations–level sanctions are extensive enough to make many firms think twice about investing, inasmuch as they both create stigma for companies involved in North Korea, and make dealing in certain types of products (namely anything to do with luxury goods, chemicals, precision machinery, or high technology) burdensome, even if they are allowed by the sanctions. Financial sanctions in particular make it difficult to transfer money into and out of North Korea.

It is not particularly surprising that North Korea would be a terrible environment for attracting and keeping foreign investors. Most totalitarian regimes with cults of personality, command economies, onerous trade and financial sanctions, and a lingering suspicion of outsiders are. The question is not whether North Korea is a terrible place to do business. Of course it is. How North Korea can be such a bad investment environment at the same time that North Koreans are increasingly entrepreneurial, outward-looking, flexible, and creative in how they do business is a much more interesting question. Being enterprising in making money does not mean being good at attracting other people with money, at least over the long term.

The paradox for both potential foreign investors and North Korean officials and entrepreneurs attempting to do business with them is this: the specific ways in which foreign investors come to grief in North Korea are in part a result of the ways in which North Korean business networks have evolved in response to the terrible environment during and since the Arduous March. North Korean trade networks have evolved not only to survive in a low-trust, poorly institutionalized environment with terrible infrastructure, but even to thrive by taking advantage of the terrible situation to provide goods and services (such as transport and finance) that are otherwise lacking, and developing the ability to do business in ways counter to regulations if they are in the right patron-client networks. The comfort North Koreans have dealing with ambiguity in business—the blurring of state and nonstate economic activity, of formal and informal business, and of licit and illicit dealings—has been an advantage for North Korean trade networks in maneuvering around an environment where private economic activity must both avoid the state and give the state its cut, and the difference between legal and illegal is not particularly meaningful.

While it is technically laws and regulations, and the state institutions that implement and enforce them, that create the investment environment for foreign investors, the manner in which North Korean trade networks survive and thrive tells us much about the difficulties that foreign businesses have in North Korea. Virtually all foreign investors must have a North Korean partner, so the experience of doing business in North Korea is the experience of interacting with North Korean business networks. The patron-client networks that provide political cover for North Korean entrepreneurs, ensure state officials their cut and the state its revenue, and cut through otherwise crippling formal laws and regulations, are difficult for foreigners to enter, and are not as effective between foreigners and North Koreans as among North Koreans themselves. North Korean trade networks also generally do not require the conditions, such as long-term credible commitments, property rights, dependable infrastructure, and an efficient supply chain, that foreign investments with high capital costs do. In fact, given that North Korean trade networks sometimes operate by exploiting these weaknesses, the strengths of North Korean business networks are often the downfall of foreign firms. At best, foreign investors are left to confront a fluid, ambiguous environment for which North Korean trade networks are suited, but which severely hamper the ability of foreign companies to operate. At worst, North Korean partners appear to turn to the task of bilking investors with the same creativity and flexibility that they have demonstrated in their trade networks.

In this chapter, I briefly look at North Korea's outreach to the rest of the world. North Korea is indeed attempting to attract investors and trade, especially with non-Chinese investors, through special economic zones, trade promotion campaigns, and regulatory and legal incentives. Some of these efforts have borne fruit, but many have not. I illustrate the frustration of many investors, and how North Korean networks' advantages can become disadvantages when dealing with non–North Koreans inside of North Korea, with a detailed assessment of the Xiyang debacle, the Chinese mining investment that publicly and spectacularly blew up in 2012. Xiyang skated on the edge between formality and informality, and attempted (to its deep regret) to build up North Korean networks through its local partner to secure its investment. It failed, in part because the North Korean side appeared to have used its monopoly on information, connections with the food chain, and the informal networks Xiyang was attempting to access as a way to enrich itself and expropriate Xiyang's investments.

Finally, I look at less disastrous, but nonetheless difficult, interactions between foreign firms and North Korean businesses. Chinese firms that insist on doing business in North Korea employ a number of strategies to mitigate risk and extract some type of profit (when possible) from the country. The successful Chinese investor's response to a country with weak property rights, a confusing and predatory political economy, and infrastructure and worker quality problems has been a combination of mimicking (if imperfectly) North Korean trade network behavior (in effect embracing the ambiguity) and structuring trade and investments to minimize dependence on any proper functioning of the North Korean economy. North Korea's entrepreneurialism has a way to go before it is a net positive for all aspects of the North Korean economy.

North Korea Looks Outward

One of the ironies of North Korea's struggle to attract foreign investment is that, for an ostensibly autarkic country, it has long been officially open to both foreign investment and foreign currency holdings. The North Korean government passed its first equity joint venture law in 1984, and passed a raft of more detailed laws governing foreign investment in the early 1990s, with updates and amendments in 1999, 2006, and 2011. North Korean laws on investment are actually fairly clear, concise, and easy to parse, particularly in terms of the advantages and inducements given to foreign investors.[6] Laws allowing for the establishment of equity and contract joint ventures, as well as, interestingly, wholly owned foreign enterprises outside of Rajin-Sonbong, were last amended in 2011. How investors are supposed to resolve disputes is less clear; the most detail North Korean law provides is that the complainants should submit their complaint to the relevant authority (often the organ that is the target of the investors' ire) and it will be dealt with within thirty days.[7] Nonetheless, there are a number of theoretical advantages for foreign investors provided by North Korean laws. In concert with these laws, North Korea's efforts to attract trade and foreign investors have come, notionally, in two prongs: promotion of trade and investment, and the creation and development of special economic zones. The primary "beneficiaries" of North Korea's honeyed enticements have, since 2006, largely been Chinese firms, leading to both North Korean concerns about being too dependent on Chinese money, and Chinese concerns about being fleeced in North Korea.

Trade Promotion

The North Korean central state has taken halting measures to attract outside investment, not only from China, but also from countries beyond. North Korean officials made presentations to Chinese investors about welcoming investment as early as 2005,[8] and seem to have kicked trade promotion activities into higher gear in 2010, with the creation of the Taepung International Investment Group, which was merged into the Joint Venture and Investment Committee (JVIC) by 2013 to form a unified trade promotion group, with a branch office in Beijing. The JVIC has indeed made contact with Chinese investors and attempted to build confidence in North Korea as a destination for capital.[9] In 2012, North Korean trade officials made trips to investment forums throughout China, and publicly made commitments to protect Chinese investors. The same year, North Korean officials also signed a tourism agreement with Dandong officials to ease the way for a daily tourist train from Dandong to Pyongyang.[10]

North Korean companies themselves also proactively advertise for business. A search of North Korean websites, especially Naenara, in April 2014, illustrates the desire of North Korean trading companies to go into business with outsiders (and specifically non-Chinese outsiders). Clearly some of the companies were just listed by North Korea as propaganda—a bid to show economic development and innovation where none was actually occurring. With that said, of the 142 companies described in Naenara and associated websites as offering opportunities for investment or joint ventures, ninety-two listed some sort of contact information—email, phone, fax, or some combination of all three—suggesting that the majority of the companies listed are relatively serious about investment with the non-Chinese outside world.[11]

North Korean companies presented themselves as already internationalized. Seventy-one companies (half of the sample) claimed to have overseas branches, investments, or collaborations, although the evidence for this was often slim. Besides China and Japan (the primary post-2006 and pre-2006 trading partners, respectively), companies from Russia, France, Taiwan, Hong Kong, Malaysia, Vietnam, and Switzerland were also claimed to have business relationships with the companies seeking investment. Separate data from the Open Source Center from before Kim Jong-il died at the end of 2011 also listed Austria, Germany, Italy, Singapore, and South Korea (outside of Kaesong) as being the origin countries of non-Chinese, non-Japanese trade after sanctions began in 2006.[12]

The categories of goods in which the companies advertised for sales and investment suggests a shift (at least in public) away from politically problematic goods. For the companies advertising a single category of goods or services, the top categories were light machinery and equipment, textiles and clothing, health products (often "natural" medicines of dubious quality), and food and beverage items (including fisheries products) (see figure 4.1). This stands in contrast to the Open Source Center report, where mining was by far the most common industry for foreign-involved joint ventures, with nearly ninety out of 351 known investments.[13] Mining, the driver of much of North Korea's exports since 2008, was only the purview of five single-category companies, suggesting that the North Korean companies that seek outside funding through the Internet may differ from the companies bringing in the majority of North Korea's "legitimate" hard currency. With the exception of some electronics and light industry, none of the offered goods would conceivably be under sanctions. Given

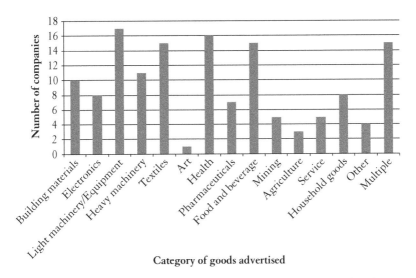

Figure 4.1.   Categories of goods advertised by North Korean companies (April 2014)
Source: http://naenara.com.kp/en and other North Korean website, April 2014.

the frequent name changes and front companies typical of North Korean enterprises, it is difficult to say whether the individuals involved or the companies themselves are under UN-imposed sanctions.

In the sample, seventeen companies claimed expertise in multiple fields, although most of these were trading companies, suggesting that they may not have been producing the goods they were advertising. Of those with known establishment dates, only two (Korea Kwangryang Trading Corporation, and Gold Cup Trading Corporation) had been created since the beginning of sanctions in 2006, suggesting that the multi-industry conglomerates may be largely traditional state-owned enterprises attempting to branch out into new markets. Taken together, there is some evidence that North Korean enterprises, particularly those not at the center of the central state's revenue strategy (that is, those not involved in mining) are indeed looking for new investors and trading partners in China and elsewhere, in industries that would not be immediately obvious as growth industries in North Korea. Whether this desire for trade is impervious to political reversals at the very top of the North Korean state is unclear, but it does suggest that North Korean companies are genuine in their search for foreign trade opportunities. The question is whether they are actually getting them; this is less clear.

Special Economic Zones

Special economic zones are perhaps the best-known examples of North Korea's fitful and at times strange relationship with formal investment promotion and economic reform. North Korea has long experimented with special economic zones seemingly inspired by (and even strongly encouraged by) China's experiences with Shenzhen in the early 1980s. Following a visit by Kim Il Sung to China, North Korea set up the Rajin-Sonbong Free Economic Trade Zone in the northeast corner of the country in 1991, followed by Kaesong Industrial Complex, the Mt. Kumgang Tourist Region, and Sinuiju Special Administrative Region in 2002. The actual development in these regions has been questionable at best. The legal framework for foreign investment in Rajin-Sonbong was not arguably developed until after 1999, the ostensible Chinese-Dutch "governor" of the special economic zone near Sinuiju was jailed on corruption charges in 2003, just weeks after being appointed by the North Koreans, and South Korean tours of Mt. Kumgang ended rather suddenly in 2008 after North Korean soldiers shot a South Korean tourist to death, although the site has hosted family reunions on and off since then.[14] For its part, the Kaesong Industrial Complex chugged along through thick and thin until North Korea closed it for several months during the 2013 Korean Peninsula crisis. It reopened in September 2013, and operated until February 2016, when South Korea pulled its companies out of Kaesong in response to the fourth nuclear test and a long-range rocket launch.[15]

With Chinese companies moving into North Korea, from 2005 China gradually began improving North Korean transportation infrastructure, and linking it with Chinese highways and railways in the border regions, particularly so that North Korea could play a role in developing the Tumen River region, and the Yalu River region. China and North Korea agreed to build a new bridge over the Yalu in 2009, and agreed to develop Hwanggumpyong and Wihwado in the Yalu River as economic zones in 2010.[16] Most of all, China focused on building up Rajin-Sonbong as an infrastructural link between the Sea of Japan and the Chinese part of the Tumen River region. While Rajin-Sonbong had been a special economic zone since 1991, it had long been moribund. A visit by Kim Jong-il in 2009 changed this. By 2011, Rason's laws and regulations were updated to encourage Chinese investment and ground was broken on a number of new projects. The next year, China and North Korea established over-sight committees and regulations for the zones, moving in a concrete way toward developing the zones. China also built a highway from Hunchun to Rason to complete the logistical link between Jilin province and the Sea of Japan, with a number of Chinese SOEs and Jilin companies involved in developing the electrical, transportation, and tourist infrastructure of Rason.[17]

Thus from 2010 onward, Rason became the locus of Chinese attempts to connect Rason and Jilin province through infrastructure (electricity and transportation) construction so as both to assure Chinese access to the region, and make North Korea potentially more dependent on China.[18] Rason itself was gifted with a number of special regulations and some mea-sure of local autonomy, including allowing fifty-year leases on property, a concessional 14 percent corporate tax rate, the ability of foreign banks to establish branches inside the zone (and consequently to conduct business in foreign currencies), and the recognition of overseas Koreans as non-North Korean citizens (theoretically protecting South Koreans and ethnic Ko-rean Chinese citizens from depredations in North Korea). Chinese citizens were also allowed to apply for visa-free permits to enter Rason, issuable by the local government within forty-eight hours, as well as drive their own cars into North Korea for tours.[19]

Rason is not the only area in which the North Korean central state has at least made efforts to attract foreign investment and trade through modi-fying regulations and granting concessions. Many of the benefits formerly enjoyed by Rason were extended to the rest of the country by the 2013 law on special economic zones: in addition, the ability of "legitimate profits" and foreign currency to move into and out of the zones was guaranteed, investment in preferred sectors received a 10 percent tax rate (compared to the standard 14 percent tax for SEZs and Rason), tariffs were lowered for investors in SEZs, and promises of easier customs and immigration regula-tions were given.[20]

The 2013 law on special economic zones enabled the creation of local zones that could theoretically encompass areas as small as individual build-ings, and that could be initiated either by the central state, or from the bot-tom, by local governments and enterprises. The twenty special economic zones announced in 2013 and 2014 after the law encompassed export processing and trade zones, industrial development zones, agricultural

development zones, tourism development zones, and economic development zones, which appeared to incorporate multiple foci from the other
development categories.[21]

A number of local governments appear to have been called upon to create development strategies that included economic openness zones, possibly in connection with the 2013 law. Among these was a document from
the Kyongwon County government in North Hamgyong province, argu-
ing for a strategy of economic development through tourism and trade,
and evincing a strong desire for foreign (specifically Chinese) investment.
The local government was enthusiastic to attract trade and investment
from directly across the border in Hunchun, but was well aware of the
area's deficiencies both in the quality of the workforce and infrastructure,
particularly in electricity generation. Aside from the usual plans for mineral extraction (coal, granite, and rare earth metals), Kyongwon County
proposed to set up an economic openness zone (*kaifa qu*) at Ryudasom-ri,
adjacent to Hunchun on the Tumen River, which would serve as the nexus
for development activities, and house both facilities and infrastructure to
attract Chinese investment and tourism. Thus it was that Kyongwon's
tourism plan consisted of building hospitality facilities in Ryudasom-ri
and attracting ethnic Korean Chinese tourists from across the border who
would visit historical sites (apparently due to a desire for ethnic solidarity),
although at that point there was no Kyongwon tourism liaison office to
solve any problems that came up.

While Kyongwon County officials had made multiple trips to Hunchun
in 2013 to encourage investment and move forward on the Ryusadom-ri
zone, the document lamented that the lack of North Korean trading companies in Kyongwon was to blame for difficulties in both attracting and
dealing with the logistics of setting up Chinese investment. When Chinese
companies came and wanted to set up a textile factory and a weaving factory, it was a North Korean food company, and a military-owned company
that served as their counterparts. In other cases, the lack of North Korean
partners and efficient implementation of regulations had caused potential
investors to go elsewhere. Coal, for example, could only be exported from
Kyongwon County with the approval of the local public security bureau,
which complicated matters.[22]

Kyongwon County's strategy was emblematic of the dilemma that local
areas in North Korea faced in attracting trade and investment. While it

was clearly imperative and encouraged for local areas to attract investment (which itself speaks against the idea of North Korea as uniquely economically autarkic), necessary infrastructure and institutions were lacking, and the county government fell back on low value-added manufacturing, tourism, and other solutions—mineral extraction—that were likely controlled by other, more powerful branches of the North Korean state.

The Chinese Connection

While North Korea's investment strategy, particularly since the fall of Jang Song-thaek, has been oriented toward attracting investment from beyond China, realistically most foreign currency continues to come from China.[23] In the past decade, much of the academic attention towards North Korea's economic engagement with the outside world has come in the form of examinations of Chinese trade with and investment in North Korea.[24] Given China's strategic alliance with North Korea, and North Korea's possession of nuclear weapons, much commentary has been focused on the wherewithal of China to influence North Korea's behavior through its aid programs and bilateral trade relationship, with the implication being that greater North Korean dependence on Chinese aid and business might translate into less provocative behavior (or even, in the faintest of hopes, denuclearization).[25]

Other studies have been more concerned with the effect of Chinese trade and investment on North Korea's political economy, in particular whether North Korea might eventually be induced to reform and open up (on the Chinese model, or in its own way) through interaction with Chinese business. Some authors have been skeptical that Chinese economic involvement in North Korea will lead to any kind of large scale reform or movement by North Korea toward more openness. The bulk of Chinese investment has come in the extraction of mineral resources, which has enriched certain political and military elites in North Korea, and has potentially enabled them to contain any transformational influences by essentially becoming a narrowly focused rentier state.[26] Chinese investment could also be seen as self-limiting in size and scope inasmuch as, absent functioning formal institutions, traders and investors operate in a low-trust environment that forces them to keep their investments small and dependent on personal networks.[27] Others are more sanguine about the potential influence of Chinese trade and investment on North Korea, seeing the Chinese as teachers who the North Koreans are slowly and tentatively emulating.[28] North Korea has also created and altered its institutions—particularly special economic zones and investment banks—to mimic Chinese institutions that have been instrumental in spurring on Chinese economic growth, and has deepened cooperation in joint development projects (such as Rason). Finally, there is some evidence that North Korean officials and businessmen have adopted ideas about market exchange that they have learned through interacting with Chinese businesses.[29]

In the 1990s and into the early 2000s, China was a relatively minor player in North Korean trade and investment (although it provided aid to North Korea). Beginning in 2004, China began shifting its relationship with North Korea from one in which it stabilized North Korea through aid (and more generally treated it as a strategic political ally outside the realm of economics) to one in which trade and investment would dominate Chinese interactions with North Korea.[30] The result was a massive increase in China–North Korea trade over the next decade (see figure 4.2).[31]

The Chinese government trade and investment strategy has been officially characterized as "government-led, enterprise-based, market-operated, win-win" (*zhengfu zhudao, qiye weihu shichang yunzuo, huli gongying*).[32] In

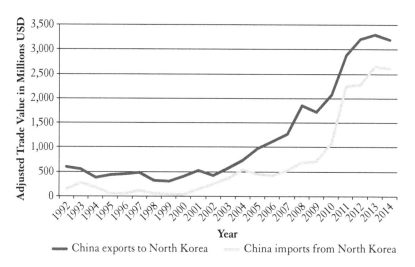

Figure 4.2. Adjusted trade between China and North Korea (1992 to 2014)
Source: UN Comtrade mirror data.

practice, this initially (from around 2003 to 2005) meant that the Chinese government, through campaigns and study tours, encouraged private traders and investors, and in some cases ordered state owned enterprises, to move into North Korea. The intent was to jointly develop resource projects (thus providing China with natural resources and North Korea with hard currency), use North Korean trade to revitalize the three northeastern provinces of China, and coordinate bilateral trade and investment at a relatively high government-to-government level, although the actual investment (outside of infrastructure) was to be by mostly profit-seeking private firms.[33]

Although there were formal joint ventures (as opposed to informal cross-border trade) in North Korea as early as 1997,[34] officially encouraged Chinese investment in North Korea began with a relatively big bang in 2004 and 2005, with high-level joint visits and investment agreements, and a North Korean trade promotion presentation. And indeed, Chinese government data suggest that there was a surge of Chinese companies moving into North Korea in 2006. The majority of companies investing in North Korea always appear to have been from Liaoning, Jilin, and Heilongjiang (see figure 4.3). While the initial surge of state-encouraged investment was headlined by large-scale state-owned enterprise investments (such as China Minmetals), in fact the majority of Chinese companies involved in

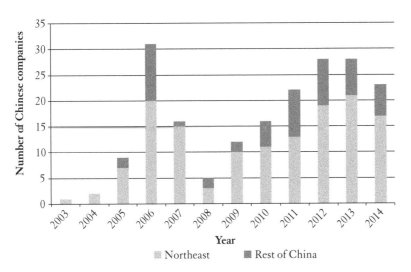

Figure 4.3. Chinese companies registered as investing in North Korea (2003 to 2014)
Source: Chinese Ministry of Commerce. The figures for 2014 are through August 2014.

North Korea from the start appear to have been small and medium-sized private enterprises based in Jilin and Liaoning.[35] They often flew under the Chinese government's radar, and were not overly solicitous of publicity. While they may have been encouraged to invest in North Korea by the central (and local) governments, most Chinese enterprises in North Korea were not controlled by the government. In fact, the overall Chinese government strategy specifically set out the terms North Korea (and Chinese companies) could expect: any trade and investment would largely be done by private enterprises, and had to be economically viable in an open market (that is, without Chinese government concessions or interventions, which were in any event not forthcoming). If anything, the *zhengfu zhudao, qiye weihu shichang yunzuo, huli gongying* strategy put businesses on notice that while the Chinese government wanted them to go into North Korea, if they did, they were on their own. Thus left exposed, Chinese firms were faced with the question of how to survive in North Korea, particularly when confronted with the ambiguity, flexibility, and (sometimes pernicious) creativity of the North Korean business environment.

The Xiyang Debacle

North Korea has a wealth of untapped natural resources. The lack of sanctions on minerals until 2016, and the country's proximity to China, which desires those natural resources (particularly minerals), have made North Korea a tempting target for mining companies looking for new investment opportunities. Private Chinese mining companies began investing in North Korea around 2003;[36] by 2008, the income North Korea derived from mining was sufficiently high that some analysts categorized it essentially as a mineral rentier state, with molybdenum production being important to China.[37] This is not say, however, that mining companies had positive experiences investing in North Korea.

One of the first mining companies that came to grief was actually the company with perhaps the most Chinese state support and prestige on the line. In 2004, China Minmetals Corporation, the largest state-owned mining company in China, was ordered by the Chinese central government to invest in North Korea as a means not only of strengthening China–DPRK trade relations, but also of increasing China's influence over North Korea's energy industry. An official intergovernmental agreement was duly signed with great fanfare in Pyongyang in October 2005 to establish joint venture coal mines in North Korea, and the North Korean government fast-tracked implementation, granting visas and moving equipment and materials with great efficiency. Soon, however, the cracks began to appear in the venture: most everything the North Korean government was supposed to provide failed to materialize. The contract called for a hundred heavy-duty trucks, but the government provided only twenty, most of which broke frequently. The government promised to build a processing plant, roads, railway sheds, and transport, none of which were forthcoming. Minmetals was forced to provide much of its equipment and materials, including paying for bridges, roads, factory construction, machinery, and trucks. Despite this, everything seemed to be in place after a year of exertion.

It was then that the investment developed even more problems. North Korean military units were moved to the vicinity of the largest Minmetals coal mine in North Korea, and began staging frequent marches and drills that interfered with the work of the mine. This gave way to a restricted military area that allowed the seizure of the entire mine. Minmetals went to the North Korean government to protest, and was told to send their people back to China while the matter was worked out within the North Korean state apparatus. Upon the Chinese workers' return to China, however, the company's North Korean contacts began refusing to talk to them, put them off, and denied them visas to return to North Korea. Everything associated with the mine was appropriated, and compensation was denied by the North Korean military. In 2010, when Premier Wen Jiabao visited North Korea and raised the issue with Kim Jong-il, a small amount of compensation was forthcoming, but not nearly enough to make up for the company's losses. Minmetals continued to invest in North Korea at the behest of the Chinese government, and the specific details of the debacle were suppressed in the Chinese media.[38]

Many of Minmetals' experiences—an impressive debut seemingly with support from the highest reaches of the North Korean state, a contract in which the North Korean partners promised the moon and then delivered very little, a gradual souring of the relationship, sudden appropriation of the physical assets that were trapped in North Korea, a struggle for compensation—are not unique among large-scale investments in North

Korea. In August 2012, Haicheng Xiyang Group, one of the largest private mining and materials conglomerates in China, issued a blistering statement on its website denouncing North Korea for deception and treachery in a failed iron ore processing deal in which Xiyang had lost more than 240 million *yuan*.[39] In a similarly unprecedented move, the North Korean government responded with its own public criticisms, claiming that the agreement that Xiyang had signed was fraudulent, and intimating that Xiyang itself had been unable to produce documents requested, and was unwilling to negotiate as things fell apart.[40] Of greater interest than the unusual publicity of the spat is the detailed account the company gave of its experiences in North Korea. It reveals exactly how and why North Korea is such a bad investment environment, and how the same conditions that allowed foreign trading entrepreneurialism to grow in North Korea also have caused foreign investors to be fleeced with abandon.

Zhou Furen, the CEO of Xiyang, admitted in later interviews that he had been overconfident in his prior assessment of North Korea as an investment environment. Although he was aware of the horror stories about North Korea, Zhou—swept up by the Chinese government's call in 2005 to invest in North Korea, hearing from investors in seafood export that there were even greater profits to be had in mining, and coming off a series of foreign business deals that had helped Xiyang grow to become one of the largest private companies in northeastern China—ignored the misgivings of his senior leadership team and powered ahead with slogans like "Nothing ventured, nothing gained."[41] After a site visit to Ongjin, a city on a peninsula on the southwestern coast of North Korea, Xiyang in October 2006 set up a company called Yangfeng Joint Venture with a North Korean company, with the contract apparently approved the following year by the North Korean government. Xiyang insisted on 75 percent ownership of the joint venture, to which the North Korean partner's representative, Ri Seong-ku, agreed. This was apparently illegal, as North Korean law states that North Korean partners can own no less than 30 percent of a joint venture, and Xiyang alleged that Ri Seong-ku forged the government approval certificate showing the 75 percent ownership stake.[42]

Construction began in October 2007, but almost immediately the company encountered nearly all of the problems about which it had been warned. It was extremely difficult to transfer money between North Korean and Chinese banks. The work site had no electricity and no food, requiring Xiyang to run on diesel generators and import food from China. Using the dilapidated North Korean rail system, moving equipment from the Chinese border to Haeju, a distance of four hundred kilometers, could take three months, as the trains moved at ten kilometers/hour when they moved at all. When Xiyang ordered cranes from Pyongyang, they were informed that the cranes would be delivered only if they also paid for new tires for the cranes.[43]

North Korea's typical suspicion of foreigners also hampered the joint venture. The Chinese workers were restricted to a small area around the worksite without escorts; they were unable even to walk on the beach (five hundred meters from the plant) after work. Given the lack of food on site, the Chinese workers wanted to travel sixty kilometers to the nearest produce market to buy food. This was at first absolutely refused with the response that foreigners were not allowed to access the markets, but after protests, the Chinese workers were allowed to travel offsite as long as there were two North Koreans accompanying them at all times. The Chinese workers were also forced to take a specific, preapproved path between Ongjin and Pyongyang, regardless of whether it was the fastest or most convenient route.[44]

At the beginning of 2009, North Korea imposed a 25 percent resource tax on joint ventures. Xiyang heard about these changes, but were not officially informed by their North Korean partners because, the North Korean partners claimed, the new regulations only applied to new joint ventures. Nonetheless, Zhou was unconvinced, and threatened to pull out. The North Korean partners pulled out all stops to convince Xiyang to stay, including providing evidence that the North Korean Supreme People's Assembly had confirmed the 2006 joint venture contract and guaranteed a thirty-year period without changes.[45]

The new facility began the full-scale processing of iron ore powder in April 2011, and Xiyang was able to produce thirty thousand tons of powder for export. Within months, however, Zhou said the North Korean workers, having learned how to process the iron ore from the Chinese technicians, progressively minimized the role of the Chinese workers in production. On 6 September 2011, Ri Seong-ku presented Xiyang with a new contract with sixteen new terms that made Xiyang's continued involvement in the project infeasible: among other things, the North Korean partners demanded a monthly salary of three hundred *yuan* (approximately fifty dollars) per worker instead of the thirty dollars originally agreed to; the cost of electricity (payable in euros) was increased; a fee for land usage was introduced; the 25 percent resource tax introduced in 2009 would be applicable after all; and, in a touching gesture toward environmental sustainability, wastewater (even treated wastewater) could no longer be discharged into the ocean.[46]

Xiyang also gradually realized that lack of transparency in their dealings with the North Koreans had allowed the emergence of a plethora of problems that threatened production. The tailings ponds agreed upon in the 2006 joint venture document had never been approved by the North Korean government (or even, apparently, submitted for approval). The port of Haeju, which was supposed to ship out the iron ore power, had limited cargo capacity, and Ri Seong-ku told Xiyang (erroneously) that he had continued shipping out iron ore powder when in fact much of the powder had not been exported and would not be marketed. The North Korean government later claimed, in fact, that the entire registration of the joint venture in 2007 had been done informally, and therefore illegally, and it had no record of a joint venture having been registered at all.[47]

Zhou let the plant fall idle, and negotiations over the new contract continued on and off. With the negotiations going nowhere, the North Koreans suddenly canceled the contract and the joint venture on 7 February 2012. By the end of February, only ten Chinese workers were left at the plant. The North Koreans adopted a passive-aggressive, and then aggressive-aggressive, strategy to get them out, sending a team of public security officers to cut off all electricity, communications, and water, smash in the windows of the living quarters, and finally order the workers to leave immediately for Sinuiju (and on to China) on a guarded bus.[48]

The North Koreans were clearly eager for foreign investment, and were willing to say whatever it took to get the contract signed, including eliding the exact status of the project vis-à-vis the legal system. Aside from agreeing to a joint venture ownership share that was (apparently) illegal, the North Korean partners rolled out the red carpet for Xiyang, hosting Zhou Furen's delegation at a reception in the North Korean Supreme People's Assembly, complete with dancing flower girls and high-level officials.[49] Although this no doubt reinforced Xiyang's impression that the project had high-level official backing, in a system where the lines between formal and informal, legal and illegal, are blurred, it would have been difficult to distinguish between high-level official backing, and backing by high-level officials who were in Ri Seong-ku's informal networks. Behaviors and practices that were individually optimal for businesspeople in North Korea's new economy were negative for the encouragement and success of foreign investment: the very characteristics, in other words, that made North Korean officials entrepreneurial also inhibited their ability to attract foreign investors for projects within North Korea. Zhou's North Korean partners, as predators within the food chain of the North Korean economy, had learned to maximize their ability to draw income from those below (and beside). Ri Seong-ku, who Xiyang noted with scorn weighed 108 kilograms, significantly more than the average malnourished North Korean, was no doubt relatively high up in the food chain and practiced in its ways.[50] Ri and his associates appear to have treated the joint venture itself, rather than just the iron ore powder produced by the joint venture, as an income stream, and a way to access foreign luxury goods.

Within North Korea, for example, Xiyang representatives were forced to stay at international hotels and guesthouses and pay for all of the expenses of two North Korean escorts who accompanied them. At one point during a Xiyang visit to the Yanggakdo Hotel in Pyongyang, Ri Seong-ku carted off twenty cases of beer from the restaurant, and charged it to Xiyang's room. He also charged Zhou Furen two thousand dollars for a visit to his own home, and bought an eighty thousand dollar Hummer in 2008. Xiyang also recounted in its statement that each time the North Korean delegation visited China, aside from insisting that Xiyang pay for the hotel, meals, and travel costs, the North Koreans also ordered alcohol at every meal, drank four bottles of wine, ordered at least ten bottles of beer for their rooms, and brought in massage girls, whether Xiyang ordered them or not. They then took the receipts and sought reimbursement for the same expenses in North Korea. When they returned to North Korea, the delegation also took back, at Xiyang's expense, suits, laptops, mobile phones, food, drinks, consumer goods, and at least forty cigarettes per person. By Xiyang's estimate, every delegation accumulated at least 200,000 *yuan* in expenses.[51] The joint venture in effect served as a way for North Korean officials to do foreign trade in luxury and consumer goods at someone else's expense within the confines of what was acceptable in the North Korean system.

While the North Korean partners demanded standard bribes for helping to grease the gears of the bureaucratic machinery, including two hundred thousand *yuan* in 2007 for bureaucrats, one hundred thousand dollars for South Hwanghae province to allow construction of the plant, and seventy thousand dollars in 2010 as a "gift to the Korean people," one of Xiyang's complaints was that they were forced to provide cash and gifts to the North Koreans for the government on the occasion of public holidays (especially those put on for Kim Jong-il).[52] While these offerings were functionally equivalent to bribes from the perspective of Chinese companies, in North Korea they are one of the primary means by which higher-level predators, and particularly the central state, receive income from lower levels, inasmuch as they serve as both income and demonstrations of personal loyalty to the central state. Xiyang's experience is similar to that of other foreigners—one foreign NGO representative recounted how he was also called on to give gifts for leaders' birthdays.[53]

Given that the focus of North Korea's trading policy (such as it is) is on acquiring foreign currency, the hierarchy of North Korean businesses is defined to a large extent by their access to foreign currency, and few people would willingly hold solely North Korean *won* after the 2009 currency reform, North Korean business partners have developed a keen sense of currency arbitrage, and have used it to their advantage. Ri Seong-ku's demand that the North Korean workers be paid three hundred *yuan* instead of thirty dollars is one such example. The fate of the refund of Xiyang's investment is another. After his workers were kicked out of North Korea, Zhou spent the next several months attempting to recoup at least part of his investment. He asked for a refund of the principal of thirty million euros plus fifteen million euros in interest in order for the North Koreans to buy out his share of the joint venture. The North Koreans at first offered thirty million euros immediately if Zhou would settle his claim. Zhou refused, having lost trust in his former partners, and believing that even if he agreed, they would come back and claim that they had in fact only offered twenty-five million euros. A few days after this offer, the North Koreans then offered thirty million US dollars, a discount of approximately 20 percent, confirming Zhou's fears.[54] In any case, the money never arrived, and Xiyang went public with its story in August 2012.

The North Korean government policy in early 2009 that imposed a 25 percent resource tax on mining investments likely rendered the Xiyang investment inherently unprofitable. Sudden changes in government policy in North Korea can be reflective of factional politics, as the central state gives credence to one faction—the military, the cabinet, or the party—over another, or as different factions jockey for positions. In the case of Musan iron mine, for instance, a number of Chinese companies were interested in investing, but soon found out that each North Korean state organization involved in the mine demanded exclusive contracts with a different Chinese company.[55]

Sudden changes can also be a way for the state to keep the population off guard and dependent on the state, or at least unable to game state policies too easily. The sudden introduction of the 2009 currency reform (which had apparently been in the planning stages for years) is one such example. While the whiplash from the inconstancy of the North Korean state is an inevitable drag on North Korean businesspeople and foreign investors, they can compensate to a certain extent by hedging their bets through establishing relationships with a variety of patrons, at least one of whom might be able to protect them from sudden changes in the environment. This is less effective for foreign investors with significant capital investments in North Korea (of which mining operations would be the primary example), inasmuch as they are unable to shift their investments out of the country on short notice, and are susceptible to being nationalized or otherwise dispossessed without recompense. In addition, given the political sensitivity of mining exports in North Korea, it is often exactly the natural resources that the factions are fighting over, rendering patrons less able to protect investors (or even themselves).

Xiyang in particular, and investors with long-term projects more generally, also faced the problem encountered by businesspeople in personalistic authoritarian regimes. Even if everyone Xiyang dealt with in North Korea had been sincere and straightforward, the business partners were unable to bind themselves, let alone the central state, to the terms of the contract over a long period of time. Even if the Supreme People's Assembly's guarantee of a thirty-year period without changes for Xiyang's contract was real, there was no way to guarantee this guarantee (so to speak) without word directly from the highest reaches of the state, and even then elite politics could have rendered the guarantee moot (as investors who had hitched their wagons to Jang Song-thaek no doubt found out in December 2013). The North Korean central state may be stable, but if it maintains that stability by shifting factions around such that no faction can gain the upper hand, this renders foreign investments hitched to one faction or another inherently unstable.[56]

The stovepiping of information that is inherent to the North Korean system leads to an inconsistency of implementation in policies, and a lack of accountability for officials even in the face of consistent law. Even North Koreans themselves may not have access to the most current information on conditions or policies outside their own areas. But this stovepiping can also enable unscrupulous (or even just confused) North Korean business partners to withhold or distort information about regulations and policies with foreign investors. Xiyang seems to have been misled about the apparent illegality of a 75 percent share joint venture, and had to learn about the resource tax imposition through the grapevine. When they confronted their North Korean business partners, Xiyang had no independent means of verifying that grandfathering their joint venture was actually possible.

Finally, it is unclear if Ri Seong-ku actually did forge all the documents necessary for the joint venture, or if the claims of the informality of the entire investment by the North Korean government were a way to save face, but that the North Korean government could make the claim at all highlights a fundamental conflict between the manner in which the North Korean economy has developed and what foreign investors need to make good investments. The de facto modus operandi for even major businesses in North Korea are de jure illegal, and business is done through a network of patron-client ties, bribes, gray markets, and informal understandings that trump whatever formal documents and relationships exist. While this provides flexibility in adjusting to market conditions and fluid power dynamics in a fractious political environment, blurring formal and informal, licit and illicit with regard to capital-intensive, long-term investments is less useful. North Korean partners are unable to provide long-term assurances. Without extremely powerful political backers (and in the end, even Jang Song-thaek was unable to protect his clients or himself), they cannot provide protection from asset seizures, and the actual terms of contracts may not matter much unless they are crystal clear.

To be sure, Xiyang seems to have handled the collapse of the investment poorly, thereby reducing to zero any chance of getting their money back. When Chinese companies lose money, they often go to Pyongyang to try to get it back. There is usually little chance of this happening, but the North Korean government lets them spend money at hotels, stores, and restaurants while they make their case. The best way to gain some recompense is to make appeals quietly, without ruffling any feathers. Xiyang complained so loudly after losing their money that they were kicked out, presumably after causing the North Koreans to lose face. Unlike many other companies, Xiyang did not go quietly into the night. Yet while Xiyang and China Minmetals were particularly egregious examples of the problems North Korea presents for foreign investment, in large part because of the sheer scale of their losses, other investors encounter barriers in their ventures that force them to adopt surprisingly complex survival strategies. Profit may be beyond the reach of many investors in such cases, and the strategies themselves may be necessary merely to keep the investments from bleeding money or disappearing entirely.

Foreign Firms' Survival Strategies

Chinese investors should in theory be the businesspeople best able to make money in North Korea. They already approach North Korea from a position of strength relative to other countries' investors: North Korea and China are long-standing allies (although in practice the overall relationship waxes and wanes with changes in the international environment and North Korea's provocations); the two countries share a long land border with a number of road and rail crossings, and there is a major Chinese seaport, in Dalian, that is just a short distance from Nampo, theoretically easing transportation costs; Chinese companies are often able to get concessional prices for goods (such as minerals) that they purchase in North Korea, because few other countries are willing to do business in the country;[57] and the Chinese government has encouraged private investment in North Korea, sometimes even to the point of running inspiring campaigns, although its follow through on advocating on behalf of jilted investors in North Korea has been somewhat less inspiring.[58] Chinese citizens are also able to get visas more easily than other nationalities to enter North Korea (particularly into Rason), and some Chinese citizens even have multiple-entry business visas.[59]

Yet in conversations with current Chinese traders and investors in North Korea in July 2014 and February 2015, many found it difficult to make a profit. One official described how repeated appeals to invest in North Korea were increasingly falling on deaf ears among businesses in northeastern China as they had more experience across the border.[60]

Haggard and Noland found in their 2007 survey that Chinese businesses in North Korea had little trust for their North Korean counterparts or North Korea's formal institutions, either to provide consistent implementations of regulations (such as they were) or resolve disputes. Firms were heavily dependent on personal networks for resolving disputes and finding investment and trade partners (and determining the reliability of partners), and circumvented the regulatory environment rather than worked through it. Payment was largely demanded on the spot using *yuan* or US dollars, with almost no extension of credit. If transactions persisted across a longer period of time, they were conducted between state-owned enterprises on both sides with high-level government support. Firms appear to keep their size small so as to avoid the "predatory state." Small firms were most likely to deal with the regulatory environment by avoiding it entirely, "focusing solely on exports [to North Korea] and avoiding contact with officials."[61] Haggard and Noland conclude that while the personal networks can allow firms to operate in a low trust environment, they cannot overcome the lack of effective formal institutions.[62]

More recent conversations with Chinese businessmen confirm many of Haggard and Noland's findings about Chinese firms' survival strategies. Chinese businesses continue to face a number of problems in North Korea. They face information problems: it is difficult to get accurate information on the business environment, investment opportunities, and relevant regulations, let alone information on how the regulations are being implemented (or not), and how to navigate the environment. They must deal with credibility issues with their North Korean partners: aside from a general lack of trust, even otherwise trustworthy North Korean partners cannot guarantee the long-term credibility of any contracts they make, since dispute resolution mechanisms are weak, the state can always change the laws or regulations (or the implementation), sometimes without warning, and the partners themselves can be purged or fall out of favor. Chinese firms also deal with labor quality and power and transport infrastructure problems like all businesses in North Korea. Understandably, this can make Chinese firms reluctant to make substantial investments that can be expropriated, regulated out of profitability, or simply stolen by North Korean partners or officials.

Chinese investors in North Korea appear to attempt to mimic many of the methods used by North Koreans themselves to survive in North

Korea's difficult business environment. Insinuating themselves into North Korean patron-client networks, and more generally building up social networks in both North Korea and China can help to resolve information problems, decrease concerns about partner and contract credibility, decrease regulatory costs, resolve disputes, and mitigate political and legal risk (to the extent that is possible in North Korea). Structuring trade and investments so as to minimize the physical footprint of the company's network inside North Korea, and thus the use of North Korean transport infrastructure and workers, can mitigate the logistical and labor quality issues in North Korea. Proper structuring of transactions, such as by insisting on deposits or pay-as-you-go in hard currency, can minimize the need for long-term contracts and defer trust issues, while private enforcement can prevent defection by Chinese firms inclined toward a softer line with North Korean firms. Strategically choosing industries in which to trade or invest can also minimize the desire or ability of rent-seeking North Korean actors to impede business, and can stymie hold-up problems by making the North Korean firms disproportionately dependent on Chinese firms. Finally, dominating the supply chain itself, both within and outside of North Korea, has emerged as an option for some Chinese firms to deal with the risks associated with doing business with North Korean firms. The extreme measures that even successful Chinese firms must take to do well in North Korea are themselves an indictment of how problematic North Korea's emerging entrepreneurial political economy is for anyone who is not North Korean, and why North Korea might still be poor, despite all its encouragement of foreign trade and investment.

Building up Social Networks

The basic building block of much of the North Korean food chain, the public-private partnership embodied in the patron-client network, is perhaps the greatest challenge for foreign investors seeking to make money in North Korea. Foreign businessmen must embed themselves in the networks to get what they need and protect their investments, but they come at it from several disadvantages. Not coming from within North Korean society, investors must rely on North Korean partners to operate in North Korea at all; these partners have significant control over many aspects of the investors' experiences. Perhaps most importantly, they can avail themselves of a relatively simple solution if disagreements arise: they can kick the investors out of the country, and disappear into North Korea's vaunted isolation.

Purely transactional payments are ineffective in North Korea's political economy. Nearly all of the Chinese businessmen who paid bribes to North Korean officials complained not only about the lavish hospitality and gifts they were expected to provide to North Korean officials and the bribes themselves, but what the bribes actually bought: very little. While it was necessary to bribe customs officers in particular, shipments were still often delayed or lost.

The bribes can be significant. One company that imports stone from North Korea estimated that bribes are approximately 3 percent of profits, all told, to both Chinese and North Korean officials, but mostly to North Korean customs and trading company officers, with additional offerings of alcohol and tobacco to the customs officials to push things through.[63] One timber company executive estimated he spent approximately one hundred thousand US dollars per year on bribes and entertainment. The North Korean trading company partner directors required food, electricity, clothes, household goods, and the like, and even their relatives had to be wined and dined when they came to China.[64] Likewise, a company that sells finished building components to North Korean companies bribes North Korean customs officers with alcohol, tobacco, and sometimes hundreds of dollars to allow cargo trucks through, but does not see a return on their investment. The company worries about entrapment from North Korean customs officials, who have been known to plant drugs on entering cargo or deliberately lose the goods.[65]

To achieve a modicum of success, Chinese companies are thus left with the task of building their patron-client networks. One way out of this problem is to establish a single North Korean point of contact, and rely on the partner, who in this respect also functions as a broker, to distribute the payouts through the relevant networks. In the case of a clothing manufacturer operating in North Korea, the company's main North Korean partner is the head of a company that specializes both in garment manufacturing and food (namely a restaurant in Rason). He is a retired military officer, but also holds a special advisory post in the local government. This partner appears to have some influence, and serves as a one-stop shop for bribes. Upon the payment of the bribe to the partner, the partner then makes sure that the relevant officials in North Korea all receive their own cut. The company estimates bribes as costing between thirty thousand and forty thousand US dollars per half year.[66]

Setting a single point of contact is not without risks, however. While a single influential contact can pave the way, the contact (like nearly all North Korean officials) is theoretically at risk of being purged at any time, which could cause the collapse of the business as well. The contact also exercises disproportionate influence over the investments, and may monopolize needed information and contacts. The most successful long-term Chinese firms thus appear to both seek out influential brokers within North Korea, and diversify their social networks so that they can attach themselves to different officials as the political and economic need arises.

One general goods trader involved with North Korea since the 1980s bases his firm's profitability on the cultivation over a long period of time of good relationships with the right North Korean officials. He has even created influential contacts himself. From a network of young North Korean officials, for example, as he expanded his business ties, the trader describes meeting a clerk in one of the North Korean trading companies. The trader spent more than one hundred thousand US dollars to buy the clerk a colonel's rank in the military. With the rank and a position in the internal security service, the clerk was able to become director of a trading company. Through his position, the contact thereafter could strike fear into the hearts of commoners in North Korea, and afford the trader smooth sailing for his business interests.[67] The trader can now simply ship his goods to Dandong, and arrange to have the goods picked up for transport to North Korea on payment of a deposit, then receive payment when the account is settled, all without a contract. While the North Korean partners offer the trader opportunities and transportation, for the most part, their most valuable commodity provided is stability and freedom from fraud.[68]

The right patrons in North Korea can open up new opportunities and allow Chinese investors to bypass North Korean laws and regulations that would otherwise strangle trade. One investing company's partner is a lieutenant colonel in the North Korean military, with a strong family background and duties in the local internal security apparatus, giving him a great deal of influence.[69] Another, the director of a timber company, had a North Korean associate who was apparently high up the food chain in North Korea. The North Korean gave him a Kim Il-sung-Kim Jong-il pin of the type worn only by high-level officials. While the businessman had been having problems going through North Korean customs in the past, with officials constantly demanding bribes, when he went through the next time with the badge, customs officials were sufficiently surprised at the badge that they fast-tracked him, and neither checked his goods, nor demanded a bribe.[70]

In another case, a leather and fur company interacts with local garrisons of the North Korean military directly. The North Korean military command tolerates soldiers using their service weapons and ammunition to engage in hunting, presumably for meat. Officers can then sell the furs as a sideline business, which have little value in North Korea, to the Chinese. By dealing directly with the military, the company is able to cut out much of the hassle with North Korean customs. Payment is in rice and other consumables, and US dollars.[71]

These well-connected businessmen tend to have discovered opportunities in North Korea from preexisting social networks. One businessman, a steel importer, had relatives in North Korea (who were nonetheless Han Chinese). Over years of visiting them, and bringing them household appliances, food and clothes, the businessman came to think it was feasible to do business in North Korea. Yet the businessman found his partners not through his relatives but through a friend in Dandong who introduced him to some North Koreans, most of whom were traders themselves. Through doing small trades with them, he gradually came to know the representatives of North Korean trading companies with access to steel, and over time built up strong relationships with them to begin doing business.[72] Another Chinese businessman was introduced to the auto repair parts business by his cousin, who imported seafood from North Korea. On a trip to North Korea with his cousin in 2007, he saw the dilapidated condition of North Korean cars in Pyongyang, and decided, after some amount of research, that this could be a lucrative market, given that Chinese investment up to that point had largely been in food, clothing, and minerals. The first shipment of parts to North Korea came in the middle of 2008, with the buyers for the parts largely coming from firms introduced to the businessman by his cousin. After the first few orders, North Korean buyers began approaching him, and as of July 2014, he was receiving orders at the rate of one per week.[73]

Once they have found trade and investment opportunities, the businessmen spend a great deal of time and effort building up the social ties with

North Korean officials to bypass much of the state apparatus and formal restrictions, much as North Korean entrepreneurs do. The steel company businessman, for instance, imports scrap steel from trading companies in North Korea, then reprocesses the scrap into new steel for buildings, doors, and windows. Success in his view relies mainly on building and maintaining the proper social relationships with various government officials and business partners in North Korea. The businessman also uses his social networks to increase the number of potential North Korean suppliers by searching for new ones through secondary ties. The North Korean companies have their own networks; a single satisfied supplier inevitably leads other suppliers to approach the steel company. The suppliers themselves are large state trading companies, local transport enterprises, and small state-approved trading firms, often with military officers as directors.[74]

North Korean trading companies generally approach the steel importer with a sample of the scrap steel. If the sample is acceptable, the steel company arranges to pick up the scrap at a border. The North Koreans accept payment in cash or in barter goods, usually food. Given a large enough cargo, the scrap may need to be shipped, and the businessman invites the partners to Dandong or Hunchun for negotiations. During these visits, he routinely lays out thirty thousand to forty thousand US dollars in entertaining the visiting North Koreans.[75] When a deal is struck, the steel company sends a truck to the border crossing to pick up the steel (calculated by truck load rather than by steel quantity), and plies the North Korean customs officers with cigarettes, food, and cash. Through building up relationships with both the customs officers and the representatives of the North Korean trading companies, the businessman hopes to avoid fraud and curry favor with the North Koreans. He sacrifices the large profits that are pursued by other Chinese businessmen who are subsequently defrauded, and is willing to accept smaller, incremental profits as a way of maintaining fraud-free business connections.[76]

Structuring Trade and Investments

The apparent bait and switch pulled on both China Minmetals and Xiyang, where North Korean officials effectively drove the investors away after equipment and infrastructure that was not easily removed from North Korea was in place, and used the opacity of the North Korean system to keep the investors from returning, receiving compensation, or even knowing who to ask, has been replicated in other circumstances.

One Chinese seafood trader recounts, for example, how in the fall of 2012, which was a particularly bountiful harvest, a large number of Chinese companies operating at the border ordered seafood from North Korea. The North Korean partners asked for the payment up front before delivery, due to security concerns. Because the Chinese companies had been cooperating with the North Korean companies for a number of years, they not only handed over the money, but did so without contracts. Soon afterward, North Korea imposed a ban on seafood exports to China, causing the Chinese companies a total loss. The ban was lifted shortly after the end of the harvest season.[77]

Similarly, in 2009, the president of a relatively large North Korean trading company came to Dandong to negotiate a deal with the steel company discussed above: the steel company would ship rice to North Korea in exchange for a large consignment of scrap steel. The company duly shipped the rice, but after two weeks, the scrap steel had not arrived. The North Koreans explained that the North Korean government had just imposed temporary steel export restrictions, and that they would pay in cash, which itself never arrived.[78] In the summer of 2013, in another case, the owner of a building component manufacturer sent three cargo trucks to North Korea with the understanding that the recipient would inspect the delivery, and either remit payment within a week, or return the cargo. The recipient instead simply disappeared, along with the three trucks, which the company could not pursue within North Korea.[79]

Other sudden changes in policy can cause financial problems for investors, even if they are not specifically bait and switches. One construction company describes how prior to 2011, his company was allowed to use Chinese workers, but at the end of 2011, North Korea suddenly changed its regulations to require North Korean workers, which created problems for the company: it was forced to compensate the Chinese workers with whom it had already signed long-term contracts.[80]

While Chinese traders cannot prevent a sudden reversal of North Korean government policy or even necessarily accurately predict them, they can structure their business deals to minimize the ability of their North Korean partners or the North Korean government to damage their business upon reversal. Often these restructured deals are detrimental to the North

Korean side because they usually minimize the use of long-term contracts, minimize capital investment in North Korea, and force North Korean businesses to front money they do not necessarily have. As a result of the 2009 incident, for instance, the steel company owner now insists on doing deals on the spot at the point of delivery from North Korean suppliers.[81]

One former Chinese Public Security Bureau officer engaged in the construction industry also demands a deposit in either Chinese *yuan* or US dollars before sending over technicians or equipment, although sometimes he will accept coal or iron ore as barter. The deposit as a condition of doing business is enforced privately. Chinese companies in the industry that do business without an initial deposit are bullied and put out of business by the businessman and other companies as a way to hold the line against North Korea attempting to encourage defections.[82] North Korean scams have in effect led to emergent behavior by their counterparties to minimize their exposure to North Korean business practices.

Some businesses combine the demand for deposits as a way of dealing with a poorly institutionalized, low-trust environment with a minimization of their physical footprint in North Korea. The auto parts supplier profits by capitalizing on the almost total lack of manufacturing capacity in North Korea, and the growing demand for parts in Rason as it develops, but by not being in North Korea at all—although the first customers were introduced to him by his cousin, eventually North Korean customers began approaching him through their representative offices in China with orders. Orders come from trading companies, civilian organizations, and the North Korean military, particularly local commanders, who are often on their own in terms of procuring parts for the vehicles.[83] He invites them to his warehouse to look over sample parts, and if they agree, he delivers the parts upon payment of a deposit of 10 percent of the total cost of the order. The Chinese company only escorts the parts through Chinese customs to North Korean customs, at which point the businessman hands over the shipment upon full payment. The businessman refuses to fulfill the order without a deposit, something that the North Koreans have objected to, after several incidents in 2008 and 2009 in which the buyers essentially disappeared after delivery of the goods without paying the majority of the amount due.[84]

Chinese companies can also, through careful choice of the industry in which they are investing, minimize the opportunities for loss from North

Korean corruption and graft, or from expropriation. Inevitably, particularly "strategic" industries for this purpose are those that add little value to products. One executive of a company engaged in light manufacturing in North Korea describes how North Korean officials require bribes, in cash, alcohol, or tobacco, for everything, including moving goods through customs, withdrawing money from banks, and passing through traffic checkpoints (under pain of looting). The amount that needs to be given depends on the time and goods being transported, and here the company is able to minimize the cost of bribes due to the mundane nature of their products. Given that none of the goods the company produces are viewed as valuable to North Korea (unlike precious metals), the bribes are not large (no more than five thousand dollars in value per year).[85]

The right investment can also turn the tables on North Korean partners. The businessman engaged in the construction industry in North Korea, for example, built up his knowledge of North Korea as an officer in the Baishan Public Security Bureau dealing with illegal immigration and smuggling from North Korea, thus giving him contacts with his North Korean counterparts. After leaving government, he leveraged this knowledge and these contacts to go into business. Although the theoretical returns were higher from mining, the businessman decided to go into high-tech engineering equipment provision to North Korea for road and tunnel construction.[86] The businessman believes that his choice of industry mitigates the risk that he will be scammed: the North Koreans obviously do not have their own construction equipment, nor do they have the ability to operate the equipment effectively without Chinese engineers. As a result, they are dependent on the Chinese company from start to finish, and have little incentive to appropriate the equipment. The businessman's North Korean counterparts are also under extreme pressure to complete construction or else, he claims, "they will lose their heads."[87] The North Koreans' need for construction equipment and technical skills changes the power dynamic, and relieves the businessman of any need to pay bribes outside of customs checkpoints.[88]

While investments can be structured to change the power dynamics between Chinese and North Korean partners, they can also be structured so as to minimize the damage done by North Korea's terrible labor and infrastructure conditions. The light manufacturer was introduced to investment opportunities in 2010 by Shenyang city officials eager to build on a sister city relationship with the Rason regional government. In this company's investments, raw materials are shipped from China to Rason, where they are put together by North Korean labor in a factory with instructions from the Chinese company. The contract he signed delineated many conditions that were never satisfied by Rason, including guaranteed water and electricity supplies, and a certain amount of labor. At the time, the North Korean partner guaranteed five heavy-duty trucks for cargo transport, but was only to come up with one heavy truck, and one old small bus that had been converted to a truck. Both of those vehicles were often broken down, with the North Korean partner forcing the investor to pay for their upkeep.[89]

The finished goods themselves, which include electronic components, cell phones, some processed wild vegetables, and wigs, are then shipped back to China (with North Korean transportation). The work itself is simple, and not dependent on just-in-time processing or delivery (as it would be for seafood, for instance). The North Korean workers themselves are incredibly inefficient. The Chinese managers can only communicate with them through translators, and their wages are paid to the government, which then pays them in food and oil.[90] To the extent that the investment is profitable, it is because the investor has chosen goods that can be produced without regard to worker productivity or logistical efficiency. While North Korea (or more specifically the government of Rason) successfully attracted the factory, the Chinese company mitigated political and economic risk by minimizing the value added by the factory, which is probably not what the government of Rason intended.

Dominating the Network

Chinese firms have occasionally found it valuable to build buyer-driven networks that maximize their control over production and distribution. In several ways, they mirror what the North Korean state did in the late 1990s and early 2000s as it trafficked in drugs, and how North Korean firms (and drug traffickers) adapted to increased foreign hostility. When the North Korean central state was directly involved in drug trafficking, it found it useful to dominate the production chain so as to minimize the costs of brokers, maximize the value it extracted from the chain, and maximize its ability to prevent discovery. After the North Korean state cracked down (and apparently removed itself from directly running drugs), the drug trafficking networks decentralized control, and moved much of it into China. More generally, North Korean firms have adapted to sanctions by offloading much of the task of running trade networks onto networks and brokers outside of North Korea. Chinese companies are not under sanctions, but their survival strategies mirror North Korean firms'. As with the North Korean central state in its drug trafficking days, Chinese companies centralize control of their trade networks, and minimize brokerage and transportation costs by cutting out the brokers when feasible. At the same time, as with North Korean firms, Chinese companies put as much of their trade networks outside of North Korea as possible.

In the case of a Chinese seafood company that imports seafood from North Korea, North Korean seafood prices are so low (sea cucumbers are one-tenth the price they are in China, for instance) that the seafood company is able to make money even with spoilage, the inability of the North Korean partners to guarantee timely transportation, kickbacks to the suppliers, and the more general need for bribes and cultivating relationships to do business at all. The partner firms themselves were previously owned by local military units, but are now under both the Sinuiju regional government as well as the central government, with considerable autonomy in setting prices, suggesting the usual confusion of ownership and management within North Korea.[91]

The company makes money by controlling nearly the entire value chain from provision of materials to distribution of finished products, thereby cutting out middlemen and exercising greater control over their suppliers. The company provides the North Korean partners in Sinuiju with seafood farming equipment, fishing nets and like at no cost, although most of the catch is wild. The partners then deliver seafood to the border every month. If the haul is too large, the seafood company sends trucks to Sinuiju to pick up the raw products, and transports them to the plant in Baishan, where they are processed, and then sold to buyers elsewhere in China, in Hebei, Henan, and Shaanxi.[92] North Korean firms are thus only involved to the extent that they physically catch the seafood and transport it to the border. Everything else is controlled by the Chinese firm so as not to leave anything to chance. The result is that North Korea's benefit from the investment itself is also minimized.

The Zen of Automobile Maintenance

One case, that of a Chinese businessman involved in auto repair in North Korea, is illustrative of what a relatively "successful" investment in North Korea looks like. The Chinese investor was alerted to the potential market for auto repair services by a friend, who mentioned that North Korean vehicles were in dilapidated condition, and that North Koreans had few repair parts. After a research trip to North Korea himself, the investor decided that there was a market for repairing the vehicles of state trading companies and civilian government officials, as they had vehicles but little access to the (barely adequate) military repair facilities, and thus were dependent on Chinese-owned shops. Eventually, he set up repair shops in Pyongyang and Sinuiju.[93]

The auto repair shop owner mitigated risk by structuring his investments to minimize financial and physical ties with North Korea. The nature of the auto repair business meant that on-the-spot payments were the norm, and thus he was not worried about not being paid, unlike traders who shipped goods to North Koreans. He also hired only Chinese workers, which eliminated his need to deal with North Korean workers and the state apparatus meant to control them. Finally, the capital investment needed for the shops was small: the parts themselves were shipped in from China, there were only four or five Chinese workers who needed to be brought in, and there was little for the North Korean state to appropriate if it came to that.[94] The structure of the investment thus made the investor largely immune from political and economic risk.

Unlike other investments, the auto repair shops allow the businessman to build the social networks that would otherwise have required bribes, and outside of customs, he claimed not to have needed to bribe anyone. On arrival, he offered services to other Chinese businessmen working in North Korea, who after six months in turn introduced him to North Korean officials, all of whom needed repair services, and who were in positions to ease the way for his business dealings in the country. This strategy seems to have paid off in some respects. In customs in Sinuiju, the businessman initially needed to provide large bribes of alcohol and cash, particularly since he was bringing in Chinese workers, but as he began repairing the cars of customs officials, they gave him contacts that he could use to avoid hassles in customs, and the need for bribes (beyond simply providing cigarettes) was lessened.[95]

At the same time, often the auto repair shops were forced to accept barter goods (such as ginseng) as payment for services rendered—this obligated the businessman to take the extra step of taking the goods back to China to sell to realize earnings—and certain government officials were allowed to have their cars repaired for free up to a certain dollar limit on a monthly basis. The businessman sees the losses incurred in the shops as a way to establish contacts with relevant North Koreans, build his networks inside the country, and gather information about business conditions in North Korea. Eventually, he sees the repair shops as opening up opportunities for larger, more profitable business in the country.[96]

The Chinese investor replicated many of the characteristics of North Korean trade networks that have made them successful at surviving in North Korea. He was entrepreneurial: he identified a market niche that was sorely needed due to the brokenness of North Korea's formal political economy, but difficult to deliver for those without access to supply chains stretching outside of North Korea. Like many North Korean traders, he was opportunistic: he saw the auto repair business as a stepping-stone to other forms of business that might be more lucrative. The success of his business relied on steady access to suppliers in China, and at least some ability to navigate the corruption of the checkpoints between North Korea and China. From the beginning, he realized that success lay with cultivating relationships with the right people within the food chain. Spot bribes alone are insufficient to guarantee the stability of a business deal in North Korea; for this the cultivation of patron-client networks is required. While the Chinese investor was unable to give high-ranking officials equity stakes in his business as North Korean hybrid firms would to establish their networks, he did build lasting relationships by providing the officials with a service that, given the wear and tear on North Korean vehicles, they would need on a not infrequent basis. At the same time, the investor mitigated political and economic risk by minimizing the physical footprint of his operation inside of North Korea to make it immune to expropriation and political reversals. Even if his entire operation in North Korea was taken, he reasoned, he would not be losing that much. He also minimized his exposure to North Korean labor; in effect, he invested in North Korea by not really investing in it at all.

It would be going too far to say that North Korea's continuing poverty in the face of the adaptability, flexibility, and creativity of North Korean state and nonstate entrepreneurs is unfathomable. The North Korean state has attempted to address its lack of economic development through new, more accommodating laws, special economic zones, and trade promotion, but sanctions and the general stigma of doing business with North Korea, terrible infrastructure, corruption, a physically weak (if educated) work force, and crippling labor laws and dispute resolution mechanisms are all strong headwinds.

Both the nature of North Korean trade networks and the business environment are arguably the result of state weakness. While one of the main effects of the food chain is that the central state profits indirectly from the informal, often "illegal" business activity in the country, a better way to think of the food chain is as an emergent by-product of state weakness, and of the business environment as the state passing laws and regulations, and being unable to bind itself to follow them, or even control implementation on an everyday basis. The food chain exists in the form it does because officials have to pay off their superiors, but have enough autonomy to go into business to pay off their superiors in the first place. The state has enough power to selectively punish people who fall afoul of the system, but not to regulate it on a daily basis. It can profit from the corruption, but not actually stop it. North Korean trade networks' flexibility, comfort with ambiguity, and ability to adapt to a terrible environment paradoxically spell trouble for the country's ability to attract and hold trade and investment. The ambiguity in which North Korean businesspeople operate—a comfort in blurring formal and informal, state and nonstate, and even legal and illegal—is ill suited to foreign firms, particularly those in capital-intensive industries in need of long-term commitments, property rights, and minimal rent seeking.

The foreign companies that had disastrous experiences in North Korea, such as Minmetals and Xiyang, seem to have borne the full brunt of North Korean business practices—both a weak state and creatively rapacious North Korean business partners—without having a way to adapt. The Chinese companies that have been somewhat more successful have adopted strategies that to a certain extent mimic North Korean practices by, among other things, inserting themselves as much as possible into the North Korean food chain, bypassing constraints on business through informal networks, minimizing the exposure of their assets and money to North Korea's domestic situation. While these strategies allows foreign firms to survive, they also diminish the benefits North Korean firms derive, and do little to make North Korea a better place to do business.

Conclusion

THE FUTURE

A portrayal of North Korea as surprisingly marketized in contrast to the public image of North Korea as a paranoid, hermetically sealed, communist state is at this point so common in academic and journalistic circles that it has become the new conventional wisdom.[1] And indeed, much in this book does confirm that conventional wisdom: North Korea has evolved into a society with markets in everything, a state of affairs that arose as a result of a struggle for survival by the vast majority of the population during the great famine and economic collapse of the mid-1990s.

Yet this is not the whole story: the Arduous March did not just precipitate a "marketization from below" or even markets in everything. The specific form that marketization took was highly entrepreneurial at nearly all levels of North Korean society: North Koreans saw opportunities (whether out of foresight or necessity) created by the collapse of the formal economy, and seized them. Those involved were adaptable and employed considerable creativity in navigating an environment where domestic and international trade was both formally illegal and necessary as a means of survival. The networks they created not only stretched throughout North Korea itself, but also, as time passed, between North Korea and the rest of the world. State trading networks, supported as they were by the assets and outposts of the state, were able to extend further around the world, but even private trading networks extended into China, South Korea, and Japan.

The adaptability of the trading networks can be seen in how they responded to the darkening environment in the mid-2000s, outside North Korea, as the world grew tired of North Korea's nuclear weapons program and provocations, and imposed increasingly harsh sanctions, and inside North Korea, as the central state attempted to reign in the excesses of the Arduous March and its immediate aftermath. State trading networks responded to greater scrutiny and active hostility by integrating, in their own way, into the global economy, adopting the mantle of private businesses, moving to do business with a variety of private and state actors, becoming brokers in their own right, relying to a large degree on commercial methods and routes (and minimizing the involvement of North Koreans), and shifting among a number of other countries in a bid to find hospitable environments for importing and exporting goods.

For their part, nonstate trading networks continued to spread through North Korean society, despite the crackdowns against private entrepreneurs and corrupt officials. Trading networks functioned most effectively in the interstices between legal and illegal, formal and informal, in some cases insinuating themselves into the state apparatus to assure their ability to continue to operate. As with state trading networks, part of the success of private and semiprivate entrepreneurialism has come from taking advantage of the deficiencies in North Korea's political economy, pushing as much of the trade network outside of North Korea as possible, and minimizing the need to deal with North Korea's environment at all.

This success has not led to North Korea's economy growing by leaps and bounds—while this book evinces a certain admiration for North Korean resourcefulness, and even grudging respect for how North Korean officials have adapted to sanctions meant to stop them, it is not an inherently optimistic book. North Korea–style entrepreneurialism allows many North Koreans, perhaps even the majority of the population, to survive, and clearly enables some even to become wealthy. But paradoxically the same ambiguous environment in which North Korean businesses are used to moving also bodes ill for North Korea's attempts to attract and keep foreign investment and trade, as Chinese investors in particular have come to grief inside the country.

Implications

What is the upshot of North Korea being an enterprising country? Generally at this point in books about North Korea, it is customary to ruminate on the implications of whatever was discussed for one or all of the three aspects of North Korea that are of greatest interest to scholars and the general public: North Korea's nuclear weapons program and the possibility of denuclearization, the potential for "real" economic reform, and the future of the North Korean state (and the end of the regime).[2]

Denuclearization

While there has been past work done on the relationship between (the potential for) denuclearization and economic statecraft, with the question of whether North Korean economic dependence on China in particular would make the regime susceptible to genuine pressure to denuclearize,[3] this book says essentially nothing about whether North Korea is or will ever be amenable to denuclearization, and very little about the intentions or perceptions of the elites at the commanding heights of the North Korean state. Yet it does provide at least a partial explanation of why North Korea has been so intransigent in its nuclear dealings since the collapse of the 1994 Agreed Framework. It is a not unreasonable assumption that North Korea builds nuclear weapons at the expense of economic development and good relations with the outside world, because weapons development invites economic sanctions and the ire of its neighbors. From that perspective, intransigence by a North Korea desiring to develop economically is surprising.

Yet unlike Iran, the other big proliferation problem country, North Korea has never been particularly eager to return to the negotiating table as a result of sanctions. If anything, sanctions against North Korea are more comprehensive and more punitive, and have been in place for longer, than those against Iran.[4] Yet Iran negotiated with those sanctioning it; North Korea has not for a long time. Given that North Korea's trade networks have developed in such hostile environments, and have perhaps become so creative and adaptable in the forms they take and the methods they use, *because* of those hostile environments, the adaptability of North Korea's trade networks may have led the central state to conclude that nuclear weapons development is compatible with economic development. Sanctions may have slowed the progress of North Korea's programs, and perhaps denied the central state some much-needed revenue (from the shipments that were intercepted and deals that were scuttled), but it is not clear that sanctions and regional anger have brought to a standstill North Korea's ability to operate trade networks that can bring the state revenue or components for its nuclear programs. Sanctions and export controls obviously did not stop North Korea from building nuclear weapons to begin with, nor did they prevent North Korea from carrying out four nuclear tests (as of the writing of this book).

North Korea's state trading networks, in searching for nuclear components and then seeking to sell North Korean sanctioned goods around the world, demonstrated a laudable (to some) and an infuriating (to others) ability to adapt to changing conditions. When the most obvious outlets for state prerogatives—diplomats, diplomatic outposts, and state trading companies—came under greater scrutiny for receiving and shipping goods to and from North Korea, those same exemplars of state prerogatives morphed into brokers themselves, buying and selling sanctioned goods without ever necessarily touching the goods themselves, thus showing a familiarity with global markets and commercial routes. They also adopted the behavior and even appearance of private companies, abandoning in some cases the advantages that state prerogatives had conveyed, and ordering (and shipping) components using commercial shipping methods and routes. North Korea has been successful in part because it has learned to let others do the hard work on its behalf.

While both Iran and North Korea preferred to use sympathetic, co-national and co-ethnic brokers to approach suppliers and other brokers to acquire goods, Iran seems to have been dependent to a greater extent on its own brokers for acquiring and transporting goods. More specifically, when Iran used Iranian nationals or ethnic Iranians as its brokers for obtaining sanctioned goods, those brokers tended to funnel those goods through transshipment and acquisition brokers located in Dubai. When Iran did use non-Iranian brokers in East Asia and Europe, those brokers were able to funnel goods through other transshipment hubs, notably Malaysia and Taiwan, and various cities in Europe.[5] By contrast, North Korea learned quickly to minimize the involvement of North Koreans in the supply chain, as much as possible pushing foreign involvement down the chain toward North Korea, and even into North Korea itself. Both countries used commercial methods and routes, which forced their logistical supply chains to follow the geography of the global cargo shipping hub-and-spoke networks. As a consequence, both North Korea and Iran had to find amenable transshipment hubs for their sanctioned goods.[6] Yet North Korea was more flexible in how it used commercial networks and hubs.

In part this was because of an unfortunate accident of geography: Iran, being in the Middle East, was surrounded not only by hostile powers, but by countries that by and large were not particularly technologically sophisticated or integrated into the global economy. As such, Iran became dependent mainly on Dubai, a single transshipment point close to its shores that, while an ally of the United States, resisted truly reining in Iranian companies for decades.[7] North Korea's trade networks, by contrast, were able to funnel goods through a larger number of transshipment countries over time, in response to changing global hostility to their trade. With that said, North Korea does not have an unlimited number of possible broker countries. That it was able to find even three countries in the region to serve as both suppliers for its weapons programs and transshipment points is a testament to North Korea's relatively fortunate geographic positioning, sandwiched as it was between more technologically advanced countries that, even when they were hostile, did not necessarily stop North Korea from engaging in otherwise sketchy trade. After first Japan and then Taiwan took notice and cracked down, and with its complicated relationship with South Korea, after around 2008, North Korea was forced to the last major transshipment point for the goods it desired—China. That it has been able to continue to use China as a transshipment point for sanctioned goods is less due to North Korean ingenuity than that continuous enforcement of sanctions is relatively far down China's list of priorities vis-à-vis North Korea. North Korea's calculation that this will remain true even in the future is likely to be put to the test as its provocations continue. The January 2016 nuclear test was followed by sanctions (and, more importantly, Chinese enforcement) that led to at least a temporary idling of mining exports from North Korea to China.[8]

In the final analysis, North Korea's entrepreneurial trade networks mean little for whether North Korean leaders are willing to denuclearize—that ultimately may be more a question of security guarantees, national identity, and geopolitical calculations—but the networks have allowed North Korean leaders to achieve some amount of leverage (inasmuch as they have been able to continue their weapons programs, both buying and selling, despite sanctions) and given them some confidence about their ability to withstand trade-based pressure from other countries.

More generally, this does suggest that the primary means of enforcing the Nuclear Non-Proliferation Treaty—export controls, supplier cartels, and sanctions meant to stop countries from acquiring, perfecting, or profiting from chemical, biological, or nuclear weapons—are problematic. While sanctions against violators of nonproliferation norms may be necessary as signals of disapproval from the international community, and more generally may be useful in preserving the credibility of the international regime (by, for example, stigmatizing doing business with proliferating states or companies), they are not necessarily particularly useful in stopping states that are both determined to acquire nuclear weapons and have found ways to integrate themselves into global trade networks in ways that call into question our understanding of the nuclear weapons trade. The existence of export controls and supplier cartels suggests that nonproliferation policymakers understand that nonproliferation is fundamentally both a security issue *and* a trade issue, but more study is needed for any given country of concern to understand how that country trades, and whether a standard approach would actually work.

Economic Reform

Much of the academic and popular debate about Kim Jong-un, at least soon after he rose to power, has been whether he differs from his father in terms of openness to economic reform, and what this portends for the future of North Korea's economy.[9] North Korea has been in a state of "transition without reform"[10] for a long time, and it is only recently that North Korean officials have publicly expressed any willingness to consider that there is something deeply flawed about their economic and political system.[11] Obviously the Chinese government would prefer that North Korea, like China before it, would follow the path toward a greater openness to formal, legal private enterprise, decollectivization of agriculture, the existence of property rights (or private property at all), transfer of much of the state-owned economy into private hands, and reliance on markets and price signals to determine the supply of goods and services.

The regime under Kim Jong-un has sent out mixed signals about openness to reform and trade, particularly as Kim has purged rivals and enemies. In the wake of Jang Song-thaek's purge, for instance, North Korean officials were quick to let potential investors know that some economic changes, such as the introduction of additional special economic zones, the welcoming of investment from any country, and the devolution of economic decision-making power to local areas, were going forward at full steam (and in fact would be able to move even faster because North Korean "unity" had been restored).[12] On the other hand, the purges led to a more difficult business environment for foreign investors as they percolated down to the level of everyday business: Chinese businessmen dealing with North Korea complained that Kim Jong-un's rise to power, and, even more, Jang Song-thaek's purge, saw the replacement of many customs and commercial liaison officials with Kim favorites, and a shift to more rigorous customs inspections, increased taxes, and application of more restrictive regulations on Chinese businesses.[13] The regime has also attempted to crack down on border crossings, and has directly attacked some of the behaviors—bribing one's way out of work, making international phone calls, and bribing one's way across the border—that made private enterprise possible.[14]

Regardless of whether the central state has initiated or plans to initiate high-level economic reforms, several insights are clear from the enterprising experiences of North Korean trade networks over the past several decades. First, what the central state says will happen, and what actually happens, are often unrelated. The very existence of marketization from below, and the continued growth of trade networks and markets after both the 2005 retrenchment and the 2009 currency reforms, are testaments to this. If anything, North Korean entrepreneurialism suggests that the ability of the North Korean central state to impose conditions that would either totally inhibit trade or the markets, or strongly encourage them, is limited. The state has survived thus far in part by throwing up its hands and having its citizens and firms go forth and make money rather than attempt to generate its own income, and it is not clear that waiting for Kim

Jong-un to promulgate some major economic reform package (or even small, incremental ones) is a valuable enterprise. Paradoxically, the relative success of North Korea's trading networks has arguably shielded the North Korean regime from having to make wholesale reforms. Since it is no longer responsible for the welfare of the vast majority of the population, the central state itself can concentrate on attracting investment in places like Rason (or more specifically, making money by hook or by crook) and building infrastructure (such as in Pyongyang) that mostly benefit the central state and its elite supporters.

Second, even if the central state were to initiate wholesale economic reforms, it is not clear that this would result in an overall improvement in the ability of North Korea to attract investment or for the formal economy to function. To the extent that North Korean trade networks and businesses have found an equilibrium with their operational environment, they have adapted to function in an environment with substantial ambiguity, where most of their activities are technically illegal, where property rights and understandings are informal at best, and with institutions that are either nonfunctional, weak, or merely capricious. As suggested in chapter 4, North Korean trading networks have successfully adapted to their environment in a way that actually could make life more difficult for foreign investors. Any further opening up of the North Korean economy that is not accompanied by wholesale changes in the very characteristics that have forced North Korean trade networks to be adaptable and creative is likely to come at the cost of leading even more foreign companies to ruin in North Korea.

It is also not clear how much North Korea's extensive "second economy" will be of help in future reform or development. Whether the informal economy in socialist and transition economies actually has a negative effect on the formal economy, or merely adds to total economic output, is ambiguous,[15] so it would be going too far to say either that North Korea's sizeable informal and dubiously legal economy is the downfall of the formal economy (and any potential for its reform) or that the informal economy is the savior of the country. There are important differences in North Korea with both Eastern Europe and the former Soviet Union, which opted for sudden "big bang" reforms, and with China, which has pursued a gradual transition, measured in decades, to a "socialist market economy," differences that are likely to have implications for any economic reform, and its consequences, in North Korea. If anything, given how North Korea's actual economy has evolved, it is possible that even if North Korea undergoes an extended process of incremental transition akin to very cautious Chinese-style economic reform, assuming North Korea itself does not cease to exist, it is likely to end up with something of a mélange of economic characteristics: an outward-looking economy, with a focus on trade rather than production, with much of the dysfunction of the former Soviet economies' "big bang" reforms, without the high economic growth or relatively predictable rules of the economic game resulting from a Chinese-style step-by-step economic transition.

First, managers and other apparatchiks in the Soviet Union were well placed to take over state assets as they were privatized, creating the oligarchs of the post-Soviet period.[16] China opted to gradually privatize much of the state-owned economy, and retain ownership of sectors (such as finance and oil) that were deemed important for national security purposes. Yet little of North Korea's state economy is worth either retaining or privatizing. The collapse of the formal, state-owned economy in North Korea in the 1990s, the subsequent looting of assets by both state officials and private actors, and the continued lack of reliable infrastructure that has rendered many state-owned factories economically inert, suggest that there may actually be less to loot by well-positioned state officials in North Korea than there was at the end of the Soviet Union. To the extent that state officials' wealth in North Korea is dependent on trade rather than merely control of factories, and because conflicts within North Korea appear to be over access to trading and export opportunities and contacts rather than simply assets, elites may have an incentive to capitalize on their business ties to the outside world, and their knowledge of formal and informal institutions rather than loot assets (aside from obvious ones such as mines).

Second, even in the event of economic reform, the entrepreneurial networks that blur formal and informal, legal and illegal, and state and nonstate may have become so pervasive that the ability of a reforming state to bring them into a formal, legal institutional framework may be limited. Peter Andreas describes an informal economy that sprang up during the siege of Sarajevo in the Bosnian War, wherein smugglers, essentially illegal and informal traders, crossed the siege lines with the knowledge and sometimes aid of UN peacekeepers and the different combatants to supply goods for people inside Sarajevo. The criminals who rose to prominence (inasmuch they allowed the besieged population to survive) during the Bosnian War often continued to be important in Bosnia's economy after the war. The economy after the war was heavily influenced by the mafia, which in turn had negative repercussions for the countries surrounding Bosnia.[17] The ambiguity of the North Korean system means that North Korean businesspeople have become masters at providing goods in a hostile environment through illegal means. A post-reform environment that attempts to rein in illegal business may find it hard going, with many businesses easily going underground. A study of former Soviet and Eastern European socialist economies, for example, found that hidden, unofficial economic activity is associated with more pervasive bureaucratic corruption, informal contract enforcement and dispute resolution, and poorly functioning institutions.[18] In Central and Eastern Europe, by 1998, overall the informal economy provided the most important source of income for a third of households across the region,[19] suggesting that even post-socialist economies retain a high degree of activity outside the formal, taxable economy. After the fall of communism, Hungary, for instance, saw a transition from a second economy, which was characterized by workers in state firms holding second, private jobs or running side businesses, to an informal economy in which the workers worked full-time in jobs or businesses that largely avoided dealing with bureaucracies and evaded taxes and regulations.[20]

Third, in the absence of functioning state institutions following the fall of the Soviet Union, businesses turned to organized crime figures to resolve disputes and enforce contracts, providing an opening for "violent entrepreneurs."[21] By contrast, while the Chinese state has never actually approached some ideal type of rule of law, there has long been acknowledgment in China that the state should be able to resolve disputes and enforce contracts in a relatively straightforward and predictable way, and that being able to do so is important for economic development.[22] North Korean state institutions are, perhaps paradoxically, strong enough to come down hard on North Koreans who get out of line (and are not sufficiently embedded in the proper patron–client networks), but not strong enough to provide an impartial process that makes North Korea credible as an investment environment. The state, in other words, is still worth co-opting and corrupting, but too weak actually to help along economic growth on a large scale.

The saving grace, if there is any, is that the "marketization from below" and the creative, adaptable, entrepreneurial trade networks that have arisen have provided North Koreans with a taste of and experience in the market economy on both a domestic and international scale. While it obviously may not be the ideal pathway to a developing market economy, a "second economy" that provides citizens with goods, capital, and knowledge about succeeding in a postsocialist environment is better than nothing.[23] Through marketplaces, North Koreans learn about price signals, and figure out what buyers demand, and how to fill holes. Through trade, North Koreans learn about international business practices, establish personal networks that can be used to source and transport a variety of goods, and practice the rudiments of a market economy (such as firms and contracts), even if expectations remain low.[24] Particularly with the trade networks that largely exist outside of North Korea, however, the value that the North Korean state can derive from them can be lost easily. Following the purge of Jang Song-thaek, for instance, not all of the North Korean businesspeople and brokers that had been sent abroad to make money and acquire goods heeded the central state's call to come home, presumably taking their knowledge about how to do international business, their contacts, and possibly a lot of money, with them.[25]

The Future of North Korea

Tied to potential economic reform is always the question of the durability of the North Korean regime.[26] Western and Chinese observers alike have tried to discern whether a particular move by North Korea—the purge of Ri Yong-ho,[27] the execution of Jang Song-thaek,[28] the (low-key) announcement of agricultural and SOE management reforms[29], the holding of Workers' Party of Korea congress in May 2016[30]—is a sign of Kim Jong-un consolidating power, losing his grip, centralizing his authority, or decentralizing the authority of the state.[31] One expert even opined in April 2015 that Kim Jong-un's palace economy, the network of state firms and agencies such as Office 39 that are used to bring income and luxury goods to dole out to elites as a means of assuring their support, was faltering. The revenue coming in was no longer so much, diminishing the ability of the regime to give out gifts, and with it, the influence of Kim Jong-un.[32] In addition, Kim Jong-un's continuing purges, including that of

Defense Minister Hyon Yong-chol in May 2015, have called into question how stable North Korea is at the top, and how much support Kim Jong-un actually has among elites.[33]

North Korea's authoritarian regime ultimately survives because there is sufficient buy-in from elites,[34] as is the case in other authoritarian states. The Chinese Communist Party's survival is, for example, predicated both on appeals to nationalism and economic growth that has lifted hundreds of millions out of poverty since 1979. More specifically, it has co-opted Chinese entrepreneurs and other business elites either directly into the party or its ancillary organs (such as the people's political consultative conferences at all levels) or made arrangements such that newly emerging business elites have incentives (such as greater access to credit from state-owned banks) to support the continued rule of the CCP.[35]

Unlike China, there is little evidence that the co-optation of business elites into the North Korean state, to the extent they were not already state officials, is part of some deliberate plan on the part of the central state to smooth the process of reform. Except for completely private entrepreneurs who somehow manage to avoid the state apparatus entirely, those involved in the upper echelons of the food chain have concrete reasons to support the continuation of the state, and the system as a whole: for officials up and down the hierarchy, much of their ability to make money, and certainly to extract rents, depends on the continuation of a system in which entrepreneurialism exists in a gray area—encouraged but formally illegal. The ambiguity of the system itself is what provides many officials with their payday.

Yet the spread of hybrid enterprises, where privately managed firms are formally owned by the state, and state officials (or their wives) run what are effectively private businesses, suggests that while association with the state is still important for many, even most, enterprises, the fundamental productiveness, even of state actors, is no longer directed or controlled by the central state. Except for the central state's desire and demand for both hard currency and sanctioned goods, nearly the entire entrepreneurial and trade system is based on things that the central state lives with, rather than has designed. The state's indifference (within very wide parameters) to where hard currency and sanctioned goods come from, and its manifest failures in providing either functioning institutions or even goods to its population, suggest that the state is not determining much of what happens in North

Korea. While the Public Distribution System continues to bumble along, it has long been certain death for anyone but the topmost elite in Pyongyang to rely solely on it for food.

Instead, entrepreneurialism provides income and more generally a livelihood for much of the North Korean population. This population is not only no longer dependent on the central state, but traders are either directly or indirectly tied into the outside world through international trade networks, and even private consumers now buy goods imported from China, South Korea, and elsewhere. The food chain rests on a tower of corruption, as those further up the chain extract rents from those below, and it is unlikely that the central state looks more legitimate to anyone involved as a result. Studies from the transition economies in Eastern Europe suggest that, not surprisingly, mass participation in the informal economy is corrosive to the political legitimacy of the state,[36] and is generally associated with declining trust in social and political institutions as able to solve problems and disputes fairly.[37]

As a result, there may come a time when both the population, no longer dependent on the state for survival, and state officials, having grown into businessmen and outgrown their dependence on rents, begin to question the legitimacy of a state, in its mix of weakness and viciousness, that forces them into the ambiguities inherent in North Korea's trade networks. As one source in North Korea noted upon China's (perhaps temporary) restrictions on importing North Korean minerals following North Korea's fourth nuclear test in January 2016, "If the long-term export restrictions bankrupt the mineral companies, many innocent workers will lose a source of income. Merchants and residents connected to the export companies in various ways will struggle to find new jobs. Kim Jong Un cannot discount the resentment that this will cause."[38] If a time comes when resentment does boil over, the North Korean state will be in danger.

NOTES

Preface

1. For an example, see the preface of Hazel Smith, *North Korea: Markets and Military Rule* (Cambridge, UK: Cambridge University Press, 2015).

2. Kyu-ryun Kim, ed. *North Korea's External Economic Relations*, KINU Research Monograph (Seoul: Korea Institute for National Unification, 2008); Stephan Haggard and Marcus Noland, "North Korea's External Economic Relations," in *Engagement with North Korea*, ed. Sung Chull Kim and David C. Kang (Albany, NY: State University of New York Press, 2009).

3. For some of the better examples of this, see Byung-yeon Kim, "Markets, Bribery, and Regime Stability in North Korea" (Seoul: East Asia Institute, 2010); Stephan Haggard and Marcus Noland, *Witness to Transformation: Refugee Insights into North Korea* (Washington, DC: Peterson Institute of International Economics, 2011); Hyung-min Joo, "Visualizing the Invisible Hands: The Shadow Economy in North Korea," *Economy and Society* 39, no. 1 (2010): 110–45; Hyung-min Joo, "Hidden Transcripts in Marketplaces: Politicized Discourses in the North Korean Shadow Economy," *Pacific Review* 27, no. 1 (2014): 49–71.

4. Gary Gereffi and Karina Fernandez-Stark, *Global Value Chain Analysis: A Primer* (Durham, NC: Center on Globalization, Governance and Competitiveness, 2011); Gary Gereffi, John Humphrey, and Timothy Sturgeon, "The Governance of Global Value Chains," *Review of International Political Economy* 12, no. 1 (2005): 78–104; Gary Gereffi and Raphael Kaplinsky, "The Value of Value Chains: Spreading the Gains from Globalisation," *IDS Bulletin* 32, no. 3 (2001).

5. Gary Gereffi, "Global Production Systems and Third World Development," in *Global Change, Regional Response: The New International Context of Development*, ed. Barbara Stallings

(Cambridge: Cambridge University Press, 1995); Gary Gereffi and Miguel Korzeniewicz, *Commodity Chains and Global Capitalism* (Westport, CT: Praeger Publishers, 1994).

6. Peter Dicken, Philip F. Kelly, Kris Olds, and Henry Wai-Chung Yeung, "Chains and Networks, Territories and Scales: Towards a Relational Framework for Analysing the Global Economy," *Global Networks* 1, no. 2 (2001): 99. See also Jeffrey Henderson, Peter Dicken, Martin Hess, Neil Coe, and Henry Wai-Chung Yeung, "Global Production Networks and the Analysis of Economic Development," *Review of International Political Economy* 9, no. 3 (August 2002): 445.

7. Henderson et al., "Global Production Networks."

8. Dicken et al., "Chains and Networks," 95.

9. Gereffi and Korzeniewicz, *Commodity Chains and Global Capitalism*, 96–97.

10. Gereffi, Humphrey, and Sturgeon, "The Governance of Global Value Chains," 83–84.

11. Ibid., 83–84.

12. Gereffi and Korzeniewicz, op. cit.

13. Henderson et al., "Global Production Networks," talk about the social embeddedness of trade networks, in which networks are enmeshed in formal and informal links with other economic and political actors, and in turn are influenced in what they produce, how they produce it, and how they capture value by the characteristics of the territories in which the nodes of the networks are located.

Introduction: The Enterprising Country

1. Kevin Rudd, "North Korean Nuclear Threat Affects Us All," *Daily Telegraph*, 27 September 2011.

2. Thomas Fuller and Sang-hun Choe, "Thais Say North Korea Arms Were Iran-Bound," *New York Times*, 1 February 2010.

3. Kevin Rudd, "Tin Pot Dictator's Son Best Hope for New Korean Calm, Writes Kevin Rudd," *Daily Telegraph*, 28 January 2012.

4. Ibid.

5. For looks at North Korean restaurants in Jakarta and Phnom Penh, see Silvia Forsman, "The Mystery of Pyongyang," *Jakarta Expat*, 24 April 2013; and Sebastian Strangio, "Kingdom Kim's Culinary Outposts: Inside the Bizarre World of Asia's North Korean Restaurant Chain," *Slate*, 27 March 2010.

6. See, for example, Nicholas Eberstadt, *The End of North Korea* (Washington, DC: AEI Press, 1999).

7. Stephan Haggard and Marcus Noland, *Famine in North Korea: Markets, Aid, and Reform* (New York City: Columbia University Press, 2007); Marcus Noland, Sherman Robinson, and Tao Wang, "Rigorous Speculation: The Collapse and Revival of the North Korean Economy," *World Development* 28, no. 10 (2000): 1767–87; Nicholas Eberstadt, *The North Korean Economy: Between Crisis and Catastrophe* (Piscataway, NJ: Transaction Publishers, 2007).

8. Author interview, South Korean economist specializing in North Korea #1, Seoul, August 2012.

9. Marcus Noland, "Hugely Important: North Korea Running a Current Account Surplus?" Peterson Institute for International Economics, 18 March 2013, http://blogs.piie.com/nk/?p=9647.

10. Andrew Scobell, *China and North Korea: From Comrades-in-Arms to Allies at Arm's Length* (Carlisle Barracks, PA: Strategic Studies Institute, 2004). But see Seung-Hyun Yoon and Seung-Ook Lee, "From Old Comrades to New Partnerships: Dynamic Development of Economic Relations between China and North Korea," *Geographical Journal* 179, no. 1 (2013): 19–31; James Reilly, "The Curious Case of China's Aid to North Korea," *Asian Survey* 54, no. 6 (2014): 1158–83.

11. Sang Hwa Chung, "Political Economy of North Korea's WMD Venture and Its Strategic Implications," *Korean Journal of Area Studies* 28, no. 2 (2010): 183–212; Steve S Sin, "The

North Korean Regime Survival: An Extortionist Rentier State Explanation" (University at Albany, SUNY, Albany, NY, March 2013).

12. Victor Cha, *The Impossible State: North Korea, Past and Future* (New York: HarperCollins, 2012).

13. Daniel Byman and Jennifer Lind, "Pyongyang's Survival Strategy: Tools of Authoritarian Control in North Korea," *International Security* 35, no. 1 (2010): 44–74.

14. Benjamin Habib, "North Korea's Parallel Economies: Systemic Disaggregation Following the Soviet Collapse," *Communist and Post-Communist Studies* 44, no. 2 (2011): 149–59.

15. Sang Hwa Chung, "Is North Korea Doomed to Die? A Politico-Economic Analysis of the North Korean Ruling System and Its Strategic Implications" (Sejong Institute, Seoul, 2012).

16. Haggard and Noland, *Famine in North Korea*; Stephan Haggard and Marcus Noland, "Reform from Below: Behavioral and Institutional Change in North Korea," *Journal of Economic Behavior and Organization* 73, no. 2 (2010): 133–52.

17. Ruediger Frank, "Economic Reforms in North Korea (1998–2004): Systemic Restrictions, Quantitative Analysis, Ideological Background," *Journal of the Asia Pacific Economy* 10, no. 3 (2005): 278–311.

18. Stephan Haggard and Marcus Noland, "Winter of Their Discontent: Pyongyang Attacks the Market" (Peterson Institute for International Economics, Washington, DC, 2010).

19. Kyung-Ae Park and Scott Snyder, eds., *North Korea in Transition: Politics, Economy, and Society* (Lanham, MD: Rowman and Littlefield Publishers, 2012).

20. Byung-yeon Kim, "Markets, Bribery, and Regime Stability in North Korea" (East Asia Institute, Seoul, 2010).

21. Kyu-ryun Kim, ed., *North Korea's External Economic Relations*, Kinu Research Monograph (Seoul: Korea Institute for National Unification, 2008); Stephan Haggard and Marcus Noland, "North Korea's External Economic Relations," in *Working Paper Series* (Peterson Institute for International Economics, Washington, DC, 2007); Kenneth Quinones, "Beyond Collapse: Continuity and Change in North Korea," in *North Korea in the World Economy*, ed. E. Kwan Choi, E. Han Kim, and Yesook Merrill (London: RoutledgeCurzon, 2003); John S. Park, "North Korea, Inc: Gaining Insights into North Korean Regime Stability from Recent Commercial Activities" (US Institute for Peace, Washington, DC, 2009).

22. Sheena Chestnut, "Illicit Activity and Proliferation: North Korean Smuggling Networks," *International Security* 32, no. 1 (Summer 2007): 80–111; Dick K. Nanto and Raphael Perl, "North Korean Crime-for-Profit Activities" (Congressional Research Service, Washington, DC, 16 February 2007); Sheena Chestnut Greitens, "Illicit: North Korea's Evolving Operations to Earn Hard Currency" (Committee for Human Rights in North Korea, Washington, DC, 2014).

23. Ruediger Frank, "The Political Economy of Sanctions against North Korea," *Asian Perspective* 30, no. 3 (2006): 5.

24. Jae Cheol Kim, "The Political Economy of Chinese Investment in North Korea: A Preliminary Assessment," *Asian Survey* 46, no. 6 (2006): 898–916; Haggard and Noland, "North Korea's External Economic Relations"; Yoon and Lee, "From Old Comrades to New Partnerships."

25. Derek Thompson, "Silent Partners: Chinese Joint Ventures in North Korea" (US-Korea Institute, SAIS, Johns Hopkins University, Washington, DC, 2011).

26. Stephan Haggard and Marcus Noland, "Networks, Trust, and Trade: The Microeconomics of China–North Korea Integration" (PIIE Working Paper 12–8. Peterson Institute for International Economics, Washington, DC, 2012); Stephan Haggard, Jennifer Lee, and Marcus Noland, "Integration in the Absence of Institutions: China–North Korea Cross-Border Exchange," *Journal of Asian Economics* 23, no. 2 (2012): 130–45; Thompson, "Silent Partners"; Heon Joo Jung and Timothy S. Rich, "Why Invest in North Korea? Chinese Foreign Direct Investment in North Korea and Its Implications," *Pacific Review* (2015) (Online First)).

27. Carla Freeman, "Fragile Edges between Security and Insecurity: China's Border Regions," in *Managing Fragile Regions*, ed. Rongxing Guo and Carla Freeman (Berlin: Springer, 2011).

28. B. R. Myers, *The Cleanest Race: How North Koreans See Themselves and Why It Matters* (New York: Melville House, 2010); Patrick McEachern, *Inside the Red Box: North Korea's Post-Totalitarian Politics* (New York: Columbia University Press, 2010); Ralph Hassig and Kongdan Oh, *The Hidden People of North Korea: Everyday Life in the Hermit Kingdom* (Lanham, MD: Rowman and Little-field, 2009); Park and Snyder, *North Korea in Transition: Politics, Economy, and Society*.

29. Cha, *The Impossible State*; Andrei Lankov, *The Real North Korea: Life and Politics in the Failed Stalinist Utopia* (Oxford: Oxford University Press, 2013).

30. Chung, "Is North Korea Doomed to Die?"

31. Author interview, South Korean economist specializing in North Korea #3, August 2012; Author interview, academic specializing in North Korea #3, Seoul, September 2012; Lankov, *The Real North Korea*.

32. Mun-su Yang, "The Institutions and the Actual Conditions of North Korean Trade," in *Korea Development Institute Research Report* (Korea Development Institute, Seoul, 31 December 2008).

33. Haggard and Noland, *Famine in North Korea*; Haggard and Noland, "Winter of Their Discontent: Pyongyang Attacks the Market."

34. See Hyung-min Joo, "Visualizing the Invisible Hands: The Shadow Economy in North Korea," *Economy and Society* 39, no. 1 (2010): 110–45; Hyung-min Joo, "Hidden Transcripts in Marketplaces: Politicized Discourses in the North Korean Shadow Economy," *Pacific Review* 27, no. 1 (2014): 49–71.

35. Jae-Cheon Lim and InJoo Yoon, "Institutional Entrepreneurs in North Korea: Emerging Shadowy Private Enterprises under Dire Economic Conditions," *North Korean Review* 7, no. 2 (2011): 82–93. See also Haggard and Noland, *Famine in North Korea*, 188–91.

36. Tim Hall, "Geographies of the Illicit: Globalization and Organized Crime," *Progress in Human Geography* 37, no. 3 (June 2013): 366–85.

37. Haggard and Noland, *Famine in North Korea*, for instance, have an appendix on "illicit activities" that is separate from the main text.

38. See Anonymous, "Health Consequences of Cuba's Special Period," *CMAJ: Canadian Medical Association Journal* 179, no. 3 (2008): 257.

39. Ariana Hernandez-Reguant, *Cuba in the Special Period: Culture and Ideology in the 1990s* (London: Palgrave Macmillan, 2009).

40. Conversations with various Chinese academics and officials revealed a near universal sentiment that their North Korean interlocutors were unwilling to discuss the idea of Chinese-style reform, at least as long as the term "reform" (*gaige*) was being used.

41. David Remnick, "Soviet Union's 'Shadow Economy'—Bribery, Barter, Black-Market Deals Are the Facts of Life," *Washington Post*, 22 September 1990; Gregory Grossman, "The Second Economy of the USSR," *Problems of Communism* 26, no. 5 (1977): 25–40; Istvan R. Gabor, "Second Economy and Socialism: The Hungarian Experience," in *The Underground Economies: Tax Evasion and Information Distortion*, ed. Edgar L. Feige (Cambridge, UK: Cambridge University Press, 1989); Steven L. Sampson, "The Second Economy of the Soviet Union and Eastern Europe," *ANNALS of the American Academy of Political and Social Science* 493 (September 1987): 120–36. For an example of this phenomenon in Asia, see Melanie Beresford and Dang Phong, *Economic Transition in Vietnam: Trade and Aid in the Demise of a Centrally Planned Economy* (Cheltenham, UK: Edward Elgar Publishing, 2000).

42. See Bruno Dallago, "The Irregular Economy in Transition: Features, Measurement, and Scope," in *Output Decline in Eastern Europe: Unavoidable, External Influence or Homemade?* ed. Robert Holzmann, János Gács, and Georg Winckler (Dordrecht: Springer, 1995).

43. Ákos Róna-Tas, "The Second Economy as a Subversive Force: The Erosion of Party Power in Hungary," in *The Waning of the Communist State: Economic Origins of Political Decline in China and Hungary*, ed. Andrew G. Walder (Berkeley: University of California Press, 1995).

44. On the problems associated with trying to come up with numbers for hidden economic activities, see Peter Andreas and Kelly M. Greenhill, eds., *Sex, Drugs, and Body Counts: The Politics of Numbers in Global Crime and Conflict* (Ithaca: Cornell University Press, 2010).

45. Bank of Korea, "Gross Domestic Product Estimates for North Korea in 2012" (Bank of Korea, Seoul, 12 July 2013). By comparison, South Korea's trade dependency in 2012 was 110% of GDP, on a GDP of US$1.2 trillion, while Australia's was 43% and the United States's was 31% (admittedly, both countries have service-oriented economies, while North Korea clearly does not). See the World Bank's estimates of trade as a percentage of GDP at http://data.worldbank.org/indicator/NE.TRD.GNFS.ZS.

46. Hall, "Geographies of the Illicit." See also Peter Andreas, "Illicit Globalization: Myths, Misconceptions, and Historical Lessons," *Political Science Quarterly* 126, no. 3 (2011): 403–25; Peter Andreas, "Illicit International Political Economy: The Clandestine Side of Globalization," *Review of International Political Economy* 11, no. 3 (2004): 642–52.

47. Phil Williams, "Transnational Criminal Organizations: Strategic Alliances," *Washington Quarterly* 18, no. 1 (1995): 57–72; Susan Strange, *The Retreat of the State: The Diffusion of Power in the World Economy* (New York: Cambridge University Press, 1996), 110–121.

48. See William Reno, "Illicit Commerce in Peripheral States," in H. Richard Friman, ed., *Crime and the Global Political Economy* (Boulder, CO: Lynne Rienner Publishers, 2009).

49. Gary Gereffi, John Humphrey, and Timothy Sturgeon, "The Governance of Global Value Chains," *Review of International Political Economy* 12, no. 1 (2005): 78–104; Gary Gereffi and Raphael Kaplinsky, "The Value of Value Chains: Spreading the Gains from Globalisation," *IDS Bulletin* 32, no. 3 (2001); Gary Gereffi and Karina Fernandez-Stark, "Global Value Chain Analysis: A Primer" (Center on Globalization, Governance & Competitiveness (CGGC), Duke University, Durham, NC, 2011); Gary Gereffi and Miguel Korzeniewicz, *Commodity Chains and Global Capitalism* (Westport, CT: Praeger, 1994).

50. Gargi Bhattacharya, *Traffick: The Illicit Movement of People and Things* (London: Pluto Press, 2005); Barnett R. Rubin, "The Political Economy of War and Peace in Afghanistan," *World Development* 28, no. 10 (2000): 1789–1803.

51. Peter Andreas, "The Clandestine Political Economy of War and Peace in Bosnia," *International Studies Quarterly* 48 (2004): 29–51.

52. Stephan Haggard, Marcus Noland, and Erik Weeks, "North Korea on the Precipice of Famine" (Peterson Institute for International Economics, Washington, DC, 2008).

53. Andrei Lankov, "Kim Jong-Un's North Korea: What Should We Expect?" *International Journal of Korean Unification Studies* 21, no. 1 (2012): 1–19.

54. Peter Andreas, *Blue Helmets and Black Markets: The Business of Survival in the Siege of Sarajevo* (Ithaca, NY: Cornell University Press, 2008).

1. Surviving the Arduous March through Enterprise

1. Victor Cha, *The Impossible State: North Korea, Past and Future* (New York: Random House, 2012); Barbara Demick, *Nothing to Envy: Real Lives in North Korea* (London: Granta, 2010); Nicholas Eberstadt, *The End of North Korea* (Washington, DC: AEI Press, 1999); Nicholas Eberstadt, *The North Korean Economy: Between Crisis and Catastrophe* (Piscataway, NJ: Transaction Publishers, 2007); Stephan Haggard and Marcus Noland, *Famine in North Korea: Markets, Aid, and Reform* (New York: Columbia University Press, 2007); Scott Snyder, "North Korea's Decline and China's Strategic Dilemmas," special report (United States Institute of Peace, Washington,

DC, 30 October 1997); Andrew S. Natsios, *The Great North Korean Famine: Famine, Politics, and Foreign Policy* (Washington, DC: United States Institute of Peace Press, 2001).

2. Charles K. Armstrong, *The North Korean Revolution, 1945–1950* (Ithaca, NY: Cornell University Press, 2004); Charles K. Armstrong, *Tyranny of the Weak: North Korea and the World, 1950–1992* (Ithaca, NY: Cornell University Press, 2013).

3. Armstrong, *Tyranny of the Weak*, 121–29.

4. Nicholas Eberstadt, Marc Rubin, and Albina Tretyakova, "The Collapse of Soviet and Russian Trade with North Korea, 1989–1993: Impact and Implications," *Korean Journal of National Unification* 4 (1995): 87–104.

5. Armstrong, *Tyranny of the Weak*, 121–29.

6. Andrei Lankov, *North of the DMZ: Essays on Daily Life in North Korea* (Jefferson, NC: McFarland and Company, 2007), 256–58.

7. Bertil Lintner, "Pyongyang's Banking Beachhead in Europe," *Far Eastern Economic Review*, 13 February 2003; Bertil Lintner, "The Macau Connection: The Former Portuguese Colony Was a Terrorist Base for Pyongyang," *Far Eastern Economic Review*, 25 October 2001.

8. Hyun Hee Kim, *The Tears of My Soul* (New York: William Morrow and Company, 1993), 64–69.

9. Don Oberdorfer, *Two Koreas: A Contemporary History* (Reading, MA: Addison-Wesley, 1997), 253.

10. Mary Beth Nikitin, "North Korea's Nuclear Weapons: Technical Issues" (Congressional Research Service, Washington, DC, 16 December 2009), 1.

11. "China Withdrew the Experts in Nuclear Technology Deployed to North Korea," *Chosun Ilbo*, 8 September 1992, 2.

12. Balazs Szalontai and Sergey Radchenko, "North Korea's Efforts to Acquire Nuclear Technology and Nuclear Weapons: Evidence from Russian and Hungarian Archives," in *Cold War International History Project* (Washington, DC: Woodrow Wilson International Center for Scholars, August 2006); Walter C. Clemens Jr., "North Korea's Quest for Nuclear Weapons: New Historical Evidence," *Journal of East Asian Studies* 10, no. 1 (2010): 127–54.

13. Cheon-seok Kang, "North Korea Acquires Nuclear Technologies through Jochongryon in Japan," *Chosun Ilbo (Seoul)*, 3 April 1990, 5.

14. Mark Hibbs, "Agencies Trace Some Iraqi Urenco Know-How," *Nucleonics Week*, 28 November 1991.

15. Joseph S. Bermudez Jr., "North Korea's Nuclear Programme," *Jane's Intelligence Review*, September 1991, 409.

16. Hibbs, "Agencies Trace Some Iraqi Urenco Know-How."

17. Lankov, *North of the DMZ*, 284–85.

18. Ibid., 230.

19. Ibid., 221–22.

20. Jane Shapiro Zacek, "Russia in North Korean Foreign Policy," in *North Korean Foreign Relations in the Post–Cold War Era*, ed. Samuel S. Kim (Oxford: Oxford University Press, 1998), 81–84.

21. Ilpyong J. Kim, "China in North Korean Foreign Policy," in *North Korean Foreign Relations in the Post–Cold War Era*, ed. Samuel S. Kim (Oxford: Oxford University Press, 1998), 108.

22. Cha, *The Impossible State*, 121.

23. Hazel Smith, *Hungry for Peace: International Security, Humanitarian Assistance, and Social Change in North Korea* (Washington, DC: United States Institute for Peace, 2005), 66.

24. Cha, *The Impossible State*, 120–24, 186–89.

25. See work on the palace economy: Sang-hwa Chung, "Is North Korea Doomed to Die? A Politico-Economic Analysis of the North Korean Ruling System and Its Strategic Implications" (Sejong Institute, Seoul, 2012); Benjamin Habib, "North Korea's Parallel Economies: Systemic Disaggregation Following the Soviet Collapse," *Communist and Post-Communist Studies* 44, no. 2

(2011): 149–59. See also John S. Park, "North Korea, Inc: Gaining Insights into North Korean Regime Stability from Recent Commercial Activities" (US Institute for Peace, Washington, DC, 2009).

26. See Paul R. Kan, Bruce E. Bechtol, and Robert M. Collins, *Criminal Sovereignty: Understanding North Korea's Illicit International Activities* (Carlisle Barracks, PA: Strategic Studies Institute, 2010).

27. Sharon A. Squassoni, "Weapons of Mass Destruction: Trade between North Korea and Pakistan" (Congressional Research Service, Washington, DC, 11 October 2006), 10.

28. Richard Paddock and Barbara Demick, "North Korea's Growing Drug Trade Seen in Botched Heroin Delivery," *Los Angeles Times*, 21 May 2003.

29. Raphael Perl, "Drug Trafficking and North Korea: Issues for U.S. Policy" (Congressional Research Service, Washington, DC, 25 January 2007), 8.

30. Haggard and Noland, *Famine in North Korea*.

31. Young Il Kim, "North Korea and Narcotics Trafficking: A View from the Inside," *North Korean Review* 1, no. 1 (2004); Perl, "Drug Trafficking," 7.

32. Dick K. Nanto and Raphael Perl, "North Korean Crime-for-Profit Activities" (Congressional Research Service, Washington, DC, 16 February 2007), 9–10; Gordon Fairclough, "Dispatch: Export Boom: Tobacco Companies Trace Fake Cigarettes to North Korea," *Wall Street Journal*, 27 January 2006.

33. Perl, "Drug Trafficking," 6–7.

34. Bertil Lintner and Suh-kyung Yoon, "North Korea: Coming in from the Cold," *Far Eastern Economic Review*, 25 October 2001.

35. Lintner and Yoon, "Coming in from the Cold."

36. Jay Solomon, "North Korean Pair Viewed as Key to Secret Arms Trade," *Wall Street Journal*, 31 August 2010.

37. Anna Wetter, *Enforcing European Union Law on Exports of Dual-Use Goods*, Sipri Research Reports (Oxford: Oxford University Press, 2009), 89–101.

38. Lintner and Yoon, "Coming in from the Cold."

39. Lintner, "The Macau Connection"; Lintner and Yoon, "Coming in from the Cold."

40. Jay Solomon and Jason Dean, "Heroin Busts Point to Source of Funds for North Koreans," *Wall Street Journal*, 23 April 2003; "100 Kiro, 3 Oku-En Taiho No Kumichou Urisabaku Kamotsusen De Kakuseizai Mitsuyu," *Sankei Shimbun*, 13 May 2006.

41. Tetsuya Suetsugu, "Risky Business Leading N. Korea to Ruin," *Yomiuri Shimbun*, 22 August 2003.

42. Perl, "Drug Trafficking and North Korea," 7.

43. ISN SECURITY WATCH, "Swiss Firm Denies 'Axis of Evil' Link" (Zurich: ETH Zurich, 4 April 2006).

44. Bertil Lintner and Steve Stecklow, "Paper Trail Exposes Missile Merchants," *Far Eastern Economic Review*, 13 February 2003.

45. Lintner and Stecklow, "Paper Trail."

46. Lintner and Stecklow, "Paper Trail"; Bertil Lintner, "North Korea's Missile Trade Helps Fund Its Nuclear Program," *Yale Global Online*, 5 May 2003.

47. Sharon A. Squassoni, "Weapons of Mass Destruction: Trade between North Korea and Pakistan" (Congressional Research Service, Washington, DC, 28 November 2006).

48. Joseph S. Bermudez Jr., "A History of Ballistic Missile Development in the DPRK," in *Occasional Paper* (Center for Nonproliferation Studies, Monterey Institute of International Studies, Monterey, CA, 1999), 24.

49. Ibid.

50. Mike Chinoy, *Meltdown: The Inside Story of the North Korean Nuclear Crisis* (New York: Macmillan, 2010), 90–91; Gordon Corera, *Shopping for Bombs* (Oxford: Oxford University Press, 2006), 94–137.

51. Adrian Levy and Catherine Scott-Clark, *Deception: Pakistan, the United States and the Global Nuclear Weapons Conspiracy* (London: Walker and Company, 2007), 260, 512.

52. Mihir Mistry, "Pak-Bound N. Korean Ship with Missile Machinery Detained," *The Times of India*, 5 July 1999.

53. Levy and Scott-Clark, *Deception*, 279–80; Julian West, "Pakistan Murder Exposes Nuclear Link," *Daily Telegraph*, 1 November 1998.

54. Levy and Scott-Clark, *Deception*, 279–80.

55. West, "Pakistan Murder."

56. "Japanese Tools Found on Detained N. Korean Missile Kit Ship," *Press Trust of India* 18 April 2009.

57. Suetsugu, "Risky Business."

58. William Bach, "Testimony of William Bach, Director, Office of African, Asian, and European Affairs, Bureau for International Narcotics and Law Enforcement Affairs, Department of State on May 20, 2003 at a Hearing on Drugs, Counterfeiting and Arms Trade: The North Korean Connection" (The Senate Committee on Governmental Affairs, Subcommittee on Financial Management, the Budget, and International Security, United States Senate, Washington, DC, 20 May 2003).

59. Brian Hsu, "Security Bureau Links N Korea and Local Gangs," *Taipei Times*, 5 January 2004.

60. Solomon and Dean, "Heroin Busts Point to Source of Funds for North Koreans."

61. Squassoni, "Weapons of Mass Destruction: Trade between North Korea and Pakistan," 10–11.

62. Levy and Scott-Clark, *Deception*, 278.

63. Kan, Bechtol, and Collins, *Criminal Sovereignty: Understanding North Korea's Illicit International Activities*, 9–10.

64. "100 Kiro, 3 Oku-En Taiho No Kumichou Urisabaku Kamotsusen De Kakuseizai Mitsuyu"; Solomon and Dean, "Heroin Busts Point to Source of Funds for North Koreans."

65. Wetter, *Enforcing European Union Law on Exports of Dual-Use Goods*, 89–101.

66. Bertil Lintner, "North Korea's Creepy-Crawly Capitalism," *Asia Times Online*, 26 May 2006.

67. "Trader Held for Shipping Dryer with Bio-Warfare Role to North," *Kyodo News Service*, 11 August 2006.

68. Other sources have Seishin Soiji as the company involved, along with another unnamed trading company (presumably Meisho Yoko). Since Seishin Soiji was also apparently involved in selling dual-use items to Iran, it is possible that Seishin Soiji is a Japanese company with limited respect for Japanese export laws rather than a North Korean front. See "Raid Targets Illegal Export to North of Freeze-Dryer," *Kyodo News Service*, 11 February 2006.

69. *R v Ta Song Wong*, VSC 126 (6 April 2006), Kellam J., Supreme Court of Victoria (2006).

70. *R v Choi (Pong Su) (No 15)*, VSC 40 (2 March 2005), Kellam J., Supreme Court of Victoria (2005).

71. Billy Adams, "Macau Boss Linked to Drug Haul," *South China Morning Post*, 23 November 2003. One of the conspirators, Lam Yau Kim, seems to have made at least one call during the operation to a Macau phone number.

72. *R v Choi (Pong Su) (No 16)*, VSC 48 (3 March 2005), Kellam J., Supreme Court of Victoria (2005); *R v Lam*, VSC 98 (15 June 2005), Kellam J., Supreme Court of Victoria (2005).

73. *R v Wee Quay Tan*, VSC 177 (8 May 2006), Kellam J., Supreme Court of Victoria (2006); *R v Teng (Pong Su)*, VSC 33 (21 February 2005), Kellam J., Supreme Court of Victoria (2005).

74. M. Collins, E. Casale, D.B. Hibbert, S. Panicker, J. Robertson, and S. Vujic, "Chemical Profiling of Heroin Recovered from the North Korean Merchant Vessel Pong Su," *Journal of Forensic Sciences* 51, no. 3 (2006): 597–602.

75. Bertil Lintner, "North Korea's Golden Path to Security," *Asia Times*, 18 January 2007.

76. *R v Ta Song Wong*.

77. Sung Chul Kim, Young Tai Jeung, Seung-Yul Oh, Hun Kyung Lee, and Gee Dong Lee, *North Korea in Crisis: An Assessment of Regime Sustainability* (Seoul: Korea Institute for National Unification, 1997), 87.

78. Ibid., 85.

79. Lankov, *North of the DMZ*, 183; Andrei Lankov, *The Real North Korea: Life and Politics in the Failed Stalinist Utopia* (Oxford: Oxford University Press, 2013), 88–89.

80. Lankov, *The Real North Korea*, 94.

81. Ibid., 90.

82. Soo Young Choi, *North Korea's Agricultural Reforms and Challenges in the Wake of the July 1 Measures* (Seoul: Korea Institute for National Unification, 2007), 1–2.

83. FAO/WFP, "Crop and Food Supply Assessment Mission to the Democratic People's Republic of Korea," (Pyongyang: FAO/WFP, 6 December 1996), 10; Soon-hee Lim, "The Food Crisis and Life of Women in North Korea" (Korea Institute of National Unification, Seoul, 2005), 38.

84. Hazel Smith, *North Korea: Markets and Military Rule* (Cambridge, UK: Cambridge University Press, 2015), 207–8, 211.

85. Ibid., 213–14.

86. Hazel Smith, "North Koreans in China: Sorting Fact from Fiction," in *Crossing National Borders: Human Migration Issues in Northeast Asia*, ed. Tsuneo Akaha and Anna Vassilieva (Tokyo: United Nations Press, 2005), 165–90.

87. Kenneth Quinones, "Beyond Collapse: Continuity and Change in North Korea," in *North Korea in the World Economy*, ed. E. Kwan Choi, E. Han Kim, and Yesook Merrill (London: RoutledgeCurzon, 2003), 163.

88. Lankov, *North of the DMZ*, 316–17.

89. Kim et al., *North Korea in Crisis*, 107–9.

90. Ibid., 77.

91. Ibid., 68–69.

92. Andrei Lankov and Seok-hyang Kim, "North Korean Market Vendors: The Rise of Grassroots Capitalists in a Post-Stalinist Society," *Pacific Affairs* 81, no. 1 (2008): 53–72.

93. Choi, *North Korea's Agricultural Reforms*, 6–7.

94. Ibid., 9, 13.

95. Ibid., 27–29.

96. Ibid., 38.

97. Ibid., 20.

98. Hazel Smith, "North Korea: Market Opportunity, Poverty and the Provinces," *New Political Economy* 14, no. 2 (2009): 231–56.

99. Byung-Yeon Kim and Dongho Song, "The Participation of North Korean Households in the Informal Economy: Size, Determinants, and Effect," *Seoul Journal of Economics* 21, no. 2 (2008): 361–85.

100. Lankov, *North of the DMZ*, 318; Smith, *Markets and Military Rule*, 214–15.

101. Hae Young Lee, "Lives for Sale: Personal Accounts of Women Fleeing North Korea to China" (Committee for Human Rights in North Korea, Washington, DC, 1 October 2009); Kathleen Davis, "Brides, Bruises and the Border: The Trafficking of North Korean Women into China," *SAIS Review* 26, no. 1 (2006): 131–41.

102. Lankov, *North of the DMZ*, 289. See also Smith, *Markets and Military Rule*, 217.

103. Lankov, *The Real North Korea*, 84–85.

104. Lankov, *North of the DMZ*, 324–26.

105. Lankov, *The Real North Korea*, 97.

106. Lankov, *North of the DMZ*, 184; Lankov, *The Real North Korea*, 90.

107. Lankov, *North of the DMZ*, 320–22; Hyung-min Joo, "Visualizing the Invisible Hands: The Shadow Economy in North Korea," *Economy and Society* 39, no. 1 (2010): 110–45; Jae Jean Suh, "Economic Hardship and Regime Sustainability in North Korea" (Korean Institute for National Unification, Seoul, 2008), 33; Smith, *Markets and Military Rule*, 217–19.

108. Lankov, *North of the DMZ*, 320–22. See also Smith, *Markets and Military Rule*, 216, 218.

109. Suh, "Economic Hardship and Regime Sustainability," 23–26.

110. Lankov, *North of the DMZ*, 320–22.

111. Author interview, retired US diplomat, New York, September 2013.

112. Jae Jean Suh, "The Impact of Personality Cult in North Korea" (Korea Institute for National Unification, Seoul, 2004), 29.

113. Suh, "The Impact of Personality Cult in North Korea," 30–31.

114. Ibid., 33.

115. See, for example, Yong Han, "The Perils of a Red Hat," *News China*, September 2013; Wenhong Chen, "Does the Colour of the Cat Matter? The Red Hat Strategy in China's Private Enterprises," *Management and Organization Review* 3, no. 1 (2007): 55–80.

116. See Dae-kyu Yoon, "Economic Reform and Institutional Transformation," in *The Dynamics of Change in North Korea*, ed. Philip H. Park (Seoul: Institute for Far Eastern Studies, 2009), 57.

117. Lankov, *The Real North Korea*, 85.

2. State Trading Networks versus the World

1. Brian Knowlton, "Ship Allowed to Take North Korea Scuds on to Yemeni Port: U.S. Frees Freighter Carrying Missiles," *New York Times*, 19 December 2002.

2. Juan Zarate, *Treasury Wars: The Unleashing of a New Era of Financial Warfare* (New York: PublicAffairs, 2013), 240, 257.

3. See Zarate, *Treasury Wars*, 219–68.

4. Jason Campbell Sharman, *The Money Laundry: Regulating Criminal Finance in the Global Economy* (Ithaca: Cornell University Press, 2011), 122–24.

5. Author interview, academic researcher on cross-border crime, Hong Kong, August 2012.

6. Security Council, "Resolution 1695 (2006) Adopted by the Security Council at Its 5490th Meeting, on 15 July 2006" (United Nations, New York, 15 July 2006).

7. Brendan Taylor, *Sanctions as Grand Strategy* (London: Routledge, 2012), 39.

8. Kenneth Quinones, "Beyond Collapse: Continuity and Change in North Korea," in *North Korea in the World Economy*, ed. E. Kwan Choi, E. Han Kim, and Yesook Merrill (London: RoutledgeCurzon, 2003), 171–72.

9. Hong Nack Kim, "Japan in North Korean Foreign Policy," in *North Korean Foreign Relations in the Post-Cold War Era*, ed. Samuel S. Kim (Oxford: Oxford University Press, 1998), 126.

10. Marcus Noland, "The External Economic Relations of the DPRK and Prospects for Reform," in *North Korean Foreign Relations in the Post-Cold War Era*, ed. Samuel S. Kim (Oxford: Oxford University Press, 1998), 192.

11. Kim, "Japan in North Korean Foreign Policy," 126.

12. Attempts by a Mongolian company that was possibly a North Korean front company were blocked by Japan in 2014. See Kosuke Takahashi, "Mongolian Firm Blocked from Buying N. Korean 'Embassy' in Tokyo," *NKNews*, 23 January 2014.

13. Yong Hun Kim, "Debts, Mergers, Collapses and Foreclosures: The Plunging Chongryun—Part 2," *DailyNK*, 23 November 2009; Yong Hun Kim, "Chongryon Feels the Pinch: The Plunging Chongryun—Part 1," *DailyNK*, 18 November 2009.

14. Security Council, "Resolution 1718 (2006) Adopted by the Security Council at Its 5551st Meeting, on 14 October 2006" (United Nations, New York, 14 October 2006).

15. Security Council, "Resolution 1874 (2009) Adopted by the Security Council at Its 6141st Meeting, on 12 June 2009" (United Nations, New York, 12 June 2009).

16. Security Council, "Resolution 2087 (2013) Adopted by the Security Council at Its 6904th Meeting, on 22 January 2013" (United Nations, New York, 22 January 2013).

17. Security Council, "Resolution 2094 (2013) Adopted by the Security Council at Its 6932nd Meeting, on 7 March 2013" (United Nations, New York, 7 March 2013).

18. "Joint Korean Kaesong Industrial Complex Reopens," *DW (Deutsche Welle)*, 16 September 2013.

19. "Japan-North Korea Relations," Japanese Ministry of Foreign Affairs, Tokyo, 20 November 2015, http://www.mofa.go.jp/region/asia-paci/n_korea/relation.html.

20. Security Council, "Resolution 2270 (2016) Adopted by the Security Council at Its 7638th Meeting, on 2 March 2016" (United Nations, New York, 2 March 2016). The resolution included a massive loophole, likely at China's instigation: the natural resource export ban mostly did not apply if the revenue was exclusively for humanitarian or livelihood purposes, or if the resources were being re-exported through Rason.

21. David Lague, "China Ends North Korea Talks Amid Delay in Return of Funds," *New York Times*, 23 March 2007. See also Zarate, *Treasury Wars*, 219–68. The money was eventually returned through the New York Federal Reserve, the Russian Central Bank, and a Russian bank that had official North Korean accounts.

22. Derek Thompson, "Silent Partners: Chinese Joint Ventures in North Korea," (US-Korea Institute, SAIS, Johns Hopkins University, Washington, DC, 2011).

23. Author interview, South Korean economist specializing in North Korea #3, Seoul, August 2012.

24. Author interview, academic specializing in North Korea #3, Seoul, September 2012.

25. Stephan Haggard, Jennifer Lee, and Marcus Noland, "Integration in the Absence of Institutions: China-North Korea Cross-Border Exchange," *Journal of Asian Economics* 23, no. 2 (2012): 130–45; Stephan Haggard and Marcus Noland, "Networks, Trust, and Trade: The Microeconomics of China-North Korea Integration" (PIIE Working Paper 12–8. Peterson Institute for International Economics, Washington, DC, 2012).

26. Author interview, foreign NGO worker in Seoul, April 2013.

27. Panel of Experts, "Report of the Panel of Experts Established Pursuant to Resolution 1874 (2009) S/2014/147" (United Nations Security Council, New York, 6 March 2014), 59.

28. Ibid.

29. Panel of Experts, "Report of the Panel of Experts Established Pursuant to Resolution 1874 (2009) S/2013/337" (United Nations Security Council, New York, 11 June 2013), 38–39.

30. Ibid., 39–40.

31. Panel of Experts, "Report of the Panel of Experts Established Pursuant to Resolution 1874 (2009) S/2010/571" (United Nations Security Council, New York, 5 November 2010), 26.

32. Panel of Experts, "Report S/2013/337," 39–40.

33. Ibid.

34. Panel of Experts, "Report S/2014/147," 20–21; "Report S/2013/337," 23–24.

35. Panel of Experts, "Report of the Panel of Experts Established Pursuant to Resolution 1874 (2009) S/2012/422" (United Nations Security Council, New York, 14 June 2012), 29; "Report S/2013/337," 36–37.

36. Panel of Experts, "Report S/2014/147," 20–21; "Report S/2013/337," 23–24.

37. Panel of Experts, "Report S/2010/571," 25.

38. Panel of Experts, "Report S/2014/147," 19.

39. Panel of Experts, "Report S/2012/422," 29.

40. Panel of Experts, "Report S/2012/422," 29; "Report S/2013/337," 36–37.

41. Panel of Experts, "Report S/2010/571," 25, 105.

42. Panel of Experts, "Report S/2012/422," 32–36.

43. Panel of Experts, "Report S/2014/147," 26–32.

44. Ibid.

45. Ibid.

46. Ibid., 25–27.

47. UKRINFOM, "Ukraine Detains North Korea's Dry Cargo Ship with Illegal Goods," *UKRINFORM*, 3 February 2010; Panel of Experts, "Report S/2014/147," 29.

48. Panel of Experts, "Report S/2014/147," 26–32.

49. Ibid., 60.

50. Ibid., 22–23. To be fair, the companies have strong incentives to have denied doing business with North Korea during the sanctions period.

51. Ibid., 24.

52. John S. Park, "The Key to the North Korean Targeted Sanctions Puzzle," *Washington Quarterly* 37, no. 3 (Fall 2014): 199–214.

53. Panel of Experts, "Report S/2012/422," 36.

54. Ibid., 31–33.

55. Ibid.

56. Much of Taiwan's trade with North Korea was likely disguised as China-North Korea trade through transshipment in China.

57. Center for Nonproliferation Studies, "Taiwan Further Restricts Trade to Iran, North Korea," *International Export Control Observer*, March/April 2007, 4–5.

58. Eugene Chien, "Beyond SARS: Give Taiwan WHO Status," *New York Times*, 16 May 2003.

59. Justin V. Hastings, "Globalization, Ma Ying-Jeou, and the Future of Transnational Criminal Networks," in *Globalization in the Shadow of Power: New Approaches to Security Relations across the Taiwan Strait*, ed. Ming-chin Monique Chu and Scott L. Kastner (London: Routledge, 2014).

60. Justin V. Hastings, "Illicit Flows in the Hong Kong-China-Taiwan Triangle," *Issues and Studies* 45, no. 2 (2009): 185–220.

61. Hastings, "Illicit Flows."

62. "Tokyo Trading Companies Raided under Suspicion of Exporting WMD-Linked Device to DPRK," *Tokyo Kyodo World Service*, 17 February 2006; "Man Held over Illegal Export to N. Korea," *The Daily Yomiuri (Tokyo)*, 11 August 2006; "Asahi: Man Sold Pyongyang Restricted Device," *Asahi Shimbun (Tokyo)*, 11 August 2006; Center for Nonproliferation Studies, "Illicit Trafficking: Japanese Export Controls under Scrutiny as Revelations of Illicit Transfers Continue," *International Export Control Observer*, March 2006, 9.

63. Togzhan Kassenova, "Policy Forum 11–30: A 'Black Hole' in the Global Nonproliferation Regime: The Case of Taiwan" (Nautilus Institute, Berkeley, CA, 8 September 2011).

64. Kyodo, "Taiwan Firm Sold WMD-Related Tech to N. Korea: Justice Ministry," *Japan Economic Newswire*, 27 November 2007.

65. Hastings, "Transnational Criminal Networks."

66. U.S. Department of Justice, "Press Release: Taiwanese Father and Son Arrested for Allegedly Violating US Laws to Prevent Proliferation of Weapons of Mass Destruction" (U.S. Department of Justice, Washington, DC, 6 May 2013).

67. See U.S. Department of the Treasury, "Press Release: Treasury Sanctions Taiwan Proliferators Linked to North Korea" (Department of the Treasury, Washington, DC, 10 May 2013).

68. *Criminal Complaint: United States of America under Seal v. Hsien Tai Tsai, Also Known as "Alex Tsai,"* Northern District of Illinois, Eastern Division, United States District Court (23 October 2012).

69. Ibid.

70. Ibid., 19.

71. Author interview, Chinese trading company representative, Dandong, November 2013.

3. Entrepreneurialism, North Korea–Style

1. Stephan Haggard and Marcus Noland, "Sanctioning North Korea: The Political Economy of Denuclearization and Proliferation," *Asian Survey* 50, no. 3 (2010): 539–68; Stephan Haggard and Marcus Noland, "Winter of Their Discontent: Pyongyang Attacks the Market" (Peterson Institute for International Economics, Washington, DC, 2010).

2. My thanks to one of the anonymous reviewers for this point.

3. Haggard and Noland, "Sanctioning North Korea"; Haggard and Noland, "Winter of Their Discontent."

4. Haggard and Noland, "Winter of Their Discontent."

5. Yonhap, "N. Korean Technocrat Executed for Bungled Currency Reform: Sources," *Yonhap*, 18 March 2010.

6. Daniel Tudor and James Pearson, *North Korea Confidential: Private Markets, Fashion Trends, Prison Camps, Dissenters and Defectors* (Rutland, VT: Tuttle Publishing, 2015), locations 237–81.

7. Alexandre Mansourov, "North Korea: The Dramatic Fall of Jang Song Thaek," 38north, 9 December 2013, http://38north.org/2013/12/amansourov120913/.

8. Sang-hun Choe and David E. Sanger, "Korea Execution Is Tied to Clash over Businesses," *New York Times*, 23 December 2013.

9. Author interview, South Korean economist specializing in North Korea #3, Seoul, August 2012.

10. Dong Yu and Yu Tian, "Chaoxian Shifang 'Bian'ge' Xinhao?" *Nanfang Zhoumo*, 11 August 2012.

11. Author interview, South Korean economist specializing in North Korea #5, Seoul, April 2013; Author interview, South Korean economist specializing in North Korea #3.

12. See Patrick McEachern, *Inside the Red Box: North Korea's Post-Totalitarian Politics* (New York: Columbia University Press, 2010) for a discussion of North Korean interest groups.

13. Korean Central News Agency, "Traitor Jang Song Thaek Executed," *Korean Central News Agency*, 13 December 2013.

14. Yaohui Wang, interview with Chinese businessman #10, Hunchun, July 2014; Yaohui Wang, interview with Chinese businessman #7, Hunchun, July 2014; Yaohui Wang, interview with Chinese businessman #6, Hunchun, July 2014.

15. Fenghuangwang, "Chaoxian: Zhangchengze Shijian Bu Hui Yingxiang Jingji Jiang Yin Waizi Fazhan Tequ," *Fenghuangwang*, 17 December 2013.

16. Yaohui Wang, interview with Chinese businessman #8, Hunchun, July 2014; Wang, interview with Chinese businessman #10.

17. Yaohui Wang, interview with Chinese Businessman #9, Hunchun, July 2014.

18. Yaohui Wang, interviews with Chinese businessmen, Shenyang, Hunchun, Dandong, and Yanji, July 2014.

19. Choson Exchange, "May 30th Measures and IFES Report," Choson Exchange, 3 December 2014, http://www.chosonexchange.org/our-blog/2014/12/3/may-30th-measures-and-ifes-report; Andrei Lankov, "Reforming North Korea: It Seems That, at Long Last, North Korea Has Decided to Begin Chinese-Style Reforms," *Al Jazeera English*, 30 November 2014.

20. Haggard and Noland, *Witness to Transformation*, 58–65.

21. Byung-Yeon Kim, "Informal Economy Activity of Soviet Households: Size and Dynamics," *Journal of Comparative Economics* 31, no. 3 (2003): 532–51.

22. Hazel Smith, *North Korea: Markets and Military Rule* (Cambridge, UK: Cambridge University Press, 2015), 220–22. See Hyeong Jung Park, "North Korean Economy as a Hybrid of Past

and Future—Segmentation of the Economy in Seven Semi-Independent Compartments Based on Diversification of Surplus Occupation and Economic Coordination Mechanism," *North Korean Studies Review* 13, no. 1 (2009): 40–41.

23. Author interview, South Korean economist specializing in North Korea #3. See also Hyeong Jung Park, "Commercial Engagements of the Party-State Agencies and the Expansion of Market in the 1990s in North Korea," *Journal of Korean Unification Studies* 20, no. 1 (2011): 231–32.

24. Author interview, South Korean economist specializing in North Korea #2, Seoul, August 2012; See also Park, "Commercial Engagements," 214–15.

25. Wha-Soon Kim, "Factors Determining the Work Type for North Korean Residents in the Period of Marketization," *Unification Policy Studies* (Korean Institute for National Uniification) 22, no. 1 (2013): 79–112.

26. Author interview, South Korean economist specializing in North Korea #2; See also Hyeong Jung Park, "Why Has North Korea Neither Collapsed nor Reformed and Opened?" *North Korean Studies Review* 16, no. 1 (2013): 51–52.

27. Ole Bruun, "Political Hierarchy and Private Entrepreneurship in a Chinese Neighborhood," in *The Waning of the Communist State: Economic Origins of Political Decline in China and Hungary*, ed. Andrew G. Walder (Berkeley: University of California Press, 1995).

28. Park, "Commercial Engagements," 214–15.

29. Kang-taek Im, Mun-su Yang, and Seoki Lee, "Study of the Status of North Korea's Official Economy for Estimation of Unification Costs/Benefits" (Korea Institute of National Unification, Seoul, 2011), 83–110.

30. Song Min Choi, "More Checkpoints, More Bribes," *DailyNK*, 23 January 2013.

31. Stephan Haggard and Marcus Noland, *Witness to Transformation: Refugee Insights into North Korea* (Washington, DC: Peterson Institute for International Economics, 2011), 82, 99.

32. Hyeong Jung Park, Hyun Joon Jeon, Young Ja Park, Cheol Ki Yoon, "The Reality of North Korean Corruption and Anti-Corruption Strategy: Groping for International Cooperation" (Korea Institute for National Unification, Seoul, 2012), 133–35.

33. Jeong-ah Cho, "The Changes of Everyday Life in North Korea in the Aftermath of Their Economic Difficulties" (Korea Institute for National Unification, Seoul, 2007), 41–46.

34. Author interview, South Korean economist specializing in North Korea #4, Seoul, September 2012.

35. Yong Jae Mok, "Crackdowns Enhancing Anti-Socialist Cycle," *DailyNK*, 23 June 2011.

36. Author interview, academic specializing in North Korea #3, Seoul, September 2012.

37. Author interview, South Korean economist specializing in North Korea #2.

38. Ibid.

39. Author interview, South Korean academic specializing in North Korea #2, Seoul, April 2013.

40. Philo Kim, "Segmentalized Marketization and Its Socio-Political Implications in North Korea," *North Korean Studies Review* 16, no. 1 (2013): 102–6.

41. Author interview, South Korean academic specializing in North Korea #2.

42. Eun-I Jung, "Research on North Korean Trade Companies: Focusing on the City of Sinuiju on the DPRK-China Border" (Ministry of Unification, Seoul, 2012), 6–10; Park, "Commercial Engagements," 220–21, 224–28, 230.

43. Jung, "Research on North Korean Trade Companies," 6–10.

44. Hyeong Jung Park, "Towards a Political Analysis of Markets in North Korea," *Korean Political Science Review* 46, no. 5 (2012): 207–24; Im, Yang, and Lee, "Study of the Status of North Korea's Official Economy," 83–110.

45. Hyeong Jung Park, "The Trend of the North Korean Military in the Process of Kim Jung-Eun's Power Settlement (2009–2013)" (Korean Institute of National Unification, Seoul, 2013), CO 13–23.

46. Mun-su Yang, "The Institutions and the Actual Conditions of North Korean Trade" (Korea Development Institute, Seoul, 31 December 2008), 18–19.

47. Author interview, South Korean economist specializing in North Korea #5; Jung, "Research on North Korean Trade Companies," 15–31.

48. Jung, "Research on North Korean Trade Companies," 15–31.

49. Yang, "The Institutions and the Actual Conditions of North Korean Trade," 18–19.

50. Jung, "Research on North Korean Trade Companies," 15–31.

51. Andrei Lankov, "How North Korean Trading Companies Make Money," *DailyNK*, 28 June 2013. See also Hyeong Jung Park and Sahyun Choi, "Fiscal Segmentation and Economic Changes in North Korea" (Korea Institute for National Unification, Seoul, 2014), 40–51.

52. Lankov, "How North Korean Trading Companies Make Money." See also Park and Choi, "Fiscal Segmentation," 40–51.

53. Jung, "Research on North Korean Trade Companies," 15–31.

54. Park et al., "Reality of North Korean Corruption," 128–31, 133–35.

55. Yong Hun Kim, "Green Shoots of Private Enterprise Growth," *DailyNK*, 17 August 2011.

56. Park et al., "Reality of North Korean Corruption," 75–81.

57. Author interview, South Korean Economist specializing in North Korea #2.

58. Andray Abrahamian, Geoffrey K. See, and Xinyu Wang, "The ABCs of North Korea's SEZs" (US-Korea Institute, School of Advanced International Studies, Johns Hopkins University, Washington, DC, 2014).

59. Author interview, South Korean academic specializing in North Korea #2; Jong-wun Lee and I-kyung Hong, "Analysis of the Reality of Economic Exchange and Transaction Practices in the Sino-DPRK Border Area" (Korea Institute for International Economic Policy, Seoul, 2 August 2013), 53–54.

60. Lankov, "How North Korean Trading Companies Make Money."

61. Lee and Hong, "Analysis of the Reality of Economic Exchange and Transaction Practices in the Sino-DPRK Border Area," 15–16, 71.

62. Author interview, academic specializing in North Korea #3.

63. Author interview, South Korean academic specializing in North Korea #2.

64. Author interview, academic specializing in North Korea #3.

65. Author interview, South Korean academic specializing in North Korea #2.

66. GoodFriends, "One Million Won Required for Obtaining a Position as a Hyesan City Police Officer," *North Korea Today*, October 2010.

67. Mi Jin Kang, "A Modern Day Gold Rush," *DailyNK*, 15 March 2011.

68. Author interview, foreign NGO worker in Seoul, Seoul, April 2013.

69. Author interview, foreign NGO worker in Beijing, Beijing, April 2013.

70. Smith, *Markets and Military Rule*, 209–93.

71. Sung Hwee Moon, "Water Trade Burgeoning in North Korea," *DailyNK*, 15 December 2008. This may have occurred in 2006.

72. In Ho Park, "2008 Top Items in the Jangmadang," *DailyNK*, 1 January 2009.

73. Cheong Ho Choi, "Fashion Also Influenced by South Korean Culture," *DailyNK*, 21 July 2011.

74. Andrei Lankov, "The Secret World of North Korea's New Rich," *Asia Times*, 10 August 2011; Kwang Jin Kim, "Seamstresses Inspired by SK Fashion Magazines," *DailyNK*, 9 November 2012.

75. Author interview, South Korean economist specializing in North Korea #4, Seoul, September 2012.

76. Gwan Hee Yoo, "Wholesalers at Forefront of Market Battle," *DailyNK*, 27 March 2010.

77. Jeong Jin Im, "Servi-Cha: The Lifeblood of the People's Economy," *DailyNK*, 28 October 2010.

78. Kim, "Green Shoots."

79. Song Ah Seol, "Servi-Cha Professionalizing for Kim Jon Eun Era," *DailyNK*, 13 March 2014; Im, "Servi-Cha: The Lifeblood of the People's Economy."

80. Seol, "Servi-Cha Professionalizing."

81. Mi Jin Kang, "Loans Creating Circle of Poverty," *DailyNK*, 16 May 2011.

82. Chico Harlan, "North Korean Defectors Learn Quickly How to Send Money Back Home," *Washington Post*, 6 February 2012.

83. Tudor and Pearson, *North Korea Confidential*, locations 341–70.

84. Jung Hyun Kwon and Dae Jung Kwak, "Tens of Thousands of Drug Addicts in Pyongyang: 'Drug Eradication Groups', Active in Three Major Cities," *DailyNK*, 19 August 2005.

85. DailyNK, "Drug Smugglers in Collusion with Cadres," *DailyNK*, 13 August 2008; Do Hyung Kim, "A Scuffle between Safety Agents and Middle School Students: A Rumor Says Pits Will Be Dug Along the Border," *DailyNK*, 28 February 2008.

86. United States Department of State, "International Narcotics Control Strategy Report 2012," (United States Department of State, Washington, DC, 2012). For more recent sources on North Korean drug trafficking, see Andrei Lankov and Seok-hyang Kim, "A New Face of North Korean Drug Use: Upsurge in Methamphetamine Abuse across the Northern Areas of North Korea," *North Korean Review* 9, 1 (2013): 45–60; Minwoo Yun and Eunyoung Kim, "Evolution of North Korean Drug Trafficking: State Control to Private Participation," *North Korean Review* 6, 2 (2010): 55–64.

87. DailyNK, "This Is All Kim Jong Il's Fault," *DailyNK*, 29 November 2011.

88. Phoenix Weekly, "Beihan Dupin Gongxian Zhongguo Dong San Shen," *Taiwan Post*, 8 December 2011.

89. Chosun Ilbo, "Crackdowns, Public Executions on Sino-Korean Border," *Chosun Ilbo*, 11 March 2005.

90. Phoenix Weekly, "Beihan Dupin Gongxian Zhongguo Dong San Shen."

91. Kwang Jin Kim, "Hyesan Sees String of Drugs Arrests," *DailyNK*, 18 January 2013; Myung O Kim, "Anti-Socialist Units Unleashed on Border Area," *DailyNK*, 7 February 2011; Gwan Hee Yoo, "North Korea Launches Drugs Crackdown," *DailyNK*, 27 August 2010.

92. Phoenix Weekly, "Beihan Dupin Gongxian Zhongguo Dong San Shen."

93. Yanbian News Network, "Wozhou Zhenpo Teda Fandu An: Jiaohuo Bingdu 1472.8 Ke," *Yanbian News Network*, 5 September 2010.

94. Dongbei Jinghuo Xinwen, "Yanbian Zhou Gong'anju Zhenpo Teda Kuaguo Zousi Fandu An," *Dongbei Jinghuo Xinwen*, 27 March 2010; He Zhou, "Yanbian Jingfang Zhenpo '9.20' Teda Kuaguo Zousi Fanmai Bingdu An," 27 March 2010.

95. Chunli Wang, "Jilin Sheng Jingfang Zhenpo '2.11' Teda Kuaguo Fandu An," Zhongguo Jilin Wang, 25 June 2009.

96. Chunlei Zhang, "Yanji Jingfang Pohuo Yiqi Teda Kuaguo Zousi Dupin An," *Beifang Fazhi Bao*, 28 April 2008.

97. Dongbei Jinghuo Xinwen, "Yanbian Zhou Gong'anju Zhenpo Teda Kuaguo Zousi Fandu An"; Zhou, "Yanbian Jingfang Zhenpo '9.20' Teda Kuaguo Zousi Fanmai Bingdu An."

98. Yanbian News Network, "Wozhou Zhenpo Teda Fandu An: Jiaohuo Bingdu 1472.8 Ke."

99. Kwon and Kwak, "Tens of Thousands of Drug Addicts in Pyongyang."

100. Kim, "Scuffle."

101. Sung Jin Lee, "Drug Prices Influencing All Corners of North Korean Market," *DailyNK*, 12 November 2009.

102. DailyNK, "Drug Smugglers in Collusion with Cadres."

103. Mok, "Crackdowns"; Hyuk Su Jin, "The Cost of Loyalty on the Day of the Sun," *DailyNK*, 15 April 2010.

104. Yanbian News Network, "Wozhou Zhenpo Teda Fandu An: Jiaohuo Bingdu 1472.8 Ke."

105. Wang, "Jilin Sheng Jingfang Zhenpo '2.11' Teda Kuaguo Fandu An."

106. Zhou, "Yanbian Jingfang Zhenpo '9.20' Teda Kuaguo Zousi Fanmai Bingdu An."

107. Zhang, "Yanji Jingfang Pohuo Yiqi Teda Kuaguo Zousi Dupin An."

108. Yanbian News Network, "Wozhou Zhenpo Teda Fandu An: Jiaohuo Bingdu 1472.8 Ke."

109. Dongbei Jinghuo Xinwen, "Yanbian Zhou Gong'anju Zhenpo Teda Kuaguo Zousi Fandu An."

110. Yanbian News Network, "Wozhou Zhenpo Teda Fandu An: Jiaohuo Bingdu 1472.8 Ke."

111. Dongbei Jinghuo Xinwen, "Yanbian Zhou Gong'anju Zhenpo Teda Kuaguo Zousi Fandu An."

112. Wang, "Jilin Sheng Jingfang Zhenpo '2.11' Teda Kuaguo Fandu An."

113. Nathan Thompson, "Inside One of North Korea's Secretive Slave Restaurants," Vice. com, 11 April 2014; Winston Ross, "I Ate Dinner in Pyongyang's Cambodian Outpost," Vice. com, 5 February 2014.

114. Adam Taylor, "North Korea Reportedly Using Sexy Waitresses in Foreign Restaurants as Spies," *Business Insider*, 24 July 2012.

115. Sebastian Strangio, "Kingdom Kim's Culinary Outposts: Inside the Bizarre World of Asia's North Korean Restaurant Chain," *Slate*, 27 March 2010.

116. Author interview, Chinese think tank researchers, Beijing, November 2012.

117. Author interview, Chinese academic specialist on North Korea #1, Shenyang, November 2013.

118. Tae-jun Kang, "New North Korean Staffed Restaurant Opens in Amsterdam," *NKNews*, 27 January 2014.

119. Author interview, foreign NGO worker in Seoul.

120. Ibid.

121. Author interview, Chinese think tank researchers.

122. Taylor, "Sexy Waitresses."

123. Author interview, Chinese academic specialist on North Korea #1.

124. Wang, interview with Chinese businessman #10.

125. Author interview, Chinese businessman, Shenyang, November 2013.

126. Author Interview, South Korean economist specializing in North Korea #4.

127. Ibid.

128. Tudor and Pearson, *North Korea Confidential*, location 456.

129. Wang, interview with Chinese businessman #10.

130. Ibid.

131. Author interview, Chinese trading company representative, Dandong, November 2013. Obviously, since the trader was based in Dandong, this was a self-serving comment.

132. Author interview, Chinese businessman #10.

133. Author interview, Chinese trading company representative; Ross, "I Ate Dinner."

134. Wang, interview with Chinese businessman #10.

135. Author interview, Chinese trading company representative.

136. Wang, interview with Chinese businessman #10.

137. Seong Hwan Kim, "20 North Korean Restaurants Overseas Close Down in the Wake of Sanctions," *DailyNK*, 29 April 2016.

138. Ibid.

139. Author interview, Chinese trading company representative.

140. Wang, interview with Chinese businessman #10.

141. Ji Jun, "Huaxi Cun Lai Le Chaoxian Nü Fuwuyuan," *Southern Weekend*, 1 August 2012. www.lnfzm.com/content/79132.

4. A Terrible, Horrible, No Good, Very Bad Investment Environment

1. Marcus Noland, "Hugely Important: North Korea Running a Current Account Surplus?" Peterson Institute for International Economics, 18 March 2013. http://blogs.piie.com/nk/?p=9647.

2. Kisan Gunjal, Swithun Goodbody, Siemon Hollema, Katrien Ghoos, Samir Wanmali, Krishna Krishnamurthy and Emily Turano, "Special Report: FAO/WFP Crop and Food Security Assessment Mission to the Democratic People's Republic of Korea" (Food and Agriculture Organisation/ World Food Programme, Rome, 28 November 2013).

3. Stephan Haggard and Marcus Noland, "Networks, Trust, and Trade: The Microeconomics of China-North Korea Integration" (PIIE Working Paper 12–8. Peterson Institute for International Economics, Washington, DC, 2012), 31.

4. Scott Thomas Bruce, "A Double-Edged Sword: Information Technology in North Korea," (East-West Center, Honolulu, 2012). Chinese-made mobile phone with Chinese SIM cards that are used near the border within reach of Chinese mobile phone towers can be used to call the outside world, of course.

5. For a short discussion of the problems investors have in North Korea, see Yaohui Wang and Justin V. Hastings, "North Korea Risky Business for Chinese Investors," East Asian Bureau of Economic Research/Australian National University, January 10, 2014, http://www.eastasiaforum.org/2014/01/10/north-korea-risky-business-for-chinese-investors/.

6. Andray Abrahamian, Geoffrey K. See, and Xinyu Wang, "The ABCs of North Korea's SEZs" (US-Korea Institute, School of Advanced International Studies, Johns Hopkins University, Washington, DC, 2014).

7. See various laws collected in *Laws and Regulations of the Democratic People's Republic of Korea Covering External Economic Matters* (Pyongyang: Legislation Press, 2012). The digitized version can be found at: kimchilaw.com/north-korean-laws-2/.

8. Seung-Hyun Yoon and Seung-Ook Lee, "From Old Comrades to New Partnerships: Dynamic Development of Economic Relations between China and North Korea," *Geographical Journal* 179, no. 1 (2013): 19–31.

9. Author interview, journalist, Beijing, November 2012.

10. James Reilly, "China's Market Influence in North Korea," *Asian Survey* 54, no. 5 (2014): 904, 910.

11. Thanks to James Goymour for his efforts in collecting the data discussed in this section.

12. Open Source Center, "North Korea—Characteristics of Joint Ventures with Foreign Partners, 2004–2011" (Open Source Center, Washington, DC, 1 March 2012), Appendix.

13. Ibid., 5.

14. Abrahamian, See, and Wang, "ABCs of North Korea's SEZs," 8–10.

15. ABC News, "South Korea Suspends Operations at Joint Kaesong Factory Complex over North Korea Missile Launch," Australian Broadcasting Corporation, 10 February 2016.

16. Yoon and Lee, "From Old Comrades to New Partnerships."

17. Reilly, "China's Market Influence in North Korea," 905–907.

18. Andray Abrahamian, "A Convergence of Interests: Prospects for Rason Special Economic Zone" (Korea Economic Institute of America, Washington, DC, 24 February 2012).

19. Abrahamian, See, and Wang, "ABCs of North Korea's SEZs," 23–25.

20. Ibid., 12–13.

21. Ibid., 14–17.

22. Chinese translation of Kyongwon County's plan for economic development, 2013.

23. Nicholas Eberstadt, "North Korea's Paradoxical Upswing in Trade," American Enterprise Institute, 4 June 2014, https://www.aei.org/publication/north-koreas-paradoxical-upswing-in-trade/.

24. Jae Cheol Kim, "The Political Economy of Chinese Investment in North Korea: A Preliminary Assessment," *Asian Survey* 46, no. 6 (2006): 898–916; Kyu-ryun Kim, ed. *North Korea's External Economic Relations*, KINU Research Monograph (Korea Institute for National Unification, Seoul, 2008).

25. Stephan Haggard and Marcus Noland, "The Political Economy of North Korea: Implications for Denuclearization and Proliferation" (East-West Center, Honolulu, 2009); Stephan Haggard and Marcus Noland, "Sanctioning North Korea: The Political Economy of Denuclearization and Proliferation," *Asian Survey* 50, no. 3 (2010): 539–568; James Reilly, "The Curious Case of China's Aid to North Korea," *Asian Survey* 54, no. 6 (2014): 1158–1183.

26. Balázs Szalontai and Changyong Choi, "China's Controversial Role in North Korea's Economic Transformation: The Dilemmas of Dependency," *Asian Survey* 53, no. 2 (March/April 2013): 269–291.

27. Stephan Haggard, Jennifer Lee, and Marcus Noland, "Integration in the Absence of Institutions: China-North Korea Cross-Border Exchange," *Journal of Asian Economics* 23, no. 2 (2012): 130–145; Haggard and Noland, "Networks, Trust, and Trade."

28. Ruediger Frank, "Why Now Is a Good Time for Economic Engagement of North Korea," *Asia-Pacific Journal* 11, no. 14 (2013).

29. Reilly, "China's Market Influence in North Korea."

30. Andrew Scobell, *China and North Korea: From Comrades-in-Arms to Allies at Arm's Length* (Carlisle Barracks: Strategic Studies Institute, 2004); Stephan Haggard and Marcus Noland, "North Korea's External Economic Relations," in *Engagement with North Korea*, ed. Sung Chull Kim and David C. Kang (State University of New York Press, Albany, NY, 2009).

31. To take into account shipping and other ancillary costs, Chinese exports to North Korea were multiplied by 1.1, and Chinese imports from North Korea were divided by 1.1. This allows for a more accurate representation of what imports actually cost North Korea, and what income North Korea actually received from exports. See Eberstadt, "North Korea's Paradoxical Upswing in Trade."

32. Yoon and Lee, "From Old Comrades to New Partnerships," 23.

33. Ibid., 23.

34. Derek Thompson, "Silent Partners: Chinese Joint Ventures in North Korea" (US-Korea Institute, SAIS, Johns Hopkins University, Washington, DC, 2011), 35.

35. Thompson, "Silent Partners," 35; Haggard and Noland, "Networks, Trust, and Trade," 5.

36. Author interview, South Korean economist specializing in North Korea #3, Seoul, August 2012.

37. Author interview, South Korean economist specializing in North Korea #3; See also Thompson, "Silent Partners," 56–62.

38. Yaohui Wang, interview with Chinese businessman #16, Changchun, July 2014.

39. Zhongguo Xiyang Jituan, "Xiyang Jituan Zai Chaozian Touzi De Emeng," Sina.com.cn, 3 August 2012, http://blog.sina.com.cn/s/blog_916fb56901017b75.html.

40. Ziran Zhou, Weidan Cheng, Gang Cheng, Xianglie Han, "Chaoxian Zhongyangshe Bochi Zhongguo Gongsi 'Touzi Chaoxian Beipian' Zhize," *Huanqiu Shibao*, 6 September 2012.

41. 21 Shiji Wang, "Xiyang Jituan 2.4 Yi Touzi Chaoxian: Zhou Furen Zishu 'Beitao' Shimo," *21st Century Business Herald*, 25 August 2012.

42. Ibid.

43. Ibid.

44. Zhongguo Xiyang Jituan, "Xiyang Jituan Zai Chaozian Touzi De Emeng."

45. 21 Shiji Wang, "Xiyang Jituan 2.4 Yi Touzi Chaoxian: Zhou Furen Zishu 'Beitao' Shimo."

46. Ibid.

47. Ibid.

48. Zhongguo Xiyang Jituan, "Xiyang Jituan Zai Chaozian Touzi De Emeng."

49. Zhongguo Xiyang Jituan, "Xiyang Jituan Zai Chaozian Touzi De Emeng"; 21 Shiji Wang, "Xiyang Jituan 2.4 Yi Touzi Chaoxian: Zhou Furen Zishu 'Beitao' Shimo."

50. Zhongguo Xiyang Jituan, "Xiyang Jituan Zai Chaozian Touzi De Emeng."

51. Ibid.

52. Ibid.

53. Author interview, foreign NGO worker in Seoul, April 2013.

54. 21 Shiji Wang, "Xiyang Jituan 2.4 Yi Touzi Chaoxian: Zhou Furen Zishu 'Beitao' Shimo."

55. Author, interview, South Korean economist specializing in North Korea #3.

56. Patrick McEachern, "Interest Groups in North Korean Politics," *Journal of East Asian Studies* 8, no. 2 (2008): 235–258; Patrick McEachern, "North Korea's Policy Process: Assessing Institutional Policy Preferences," *Asian Survey* 49, no. 3 (2009): 528–552; Patrick McEachern, *Inside the Red Box: North Korea's Post-Totalitarian Politics* (New York: Columbia University Press, 2010).

57. See Reilly, "The Curious Case of China's Aid to North Korea," 1175–1177.

58. Several Chinese investors interviewed said that they had little hope of ever receiving help from the Chinese government if their businesses failed in North Korea.

59. Yaohui Wang, interview with Chinese businessman #1, Shenyang, July 2014.

60. Yaohui Wang, interview with government official #1, Baishan, July 2014.

61. Haggard and Noland, "Networks, Trust, and Trade," 12.

62. Ibid.

63. Yaohui Wang, interview with Chinese businessman #3, Shenyang, July 2014.

64. Yaohui Wang, interview with Chinese businessman #9, Hunchun, July 2014.

65. Wang, interview with Chinese businessman #1.

66. Yaohui Wang, interview with Chinese businessman #5, Shenyang, July 2014.

67. Yaohui Wang, interview with Chinese businessman #13, Yanji, July 2014.

68. Ibid.

69. Yaohui Wang, interview with Chinese businessman #4, Shenyang, July 2014.

70. Wang, interview with Chinese businessman #9.

71. Yaohui Wang, interview with Chinese businessman #7, Hunchun, July 2014.

72. Yaohui Wang, interview with Chinese businessman #8, Hunchun, July 2014.

73. Yaohui Wang, interview with Chinese businessman #6, Hunchun, July 2014.

74. Wang, interview with Chinese businessman #8.

75. Ibid.

76. Ibid.

77. Yaohui Wang, interview with Chinese businessman #14, Baishan, July 2014.

78. Wang, interview with Chinese businessman #8.

79. Wang, interview with Chinese businessman #1.

80. Yaohui Wang, interview with Chinese businessman #15, Baishan, July 2014.

81. Wang, interview with Chinese businessman #8.

82. Wang, interview with Chinese businessman #15.

83. Wang, interview with Chinese businessman #6.

84. Ibid.

85. Wang, interview with Chinese businessman #4.

86. Wang, interview with Chinese businessman #15.

87. Ibid.

88. Ibid.

89. Wang, interview with Chinese businessman #4.

90. Ibid.

91. Wang, interview with Chinese businessman #14.

92. Ibid. Local hotels and restaurants in Liaoning and Jilin generally have their own brokers who acquire fresh seafood directly from North Korea.

93. Yaohui Wang, interview with Chinese businessman #11, Hunchun, July 2014.

94. Ibid.

95. Ibid.

96. Ibid.

Conclusion: The Future

1. Hazel Smith, *North Korea: Markets and Military Rule* (Cambridge, UK: Cambridge University Press, 2015); Daniel Tudor and James Pearson, *North Korea Confidential: Private Markets, Fashion Trends, Prison Camps, Dissenters and Defectors* (Rutland, VT: Tuttle Publishing, 2015); Stephan Haggard and Marcus Noland, *Famine in North Korea: Markets, Aid, and Reform* (New York: Columbia University Press, 2007); Stephan Haggard and Marcus Noland, *Witness to Transformation: Refugee Insights into North Korea* (Washington, DC: Peterson Institute for International Economics, 2011).

2. See, for example, the closing chapters of Victor Cha, *The Impossible State: North Korea, Past and Future* (New York: Random House, 2012); Andrei Lankov, *The Real North Korea: Life and Politics in the Failed Stalinist Utopia* (Oxford: Oxford University Press, 2013).

3. Stephan Haggard and Marcus Noland, "The Political Economy of North Korea: Implications for Denuclearization and Proliferation," in *East-West Center Working Papers: Economic Series* (Honolulu: East-West Center, 2009); Stephan Haggard and Marcus Noland, "Sanctioning North Korea: The Political Economy of Denuclearization and Proliferation," *Asian Survey* 50, no. 3 (2010): 539–68.

4. Not everyone agrees that North Korean sanctions are particularly harsh. See, for example, Joshua Stanton, "You'd Be Surprised How Much Tougher Our Zimbabwe and Belarus Sanctions Are Than Our North Korea Sanctions," One Free Korea, http://freekorea.us/2014/07/15/youd-be-surprised-how-much-tougher-our-zimbabwe-and-belarus-sanctions-are-than-our-north-korea-sanctions/; Joshua Stanton, "Obama Administration Sanctions Everyone except Kim Jong Un," One Free Korea, http://freekorea.us/2014/07/10/obama-administration-sanctions-everyone-except-kim-jong-un/.

5. Justin V. Hastings and Adam N. Stulberg, "Technology and Knowledge Transfer in Nuclear Proliferation Networks: An Iran Case Study," in *International Studies Association 2015 Annual Meeting* (New Orleans, LA, 18–21 February 2015).

6. Justin V. Hastings, "The Geography of Nuclear Proliferation Networks: The Case of AQ Khan," *Nonproliferation Review* 19, no. 3 (2012): 429–50.

7. Bryan Early, *Busted Sanctions: Explaining Why Economic Sanctions Fail* (Stanford, CA: Stanford University Press, 2015), chapter 5.

8. Song Ah Seol, "Trucks Loaded with Mineral Extracts Blocked from Entering China," *DailyNK*, 7 March 2016.

9. Andrei Lankov, "Kim Jong-Un's North Korea: What Should We Expect?" *International Journal of Korean Unification Studies* 21, no. 1 (2012): 1–19; Victor D. Cha and Nicholas D. Anderson, "A North Korean Spring?" *Washington Quarterly* 35, no. 1 (2012): 7–24.

10. Haggard and Noland, *Famine in North Korea*; Stephan Haggard and Marcus Noland, "Reform from Below: Behavioral and Institutional Change in North Korea," *Journal of Economic Behavior and Organization* 73, no. 2 (2010): 133–52.

11. James Reilly, "China's Market Influence in North Korea," *Asian Survey* 54, no. 5 (2014): 894–917.

12. Fenghuangwang, "Chaoxian: Zhangchengze Shijian Bu Hui Yingxiang Jingji Jiang Yin Waizi Fazhan Tequ," *Fenghuangwang*, 17 December 2013.

13. Yaohui Wang, interview with Chinese businessman #14, Baishan, July 2014; Yaohui Wang, interview with Chinese businessman #12, Yanji, July 2014.

14. Joshua Stanton, "N. Korea Perestroika Watch: 'Gunfire Must Be Made to Resound,'" One Free Korea, http://freekorea.us/2014/07/10/obama-administration-sanctions-everyone-except-kim-jong-un/.

15. Friedrich Schneider and Dominik H. Este, "Shadow Economies: Size, Causes, and Consequences," *Journal of Economic Literature* XXXVIII, no. 1 (2000): 77–114.

16. Marshall Goldman, *The Piratization of Russia: Russian Reform Goes Awry* (New York: Routledge, 2003).

17. Peter Andreas, "The Clandestine Political Economy of War and Peace in Bosnia," *International Studies Quarterly* 48 (2004): 29–51; Peter Andreas, *Blue Helmets and Black Markets: The Business of Survival in the Siege of Sarajevo* (Ithaca, NY: Cornell University Press, 2008).

18. Simon Johnson, Daniel Kaufmann, John McMillan, and Christopher Woodruff, "Why Do Firms Hide? Bribes and Unofficial Activity after Communism," *Journal of Public Economics* 76, no. 3 (2000): 495–520.

19. Claire Wallace, Christian Haerpfer, and Rossalina Latcheva, "The Informal Economy in East-Central Europe 1991–1998" (Inst. Für Höhere Studien, Vienna, 2004), 28–29.

20. Endre Sik, "From the Second to the Informal Economy," *Journal of Public Policy* 12, no. 2 (1992): 153–75.

21. Vadim Volkov, *Violent Entrepreneurs: The Use of Force in the Making of Russian Capitalism* (Ithaca, NY: Cornell University Press, 2002).

22. Randall Peerenboom, *China's Long March toward Rule of Law* (Cambridge, UK: Cambridge University Press, 2002).

23. Endre Sik, "From the Multicoloured to the Black and White Economy: The Hungarian Second Economy and the Transformation," *International Journal of Urban and Regional Research* 18, no. 1 (1994): 46–70.

24. Organizations like Choson Exchange, which teaches North Koreans about entrepreneurship, also do this more directly.

25. Joshua Stanton, "North Korea's Overseas Money Men, Called Home, Go to Ground Instead," One Free Korea, http://freekorea.us/2013/12/16/north-koreas-overseas-money-men-called-home-go-to-ground-instead/.

26. Daniel Byman and Jennifer Lind, "Pyongyang's Survival Strategy: Tools of Authoritarian Control in North Korea," *International Security* 35, no. 1 (2010): 44–74. See also the final chapter of Haggard and Noland, *Famine in North Korea*, as well as Haggard and Noland, *Witness to Transformation*, and Bruce W. Bennett and Jennifer Lind, "The Collapse of North Korea: Military Missions and Requirements," *International Security* 36, no. 2 (2011): 84–119.

27. Dong Yu and Yu Tian, "Chaoxian Shifang "Bian'ge" Xinhao?" *Nanfang Zhoumo*, 11 August 2012.

28. Fenghuangwang, "Chaoxian."

29. Andrei Lankov, "Reforming North Korea: It Seems That, at Long Last, North Korea Has Decided to Begin Chinese-Style Reforms," *Al Jazeera English*, 30 November 2014.

30. BBC, "N Korea Congress: Kim Jong-un Praises Nuclear Tests," British Broadcasting Corporation, 6 May 2016.

31. See Ken E. Gause, "Coercion, Control, Surveillance, and Punishment: An Examination of the North Korean Police State" (Committee for Human Rights in North Korea, Washington, DC, 2012), 159–77.

32. Jae-soon Chang, "N.K. Leader Has Yet to Consolidate Power, Could Be Marginalized into 'Puppet': U.S. Expert," *Yonhap News Agency*, 14 April 2015.

33. Michael Madden, "N Korea 'Execution' Highlights Kim's Insecurity," *British Broadcasting Corporation*, 13 May 2015.

34. Scott Thomas Bruce, "A Double-Edged Sword: Information Technology in North Korea," in *Asia Pacific Issues* (Honolulu: East-West Center, 2012); Byman and Lind, "Pyongyang's Survival Strategy: Tools of Authoritarian Control in North Korea."

35. Xin Sun, Jiangnan Zhu, and Yiping Wu, "Organizational Clientelism: An Analysis of Private Entrepreneurs in Chinese Local Legislatures," *Journal of East Asian Studies* 14, no. 1 (2012): 1–29; Ying Chen and David Touve, "Conformity, Political Participation, and Economic Rewards: The Case of Chinese Private Entrepreneurs," *Asia Pacific Journal of Management* 28, no. 3 (2011): 529–53; Jonathan Unger and Anita Chan, "State Corporatism and Business Associations in China: A Comparison with

Earlier Emerging Economies of East Asia," *International Journal of Emerging Markets* 10, no. 2 (2015); Ying Sun, "Municipal People's Congress Elections in the PRC: A Process of Co-Option," *Journal of Contemporary China* 23, no. 85 (2014): 183–95.

36. Claire Wallace and Rossalina Latcheva, "Economic Transformation Outside the Law: Corruption, Trust in Public Institutions and the Informal Economy in Transition Countries of Central and Eastern Europe," *Europe-Asia Studies* 58, no. 1 (2006): 81–102.

37. Ibid.

38. Seol, "Trucks Loaded with Mineral Extracts Blocked from Entering China."

INDEX

www.ingramcontent.com/pod-product-compliance
Ingram Content Group UK Ltd.
Pitfield, Milton Keynes, MK11 3LW, UK
UKHW040828090225
454781UK00003B/186/J